Love, Activism, and the Respectable Life of Alice Dunbar-Nelson

Love, Activism, and the Respectable Life of Alice Dunbar-Nelson

Tara T. Green

BLOOMSBURY ACADEMIC
NEW YORK • LONDON • OXFORD • NEW DELHI • SYDNEY

BLOOMSBURY ACADEMIC
Bloomsbury Publishing Inc
1385 Broadway, New York, NY 10018, USA
50 Bedford Square, London, WC1B 3DP, UK
29 Earlsfort Terrace, Dublin 2, Ireland

BLOOMSBURY, BLOOMSBURY ACADEMIC and the Diana logo are trademarks
of Bloomsbury Publishing Plc

First published in the United States of America 2022

Cover design by Eleanor Rose
Cover photograph used with permission: Alice Dunbar-Nelson papers, Special Collections,
University of Delaware Library, Newark, Delaware

Library of Congress Cataloguing-in-Publication Data

Names: Green, Tara T., author.
Title: Love, activism, and the respectable life of Alice Dunbar-Nelson / Tara T. Green.
Description: New York: Bloomsbury Academic, 2022. | Includes bibliographical
references and index.
Identifiers: LCCN 2021026021 (print) | LCCN 2021026022 (ebook) | ISBN 9781501382314
(hardback) | ISBN 9781501382307 (paperback) | ISBN 9781501382321 (epub) |
ISBN 9781501382338 (pdf) | ISBN 9781501382345
Subjects: LCSH: Dunbar-Nelson, Alice Moore, 1875-1935. | African American feminists–
Biography. | African American women civil rights workers–Biography. | African American
women authors–Biography. | African American sexual minorities–Biography. |
African American women–Public opinion. | African American women–Social conditions–
19th century. | African American women–Social conditions–20th century. |
African Americans–Race identity. | United States–Race relations.
Classification: LCC E185.97.D838 G74 2022 (print) | LCC E185.97.D838 (ebook) |
DDC 811/.54092 [B]–dc23
LC record available at https://lccn.loc.gov/2021026021
LC ebook record available at https://lccn.loc.gov/2021026022

ISBN: HB: 978-1-5013-8231-4
PB: 978-1-5013-8230-7
ePDF: 978-1-5013-8233-8
eBook: 978-1-5013-8232-1

Typeset by Deanta Global Publishing Services, Chennai, India
Printed and bound in the United States of America

Photos used with permission: Alice Dunbar-Nelson papers, Special Collections,
University of Delaware Library, Newark, Delaware.

To find out more about our authors and books visit www.bloomsbury.com and
sign up for our newsletters.

To survivors of domestic assault and the ones who tried.

CONTENTS

PREFACE

Late one night in early 2011, I remembered a writer I had met the first time at least fifteen years before in an American literature class at Dillard University. She had written a story of a New Orleans I did not recognize, but that had wedged itself into my memory. That night I decided to find a bit more about her and learned that her papers were housed in Delaware, where she had lived. I had one question that would, a month or so later, lead me to the University of Delaware: Why did a Creole woman leave New Orleans to marry a dark-skinned man and live in Delaware? What follows is the answer to that question.

For a variety of reasons, it would take me a decade to write and rewrite this study of her life. Since 2011, President Barack Obama was reelected in 2012, the Black Lives Matter movement emerged in 2013, and I continued to write as one incident after another fueled more protests from the killing of a Black boy named Trayvon Martin to that of a Black man named George Floyd (2020). I am now submitting the manuscript on the second Monday of the trial of Derek Chauvin, the ex-police officer who knelt on Mr. Floyd's neck for nine minutes and twenty-six seconds. Adding to this, a pandemic started in one country in 2019 and spread to others and left the human race fearing for its survival. And then, in 2021 Vice President Kamala Harris was inaugurated, making her the first woman and the first person of color to hold that office. She is a direct descendant of the work that Alice Dunbar-Nelson did as a suffragist. LGBTQ+ rights, including same-sex marriage, also expanded.

The work for equal rights and social justice continues as it did during her lifetime. This is as much a book about the past as it is a book about the present that nods to the future.

ACKNOWLEDGMENTS

Writing this book was a ten-year journey. Many thanks for the enormous support I received from the Linda Carlisle Excellence Professorship, including the assistance of the brilliantly gifted Carlisle Scholars: Chase Hanes, Danielle LaPlace, and Taylor Steadman. My colleagues of Women's, Gender, and Sexuality Studies (WGSS), including past director Mark Rifkin and current director Lisa Levenstein, have gone beyond expectations to support my research. And, to Sheila Washington, the extraordinary program coordinator of WGSS who made sure I had what I needed, when I needed: "Thank You" for all that you do to keep us going.

Thanks, also, for the generous support of Vanderbilt University's Callie House Research Center for the Study of Global Black Cultures and Politics and the invaluable illuminating discussions provided by Black feminist scholars at our annual Fugitives Writing Retreat. Your advice gave me consistent direction and encouragement.

In its earliest stages, when I was the director of African American Studies, I had the assistance of a talented administrative assistant, Bruce Holland, who ordered books and made my travel arrangements. As you rest in eternity, I hope you know that you have not been forgotten.

Many thanks to the Black community of Wilmington, who with the introduction of Carol E. Henderson, my faithful tour guide, welcomed me to their community gatherings, including services at Bethel AME.

I appreciate conversations, ideas, and academic references gifted to me by E. Patrick Johnson, Joycelyn Moody, P. Gabrielle Foreman, Valerie Johnson, Dana Williams, William "Bill" Hart, Sheila Smith McKoy, Maryemma Graham, Sally Ann Ferguson, Sharon Lynette Jones, R. Baxter Miller, Willi M. Coleman, Jen Feather, Sarah Cervenak, Duane Cyrus, N. Frank Woods, Elizabeth West, Robin Adams, and Karen Kilcup. You may not remember what you said but do know that I was listening.

Where would any researcher be without librarians? I acknowledge with sincere gratitude the consistent kindness and patience of archivists (namely, Rebecca Johnson Melvin, Tim Murray, and Curtis Small) at the University of Delaware, who answered emails at all hours, even during the pandemic, and made sure that I had pieces of a rather large puzzle. Thanks also to archivists at Dillard University, Amistad Research Center, the

Library of Congress, Robert W. Woodruff Library at AUC, the Schomburg Center, Emory University's Rose Library, the Delaware Historical Society, and Howard University. I also acknowledge the work of UNCG's librarian Gerald Holmes, who always found answers to my many research questions.

I am grateful to all the students who asked the question: Is there a book about her life? And for those who wanted to be involved, Tonya Doane, Yasmeen Chism, and Aries Powell, and for Suquanna Butler, who just wanted to know more.

Gratitude also to my Sorors of Delta Sigma Theta Sorority who continue to show the patience of my endless reminder: she was the one who wrote the lyrics to our Delta Hymn.

Her voice is being heard because an editor and reviewers saw the significance of telling a Black woman's story. Thank you, Haaris Naqvi, for believing in this work, and to the staff at Bloomsbury, including Rachel Moore, for moving it forward.

Thank you with hugs to my "New Orleans crew": Jerry Ward, Brenda Marie Osbey, and Charles Nero. Our conversations helped me to further understand this woman's journey.

Hugs, kisses, and love to my mother, father, and my family, who make me want to return to New Orleans and our Westbank home, always.

Introduction

Introducing a Respectable Activist

"I am of the latter class, what E. C. Adams in 'Nigger to Nigger' immortalizes in the poem, 'Brass Ankles.' White enough to pass for white, but with a darker family background, a real love for the mother race, and no desire to be numbered among the white race."[1] Perhaps no other sentence in her body of work captures the identity politics of women's-rights and racial-equality advocate Alice Ruth Moore Dunbar-Nelson more than this one taken from her essay "Brass Ankles Speaks," written around the year 1929 under the pseudonym of Adele Morris.[2] Among others, there are two prominent issues that emerge in her honest critique of being a Black[3] woman who could pass for White.

The first is the issue of racial identity. Born just ten years after slavery ended, one Black parent (or any parent thought to have African ancestry) meant the child was relegated to the legal assignment of Negro. It did not, however, mean that acceptance by other Blacks was certain. While acknowledging the secrecy associated with "white skin," Alice[4] declared her preference for identifying with her maternal heritage—that of her formerly enslaved Black Southern mother. Denying or erasing the father would not and did not save her from societal criticism, a fact she learned very early in life as she felt wounded by darker-skinned peers who taunted her as a child for being what they called a "yallar" or a "half white nigger." Implied but not stated, "white enough to pass for white" is a slight reference to the father who is absent in her biographical references, leaving her mother to serve as the major influence over her racial identity. Who exactly her father was and what his racial background was, we may never know, as the Moore women kept this secret, only to reveal that he was a seaman. His absence marked her as "different" in a variety of ways.

Second, she certainly saw herself as different within the Black community, not only because of her skin color but because of her sexual identity as well. Under the guise of a pseudonym, she compared intraracial identity with sexuality.

a small wonder then that the few lighter persons in the community drew together; we are literally thrown upon each other, whether we liked it or not. But when we began going about together and spending our time in each other's society, a howl went up that we are organizing a "blue vein" society. We were mistresses of white men. We were lesbians. We hated black folk and plotted against them.[5]

Although she stated that the group was comprised of "lighter persons," it is clear from the use of two gender categories—mistresses and lesbians—that this was a group of women. Here, she positioned sexual identity with the complicated feelings she had about being a light-skinned African American woman. Cheryl Wall has convincingly observed, "Adopting a pseudonym . . . constitutes a form of passing for a writer" that may be used to "explore forbidden issues or emotions."[6] Wall's observation proves accurate when applied to "Brass Ankles Speaks." If the young Alice Moore's authenticity as a Black person was questioned by the members of her community because of her light skin, she most certainly would not have felt comfortable publicly embracing her attraction to women.

In her research of this essay, Gloria (Akasha) Hull posited that "she sent the ten-page typescript signed 'Adele Morris' to *Plain Talk* magazine."[7] In response, the editor G. D. Eaton objected to publishing it "anonymously" and further stated, "Yet I realize the danger to you if you put your name under the title."[8] Five days later he wrote, "your document is a personal one, and that is the more reason it should carry your own name."[9] Alice "would never consent to such public unmasking," concluded Hull.[10] Publicly revealing the intricate details of her identity was not something she was ever willing to do. If she had dared to, she would have "threatened mainstream Black political and cultural narratives of racial uplift and achievement, respectability and civility."[11] As a result, the author who frequently failed to find venues to publish her work kept the revelations she made in this essay private.

Living with secrets to avoid public scrutiny was something that she learned to do at an early age. Born in New Orleans on July 19, 1875, Alice Ruth Moore was the second daughter of Patsy Wright and a Mr. Moore. Alice's father was likely a White man, considering that different names appear on public documents (e.g., US Census, birth and marriage certificates). Although Patsy Wright went by the name of Patsy Moore in the US Census after her daughters' birth, there is no evidence that she ever lived with or was ever legally married to her daughter's father, making it unlikely that her daughters had a sustained relationship with their father. In fact, besides the census, marriage, and birth records, his name does not appear in any of Alice's surviving personal documents. Covering the absence of this man, his identity, and the relationship he had with her mother became a family secret that Alice took to her grave. And, I argue that his absence as much as presence (in whatever capacity) had a major impact on the decisions she made as a woman primed to become a wife but with attractions to other women. Alice was always influenced by the specter of Victorian morals that demanded she lead a respectable life as a heterosexual woman dedicated to her husband. But Alice would never fit neatly into prescribed social roles.

Instead, she was a woman who tested boundaries in a variety of ways as she carefully projected a "respectable" public persona. In her overview of studies dedicated to Black women's sexuality, Michelle Mitchell finds "The notion that African-American women developed a code of silence around intimate matters as a response to discursive and literal attacks on black sexuality has influenced studies of turn-of-the century club women, reformers, and workers."[12] Mitchell's observation is applicable to Alice. According to Evelyn Brooks-Higginbotham, nineteenth-century politics of respectability

> equated public behavior with individual self-respect and with the advancement of African Americans as a group. [African American women] felt certain that "respectable" behavior in public would earn their people a measure of esteem from white America, and hence they strove to win the black lower class's psychological allegiance to temperance, industriousness, thrift, refined manners, and Victorian sexual morals.[13]

Alice's standard of respectable living most certainly had its origins in her mother's relationship with her mysterious father, which likely led her to engage in the work of the Black clubwomen's movement, a national coalition of Black women's clubs led by middle-class African American women intent on upholding the very standards that Brooks-Higginbotham describes.

While she would later become associated with the Harlem Renaissance, Alice most certainly derived her moral judgments from Victorian values as she came to know during the late Victorian age. Shirley J. Carlson provides characteristics of "Black Victorian women."[14] Influenced by the "cult of true womanhood," Black Victorian women, like their White counterparts, were "committed to the domestic sphere" as "wife and mother." Such women were "morally unassailable," "virtuous and modest." In physical appearance, her "hair and costume" were "immaculate" and in public she wore "a floor-length dress, with fitted bodice, a full skirt, and puffy sleeves." As one who upheld the "expectations of true womanhood," she was a "true lady." For Black women in particular, they were also "race conscious," "well-educated," and "self-confident." Intelligence was seen as necessary and not regarded as a characteristic only reserved for men. These women were the gems of the race.

Yet, in many ways, Alice resisted the group's "allegiance to temperance, industriousness, thrift, refined manners, and Victorian sexual morals."[15] Starting with her fiction *Violets and Other Tales* (1895), she questions the meaning of women practicing such refined manners when sexual exploitation and social restrictions, particularly targeting Black women, were prevalent during her lifetime. In fact, as the daughter of an unknown man, it is likely that she knew exploitation all too well. While Brooks-Higginbotham emphasizes the expectations of public behavior, *Love, Activism and the Respectable Life of Alice Dunbar-Nelson* allows for a sustained look into the private behavior of one woman in a growing educated Black middle-class society that prescribed to respectability. Alice lived within the protective covering of respectability, where she could at times critique, navigate, uphold, and defy societal expectations. When marriage was the mark of respectability and divorce was rare, she married three times and divorced once. When same-sex relationships were illegal and considered lascivious, she had at least three women lovers. From the Progressive Era of the late nineteenth century to the Harlem Renaissance of the 1920s–1930s, she became increasingly comfortable with her identity as a Black same-sex loving woman who also loved men. Notably, however, her attraction to women was part of her identity that remained private or hidden from public view and scrutiny, including from her family.

To expand this further, respectability politics is at the root of the "politics of silence," that is, a culture of practice that involves people of an underprivileged class or social status being themselves forced—either by some form of social threat—to not engage in the public act of "telling" or "revealing" private relations with the privileged class, making the secrecy possible and necessary. Such silences empower a paternal society where White fatherhood equates to power. Hortense Spillers emphasizes this: "Fatherhood, at best a supreme cultural courtesy, attenuates here on the one hand into a monstrous accumulation on the other hand. One has been made and bought by disparate currencies, linking back to a common origin of exchange and domination."[16] Critiquing the problem of silences for Black women and its impact on Black queer women, Evelynn Hammonds concludes, "in choosing silence Black women also lost any conception of their sexuality."[17] Alice's life exemplifies the possibility of recovery.

A study of Alice Ruth Moore Dunbar-Nelson's life shows the rootedness of silence as a means to uphold expectations while simultaneously subverting them. As a child born to a formerly enslaved woman who gave birth to two daughters—women who did not leave a consistent, clear record about the identity of their biological father—silence was a way of life for the Moore women. In the absence of a father that she could publicly claim, she had to live with "fatherhood" denial—his denial of her and her of him—and the protection that public identity could afford her. How the adult Alice upheld respectability, at least in public, allowed her an opportunity to redeem the lost narrative of her life, to resist repeating the history that had been her mother's. Maybe.

Through Black feminist studies, literary analysis, queer and sexuality studies, and historical and cultural studies, I offer a curated analysis of Alice Dunbar-Nelson's archive that shows the role respectability played in her projection and definition of an upstanding public persona and its intersection with a private self that may not have met the standards of respectable behavior. My approach also means that not all her literature is analyzed here or even referenced. Instead, I focus on showing a progression from her early publications through the work that is often neglected, her later work. These select representative pieces not only reflect specific times in her life and career but also give voice to her sustained activist interests.

Love, Activism and the Respectable Life of Alice Ruth Dunbar-Nelson is an examination of the life of a respectable activist—a Black woman activist and writer who in her public and private lives navigated complex questions of racism, women's rights, and sexual agency and found ways to resist restrictions to who she was as a creative Black woman. Alice Dunbar-Nelson's life as a respectable activist demonstrates the influences of Victorian values on middle-class African American Southern women of the late nineteenth century, as well as the evolving values and expectations related to politics of respectability of the time as they emerged in the late nineteenth century and shifted as she, like some African American women of the day, moved from the South to the North and from one century to the next. In her papers, I found a woman who lived and wrote *within* respectability by testing, teasing, expanding, and disregarding social and political boundaries as she matured from one marriage to another and one historical era to another.

Taking my cue from her archival documents, I advance the idea that as a respectable activist Alice was an early Black feminist who tried to balance her feminist leanings as an advocate for women with her racial politics, commitment to educating youth from/in marginalized communities as well as through her search for a socially acceptable husband and her relationships with women. I hear Alice's proclamation of a "real love for the mother race" affirming her position as a nineteenth-century Black feminist who primarily defined herself through her activism, included but not limited to securing women's right to vote, protecting African American girls from sexual exploitation, and advocating for equal roles in marriage—actions that were presented in her many forms of writing as well as her career as an educator. Even more importantly is her insistence that she be heard as a social justice and politically informed talented writer and galvanizing speaker. She learned from a community of Black women who loved their "colored" selves how to use her voice and talents. In the age of the New Woman and the "New Negro Woman," as Margaret Washington or Mrs. Booker T. Washington preferred to refer to herself and her sister activists, Alice walked in the footsteps of older Black female activists of the nineteenth century, such as Maria Stewart and Anna Julia Cooper.[18] At the age of twenty, Alice Moore inserted herself into this history when she became a leader in the Black clubwomen's movement.

Beyond the activism, Alice's construction of a respectable life shows the limits of love for the race and its intersection with the need to be loved by members of the race. Through her three marriages, which was unusual for any woman of the era, she learned more about who she was as a woman, a wife, and an activist. While she went into each marriage certainly hoping to prove that she was a moral, upstanding African American woman, make no mistake that she was a woman who believed in love and romance. Her letters and diaries reveal how much she greatly respected the moral exigencies required of middle-class Black people and did her best to publicly uphold the sanctity of respectability. Notably, she never returned to her maiden name—that of the missing father—after marrying Dunbar; we may assume that she felt moving forward, with an augmented identity, was the best way to proceed into each phase of life. If marriage could give her an identity that her father's absence did not and if it could correct the wrongs of the past in which her mother strove to shield herself behind the mask of marriage, then by her third marriage Alice succeeded, on some level, at achieving the level of respectability that the women of her family had tried so hard to project.

Respectability (as in the *Respectable Life*) is used here to show the fluidity of the meaning of the word and its emphasis on public performance but an insistence and dedication to enjoying the intimacies of a private life. In other words, Alice exemplifies the importance of self-definition. According to Brooks-Higginbotham, "Your definition of yourself, the worth of who you are isn't determined in these contexts of racial discrimination. If you believe that you are worthy of respect and if you live a life that is worthy of respect, then nothing anybody else can say about you can define you."[19] Therefore, living a life in public means pushing back against the possibility of controversy, but private contradictions and ironies are most certainly present. Same-sex romances were to be kept quiet, but to pretend as if they were not known intimately to Alice and her proper Black peers, as archives show, would be a silencing of beautiful lives lived. In this, she defined a life that was not fully suppressed by a past that dictated how Black women should explore their sexual desires.

We are indebted to another Black woman activist who understood the value of knowing the life of a Black woman activist. Pauline A. Young, Alice's niece, stored a rich collection of documents that preserved her famous aunt's voice. Young, a librarian by training who later worked at her alma mater Howard High in Wilmington, Delaware, shared the documents that chronicled the life of her famous aunt with Gloria Akasha Hull. Hull, at the time an English professor at the University of Delaware, had the honor of being the first scholar that Young introduced to this archive, which she had kept in her house. Recounting her first visit in her 1980 essay, "Researching Alice Dunbar-Nelson: A Personal and Literary Perspective," Hull recalls:

There in the small cottage where she lived was a trove of precious information—manuscript boxes of letters, diaries, and journals; scrapbooks on tables; two unpublished novels and drafts of published works in file folders; clippings and pictures under beds and bookshelves.[20]

Although Hull believed the documents would be housed in the Moorland-Spingarn Institute at Howard University, Young sold most of the collection to the University of Delaware in 1984 where the documents are still housed, about thirty minutes away from where Alice lived most of her life and built her career. Young would donate other valuable documents about both she and her aunt to the Atlanta University Center's Robert Woodruff library.

While there are layers of her life available in the various forms described above, there are some missing pieces that cause challenges for researchers of her exciting life. As expected, there are times when letters do not have responses. Two examples are letters to Dunbar during an early separation and letters from Edwina Kruse. Letters also are written doing periods of distance and are not necessary when Alice is in close proximity to a person. As a result, the time they lived in Colorado is not recorded to any significant extent in her archive. This also takes us to whose letters are not included, such as correspondence between Alice and most of her female lovers, which are alluded to in her diaries. Curiously, what we know about her relationship with her sister largely comes from the diaries she wrote during the 1920s. Thanks to Pauline Young, she kept letters written by her mother to her the last year or so of her aunt's death. These became central in learning more about the sisters' dedication to one another from Leila's perspective as well as her love for her only surviving daughter of whom both women relied on tremendously. There are also silences related to her time in Washington, DC. It is not clear if she was involved with any of the Black women's clubs or any other organization in the area, but her collection and the newspapers show that she did not rest once she moved to Wilmington. These silences in the archive during her marriage to Dunbar suggest something about her state of mind regarding their relationship that I discuss in the chapters to come.

It is difficult to believe that she did not keep a diary more consistently than those found in the archive. Nevertheless, one of the most valuable and informative intimate pieces of the Delaware collection are her diaries. When reading a diary, it is difficult to know how much of the diary is fact and, especially in the case of a fiction writer, how much of it is embellished. For Alice, her diaries (covering periods between 1920, 1921, 1926–7, 1928, 1929, 1930, and 1931) were a way in which she could express herself without interruption, and, at times, the diaries were part of a meditative and spiritual ritual that she attempted to immerse herself into on a daily or weekly basis, depending on her schedule. Within these pages, we learn not only how much time she dedicated to improving the social and political condition of "the mother race," but we also understand that she dedicated much of her personal and professional self to improving the conditions of women, even when she was often too helpless or too ill to advance herself financially and socially. Literally writing her life, she recorded respectability politics as the tug between her private desires and public image. Her diaries reveal what occurs beyond respectability, as argued by Brittney Cooper: "Though many

Black women practiced a culture of dissemblance in public, in their textual work and on the lecture stage, they frequently pulled back the cloak of Black female pain and frustration, exposing the personal nature of the struggles they experienced, even as they worked to make the world safer for Black women."[21] When reading Alice's diaries, Cooper's words prove instructive.

Future readers of her diaries learn how Alice felt in response to the challenges that she faced as an activist, a wife, a daughter, and a supervisor—roles that she managed while caring for family members as well as her own ailments. We hear the creeks and moans of an aging body that gives out only four years after the death of her beloved mother. Her ability to write—to capture an audience by telling a story and casting herself as the star of her dramatic life—is ever present in the diaries. To be sure, each diary serves as the only definitive evidence, from her own perspective, that she immensely enjoyed intimate relationships with women and with her husbands. And, like any sister, she expressed her annoyance of her older sister more than her love, even as the two leaned on one another for support until Alice's death in 1935. Alice's relationships with her sister, mother, and clubwomen may best be expressed by Audre Lorde, who states, "As a Black lesbian feminist, I have a particular feeling, knowledge, and understanding for those sisters with whom I have danced hard, played, or even fought."[22] A woman who worked most of her life with women, Alice's diaries place Lorde's assertion in motion. Lastly, the diaries serve as a supplement to her work as a columnist who documented her political activities and her many jobs. Ultimately, we cannot understand Alice Dunbar-Nelson without looking at all the layers of her life, namely her "gender and sexual desires cannot be understood apart from her particular family history, racialized and gendered discourses of respectability and normalcy."[23]

Despite the existence of these papers, there has been no full-length study dedicated solely to her life. Yet, Alice has never been forgotten as the wife of Paul Laurence Dunbar. For his 1973 dissertation project, Eugene Metcalf transcribed the handwritten letters between the Dunbars and provided notes for readers. Going further with a particular focus on Alice, Hull's recovery work involved editing her diary and novels and some of her published and unpublished fiction, essays, drama, and poetry. In 1987, Hull also published a comprehensive chapter on Alice's life and work in her book *Color, Sex, and Poetry*. As Adenike Marie Davidson points out, "Hull's recovery of Dunbar-Nelson serves to convince today's readers of the importance of examining her apart from the Dunbar mystique, but Hull confines much of her discussion of the author's production to the historical period of the Harlem Renaissance."[24] Nevertheless, Hull's work stands as foundational in Dunbar-Nelson studies and opened the door for Eleanor Alexander's 2001 historical study of Paul and Alice Dunbar's courtship, marriage, and separation. Recovering her identity irrespective of Dunbar, however, has prompted other scholars[25] to focus their efforts exclusively on her.

I use the archives to trace Alice's life as a respectable activist and how she loved from her childhood through her death. This work relies primarily, but not solely, on the archives at the University of Delaware. However, I am also indebted to Black newspaper collections that told the stories of Black people, celebrated Black accomplishments, and lamented the loss of some of its members. The Negro Press provided a counter-narrative to other presses that either made Black people invisible or persisted in presenting reasons for the negative treatment of Black citizens. Instead, the Black press made Black folks be seen. As a result, they live on in the archive as ancestral voices with names associated with places and events. Whether she was contributing as a member of the press or she was featured in an article, Alice's travels, insight, and contributions are recorded and lend themselves to our understanding of the respectable activist.

"God, don't let me die before I do something useful," wrote Alice Ruth Moore Dunbar-Nelson in one of her diary entries. Written when she was just forty years old, she appeared to have found herself at a crossroads. On one side, she saw herself as not having made much of a contribution to society, in effect, underestimating the tremendous amount of work she had done and the life she had led. On the other, she could not be satisfied with those accomplishments and steadily tried to do much more. And, she did. I bring you the complicated love story of a respectable activist.

1

A Respectable Activist Is Born

Known for Creole culture, Mardi Gras celebrations, and myths of wild Voodoo ceremonies, New Orleans is a mixture of nations and cultures from Africa, Europe, the Caribbean, and the Americas. New Orleans is also the home of one of its most respected African American writers, Alice Ruth Moore. Born in New Orleans on July 19, 1875, to Patsy Wright, a formerly enslaved woman, and a Mr. Moore of unknown background and origins, Alice entered that world at a pivotal time in history. Only ten years before her birth, the Confederate South had fallen to the Northern Union, ushering in the period known as the Reconstruction Era, which some argue ended in 1877 when the Union troops pulled out of the South. Hope ebbed and flowed as voting rights for Blacks were granted and then restricted. Louisiana was the location of the successful rise of P. B. S. Pinchback, a Creole man of African and French ancestry who served as governor for thirty-five days and later in Congress. New Orleans, where Pinchback worked and studied law, was a hotbed for politics, racial progress, and challenges. A city with a reputation for class distinctions based largely on racialized categories of Creoles, Black and White, of mixed ancestries, Alice's New Orleans was a city famously influenced by the uniqueness of its ethnic and cultural diversity, making it the prime setting for much of the fiction she published.

By the time Alice was born, the Black population in New Orleans had nearly doubled, making it a much different city than the one that her mother would have known prior to the birth of her daughters. According to the census, the "Number of Negroes in New Orleans increased from 25,423 in 1860 to 57,617 in 1880."[1] Within this demographic shift was a diverse population of Black people:

Composed of a large number of antebellum free Negroes, urbanized former slaves, and freedmen who came directly from Louisiana's plantations, the Negro population contained the highly skilled and the unskilled, the educated and the densely ignorant, the religious and the superstitious, and mulattos and blacks.[2]

As a formerly enslaved woman, Alice's mother was part of this diverse population. According to Alice in a letter she wrote to Paul Laurence Dunbar, her mother confessed to her daughters that she and her fellow enslaved community learned about the Emancipation Proclamation from their owner, an old judge who tried to keep them enslaved. In an effort to avoid compliance, he took his people and "fled to a wild district in Texas and there held out against the law."[3] Under the orders of Yankee soldiers, he read the Proclamation to them, asked for forgiveness, and gave them the option of returning with him to Opelousas, Louisiana, where he promised to pay them wages.[4] Apparently, Patsy Wright returned on the three-month trip from Texas and later migrated from the southwestern part of the state to the southern part with her mother who helped to raise her daughters.[5] New Orleans was a changing city, which, for Blacks who had moved out of rural areas and for those who had been in the city for generations, meant that race relations would become tense as the old practices were challenged by a city that was now predominantly Black.

Among the old practices was the mixing of races on intimate levels. Census data reveals, that, when compared to most Southern states, there was undoubtedly more culturally accepted sexual intimacy between the races in New Orleans.[6] Alice's own familial background may be a testament to this form of "intimacy." Her birth certificate lists a man named Monroe Moore as her father, but there are scant records of a man by this name in New Orleans. As Eleanor Alexander points out, there is a man by this name listed on ship records. Census records show that a Monroe Moore, who was around the probable age of Alice Moore's father, was married, but not to Patricia Wright. To add to the mystery surrounding the identity of Alice's father, Mary Leila Moore, born on December 25, 1869, has the name of John Moore listed as her father on her birth certificate. A third iteration of the name Moore as Joseph Moore appears on Alice's marriage certificate to Henry Arthur Callis in 1910. For reasons that were not made known, the family, or perhaps Patsy herself, was not interested in making public the identity of Alice and Leila's father. Although she took the name of Moore, what is likely is that Patsy Wright never legally married the man, even though early-twentieth-century census documents record that she claimed to have been married and later widowed. It is a mystery that would be passed from one generation to the next as Pauline Young, Alice's niece, would write in a letter to a publisher that Alice and her mother's parents "were American-born middle class Negroes. Her father was a seaman, and her mother a seamstress."[7] If Patricia was married, she was abandoned by the time Alice began to document her career in 1895 for census records show no mention of her father and no record of him living with the mother at any of their New Orleans residencies. John Wesley Blassingame comments on the human factors that affect the accuracy of census data: in order for them to be accurate, people must tell the truth.

> The data on heads of families is a case in point. It is impossible to tell, for instance, how many couples who told the census taker they were married were, in fact, legally married. In all censuses people *tend to lie* about this because of the stigma attached to illegal unions. Women lie about it much more frequently than do men; consequently, there are usually more women than men listed as married in any census.[8] (italics mine)

In other words, politics of respectability, as well as the politics of silence, played a major role in the creation of census information and corresponding public narratives. Patsy Wright was of the generation of Black women who greatly valued privacy regarding her intimate choices. Bringing light to the position of women during this era, Blassingame notes, "Violating Negro women, encouraging immorality, and separating families with impunity, the planters had created in the freedmen a deep hunger for stable family relations."[9] Scholars surmise that Patsy Wright was part of "Plaçage, in which women of mixed race were kept as mistresses by wealthy white men."[10] According to Joan Martin, "Plaçage was the practice that existed in Louisiana (and other French and Spanish slaveholding territories) where women of color—the option of legal marriage denied them—entered into long-standing formalized relationships with White European men."[11] However, the existence of plaçage is in question.[12] Instead, Patricia Wright may very well have been a mistress to a man, possibly a married White man, but not one that she met at any sort of ball or that involved a relationship brokered by her mother as part of the believed plaçage custom. Alice's mother's decisions were most certainly a means of survival and prompted Alice and her sister to hold close the identity of an absent father and the story of their unmarried mother. Family secrets had such a lasting impact on her daughter that they nearly dominated Alice's early literature, which was largely focused on mixed-race people of New Orleans, her activist work related to protecting young Black women from sexual exploitation and social stigma, as well as the choices she made about her own romantic relationships.

Whatever relationship she had with Mr. Moore, she may have gotten out of it what she intended. Patsy Wright was able to provide her two daughters with an education, an opportunity that was not available to her. Given the fact that it appears that the mysterious Moore fathered both of her children, it is possible that he supported her financially as well. And, for all we know, he may have had a limited relationship with his daughters. Whatever may have been the arrangement, Alice's mother made sure that her daughters were well-educated. Little Alice began to develop her oratory skills at an early age. At twelve years old, she received recognition for a "recitation" at school.[13] After maintaining honor roll status at Fisk School,[14] Alice went on to attend her high school years and take precollege classes at Southern University where she was on the honor roll. Of her school years in "Brass Ankles Speaks," she referred to having Black classmates of various hues at a "monster public school, which daily disgorged about 2500 children . . . of all shades and tints and degrees of complexions from velvet black to blonde white."[15] There, she was encouraged by her teachers to continue her education. Depending on men for financial support, however, was not an option that Patsy encouraged her daughters to pursue.

In just one generation, Alice and her older sister, Mary Leila, were able to avoid domestic work and earn teaching certificates. Due largely to the emergence of colleges and universities in the South for African Americans that provided opportunities for Black women to expand their career choices, Black women became teachers, like Alice and her sister, or nurses, secretaries, and newspaper editors, while the less educated mostly worked as field laborers and as domestics, especially in the South. Alice found her place among this growing new class when she attended and graduated from the Straight College's teacher's training program in 1892 with an AB degree.[16] Established in 1869 by the American Missionary Association, the aim of the institution was to provide "education and training [in] Christian principles of young men and women."[17] Further its aims were to produce "colored" people who would be successful upon graduation; therefore, they aimed to "build character and to lay foundation for large achievement."[18] The small college of "about four acres" had a College of Arts and Sciences and a Teachers College. Without question, there was a need at this time for qualified and educated Blacks to occupy all levels of society following the slavery era. Straight, like many other academic institutions for "colored students," emphasized the need for Black educators:

> Our schools must have well trained and efficient teachers. The public and its leaders, many of whom are college graduates, must have a large and intelligent educational interest and spirit or our schools and all they mean will suffer. Educational institutions must provide these teachers and arouse this interest and spirit. Large numbers of teachers in the city and rural schools are graduates of this College.[19]

Projecting a sense of pride for its contribution to the development of African Americans who were from Louisiana and other Southern states, Straight College gave Alice the tools she needed to provide a great "service" to the race. Earning this degree at the age of seventeen placed her in a rare and elite group. "By 1890, only 30 black women held baccalaureate degrees, compared to over 300 black men and 2,500 white women."[20]

With her teacher's training, Alice began her career as an educator in a New Orleans public school. Public schools in the city had a long history during the Reconstruction Era that involved failed attempts to integrate Blacks into the system. "By December 1867 there were about 5,000 Negro students in school."[21] White parents who believed that God had made Blacks inferior to Whites enrolled their children into private schools as newspapers incited fear of integration. Ultimately, "the reticence of many black parents and the overly cautious policy of school board officials prevented extensive integration."[22] By the time she began her teaching career, she was employed in a segregated school; it would not be until she taught in Brooklyn, New York, that she would teach students who were not Black, but were Jewish (yet another segregated group in the late nineteenth century).

Black colleges, like Straight, prepared teachers as a way to socially and economically advance the race; the result was that they produced community leaders. Responding to the restrictions imposed on African Americans in the South, Alice became active in developing the Black clubwomen's movement of the late 1800s and remained an active clubwoman for most of her life. Paula Giddings reports, "A profile of 108 of the first generation of clubwomen revealed that most had been born in the South between 1860 and 1885 and had moved North before the mass migration of the late nineteenth century. About 67 percent of the clubwomen were teachers themselves."[23] Evelyn Brooks-Higginbotham states further,

> There's something about the word respectability that I think does conjure in people's minds this front, this facade of feeling that you are better than other people when, in fact, that's not really the meaning of respectability. When I was writing about it, I was interested in how these people who were primarily maids and teachers, [sic] for the most part this is a movement made of low-income women, how do they fight for their civil rights?[24]

Alice and her sister certainly fit this profile. Black women involved in these clubs were not opposed to well-known Victorian virtues of purity and piety, but they were opposed to the implications that the virtues were only applicable to White women. They felt that there was pressure to prove that they too were ladies worthy of respect. The rise of Black women's organizations reflects this awareness: "In part, the proliferation of Black ladies' literary, intelligence, temperance, and moral improvement societies in this period was a reaction to that pressure."[25] But, as Giddings and Floris Barnett Cash have proven, the club women went far beyond their concern with society's perceptions and treatment; they also developed projects to assist members of the Black "lower class."

Among their accomplishments was to establish *The Women's Era* (TWE) in 1894, the first newspaper published for and by African American women.[26]

As a woman-centered paper for a national audience, it boasted that it was "the organ of the colored women's clubs [that] has a large circulation on many of the largest cities." For the most part, *TWE*[27] espoused pride in "colored women" and their communities. In establishing its legitimacy as a reputable paper and to attract advertisers to pay for the printing and circulation, the editor stated, "The Literary, Musical and Domestic Departments are under the control of competent writers and critics" and that it was circulated among "refined and educated classes" of women.[28] At the age of nineteen, Alice as well as other Black women were given a voice in this unique national publication.

To address disparities among Blacks in her hometown, Alice became a charter member of the Phillis Wheatley Club (PWC) in New Orleans. Named for the renowned enslaved African poet, the purpose of the PWC was to provide needed services for African Americans. There were PWC chapters in different parts of the country that served communities in various ways by providing housing alternatives for Black women, similar to those offered by the segregated YWCA. Chartered in 1894 under the leadership of Sylvanie Williams, the club's primary purpose was to "do all that our hands find to do toward elevating and helping our women."[29] Alice would begin to find her writer's voice for a national audience through this publication. In one of, if not, the earliest articles written by Alice for the *TWE* she introduced the PWC to a national readership. After establishing that the members formed the club because other clubs "are opened only to the favored sisters," she goes on to state, "After many years of waiting, the colored women of New Orleans have at last organized a Woman's Club."[30] She seemed aware that she was recording history as she gave the minutes of the meeting of October 6, 1894, that included nineteen women "old and young" who met in a Baptist church to discuss their plans, to elect officers, and to form eleven committees. All had committee chairs, except the Suffrage committee, because "The brave mortal" had not been identified.[31] Considering the location of the newly formed group, "brave" was probably the best word to describe the challenges such a woman would have to endure in the South.

According to Sylvanie Williams[32] in her own article contribution, she felt inspired to establish the club based on her observations as principal of the girls at Fisk School[33] before becoming principal at Thony Lafon School. Alice had been one of her pupils at Fisk and may have taught at one or both of the schools.[34] Williams, who felt she was unable to satisfactorily effect change in the lives of the children, set out to work "upon the morals of the mothers, the majority of whom were poor and ignorant and could not give to their girls the home culture proportionate to their educational advantages."[35] Ultimately, Williams and the women, influenced by Christian doctrines, hoped to advance the race by imposing respectability standards on society's most vulnerable—the Black uneducated poor. Recording growth from the more modest number of nineteen, she reported organizing seventy women to participate in one or more of eleven committees to achieve their goals. All of the committees, each chosen by the woman rather than assigned, were designed to help those in need and to equip the club members with knowledge of what needs might exist. In her article on the vision of the club, she named the committees as follows:

> The Temperance, Anti-Cigarette, Suffrage and Social Purity committees preach their respective doctrines, scatter reading matter and form leagues of all who take any one of the pledges. The Literature, History and Law committees form classes in the club, for our own benefit and improvement. The Self Help committee are [sic] organizing free sewing schools all over the city to teach poor girls how to sew. The Philanthropy committee devote their [sic] time to prisons and houses of correction; they give sympathy, advice, and reading matter to the inmates. We propose to enlist the interest of the colored lawyers to look into cases where we have reason to believe that injustice or undue severity has been exercised in their sentences. The Hospital committee has charge of visiting the sick in the hospital and at their homes, where they give whatever aid they can. The Committee on Newspapers and Current Events search the papers and magazines for all articles, either commendatory or derogatory to us as a race or as women. These are brought to the notice of the club, which endorses them as the case requires.[36]

Organized around contemporary social and political issues, the women were intent on strengthening perceived weaknesses among the "colored" community by placing the educated in service to those in need. Theirs was an attempt to advance respectability through education, the arts, and activism. In addition to these committees, each club member was responsible for providing two garments during the year and to solicit donations of a new garment to provide to the poor. Club meetings consisted of informing members of issues related to the Black community in the city and across the country and making plans to address various needs. Indeed, those women had an ambitious agenda. Undoubtedly, the New Orleans club women had a vision for a better, inclusive New Orleans and like other clubwomen, they had a futuristic outlook they hoped would move beyond local efforts to advance the entire race.

Soon Alice would agree that community-building and the interests of Black women and families did not have to be restricted to local communities, leading her to become a part of a national movement of Black women freedom fighters. During this period, Black women's club chapters began to become affiliated with larger organizations in order to broaden their network and social capital. For Black women's clubs, in particular, connections to national networks gave them opportunities that might help with their efforts to gain racial respect and gender quality. As they served the "least of these," they also hoped to uplift themselves. One of the most influential club leaders, Josephine St. Pierre Ruffin,[37] founder of Boston's Women's Era Club established in 1893 and *The Women's Era*, became prominent in the national Black clubwomen's movement. Ruffin intended for African American women to strengthen their voice and to have the needs of the race, especially those of women, recognized beyond the local levels. She would work to convince Black women that they had the power to advance their social status by agitating for policies and practices that would improve their circumstances for the better. In response to racial violence, the Woman's Era Club spoke out against lynching and pushed for civil rights in the *TWE*.

At its earliest stages, feminist ideologies associated with self-determinism corresponded with the politics of respectability. Their club movement emerged as early Black feminist organizations focused on the concerns identified as central to women as they pooled their financial and educational resources to address problems in Black communities. Floris Cash observes, "Feminism was part of the clubwomen's self-perspective, and consciousness of gender and race compelled their activism."[38] Much of what was taking place in Black churches such as making "demands for anti-lynching legislation and an end to segregation laws," as Brooks-Higginbotham observes, was echoed by those women involved with the club movement: "During the late nineteenth century they developed a distinct discourse of resistance, a feminist theology," or for our purposes, a feminist ideology that simultaneously overlapped and clashed with respectability politics.[39] Alice's involvement with the PWC and its affiliation with the Women's Era Club gave her a clear sense of how Black women, even the most respected in the Black community, were mistreated because of their gender and race.

However, respectability politics certainly had its share of contradictions. As a means for advancement, one segment of the Black community pooled its resources to help another segment of the community. Some of the results were the establishment of various businesses. Unfortunatley, this caused class tensions among Blacks where one segment viewed itself as the models for proper living. It also meant that no matter how well-meaning these women tried to be, to some extent, they modeled themselves after their White counterparts in an effort to prove themselves valuable members of society. Further, it was not uncommon for the middle-class educated elite to show preference for women who were light enough to pass for White. Consequently, the tensions within the community had also to do with colorism, a form of intraracial preference for one group based on skin color. In fact, Alice had a preference for lighter-skinned people whether she was willing to acknowledge it or not.[40]

Ruffin's vision for providing Black women with a space to share their observations was probably influenced by her own biracial background as the daughter of a White English mother and a Martiniquean father; she was unwilling to accept racial boundaries. Though she aspired to form an interracial organization, the Women's Era Club remained a Black woman's club. Ruffin intended for African American women to strengthen their voice and to have the needs of the race, especially those of women, recognized beyond the local levels. She would work to convince Black women that they had the power to advance their social status by agitating for policies and practices that would improve their circumstances for the better. Cash observes, "Prominent black club leaders believed that the myths of black female promiscuity would impede race; advancement and progress."[41] Highly influenced by violent crimes that were meant to terrorize African Americans in the South and left Black families fractured, women took up the charge of speaking out against such crimes, namely lynching. Ida B. Wells-Barnett, as her biographer Paula Giddings has established, was tired of the brutal treatment of Black men who were accused of raping White women. Her work, "Southern Horrors" and "Red Record," not only recorded arrests, racial violence, and consensual interracial relationships between Black men and White women but also the life-threatening lengths that she was willing to go through to expose Southern ways.

Wells-Barnett's activist work made her vulnerable to threats to her life and to what was just as important—her reputation as a moral woman. She and other women who were involved in the anti-lynching campaign saw a direct correlation between lynching Black men and the ways in which Black women were Villainized as immoral. Infuriated by her well-known successful anti-lynching campaign, the male president of the Missouri Press Association published an open letter accusing Black women of "having no sense of virtue and of being altogether without character."[42] When Ida B. Wells confronted the minister who publicly labeled her as immoral and had him publicly renounce his impugning remarks, Ruffin responded by calling for Black women to organize, resulting in the local Black women's clubs joining together to mount a national movement poised to uplift various segments of Black life in America.

The letter's attack on the virtue of a Black woman was representative of a long line of attacks that were meant to control Blacks by calling into question their sexual morals. Though largely focused on violence toward men, Wells-Barnett's work exposed the sexual abuse of African American women by men in the New South. While African American men were commonly accused of raping White women, giving cause to pull them from their homes or jail cells by angry White mobs and lynched, African American women who accused White men of rape were not provided with protection. Chrystal Feimster identifies a rape lynch narrative that Wells-Barnett uncovered through her investigative journalism: "the chaste and dependent white women; the sexually violent black man; the immoral and unredeemable black woman; and the honorable and civilized white man."[43] These players are present in several cases where Black women are sexually violated and receive no recourse for the treatment. In one such case, Maggie Reese accused Lem Thompson Jr. of raping her. When Black men organized to confront the man, they were threatened by the mass organization of White men. A jury found Thompson not guilty. In the same town, two Black brothers accused of raping a White woman were lynched by a White mob.[44] Alice would learn the various ways that sex and race collided in the South.

She and the other women agreed that one way to prove that Black women were respectable women was through their public deeds. Black women carried the burden of uplifting the race by implementing strategies to improve and solidify its moral image. As Deborah Gray White discusses, "Since, in their minds, 'a race could rise no higher than its women,' they felt that when they improved the condition of black women, they necessarily improved the condition of the race."[45] By the time the National Association of Colored Women emerged, Black women's clubs had formed in the deep South, the Northeast, and Midwest and had been forming since post-antebellum. Surely the development of clubs on local levels and the development of a national organization were due to the fact that there had been 2,018 separate incidents of lynching, resulting in the deaths of over 2,000 African American men, women, and children between 1880 and 1930.[46] Perhaps if the women could succeed in changing public perception about Black people, they may be able to save lives. Of course, taking on this responsibility for advancing a respectability agenda to refine the moral foundation of an entire race of people meant that when someone did not measure up Black women were to blame. Their desperate hope that they could solve the problems of racism by teaching the targets of the violence to act according to the aggressor's expectations would only prove how deeply entrenched racism was in the American psyche. Unfortunately, Alice Dunbar-Nelson would spend most of her life responding to these ideal standards one way or another.

In New Orleans, she promoted living a respectable life as a "sermon" she "preached" to her male peers in New Orleans, even, as I will discuss, as she wrote about the problems women faced in their attempt to comply with the ideas of respectability. In an address to Mount Zion Church on October 28, 1895, she began by telling the men, "It is not my intention to preach any sermon to-night; you can hear one of them any Sunday night that you choose to spend in church, and sermons too often are unheeded."[47] She then went on to admonish the "single" men about their habits of spending money that they had earned from hard work. Their behavior was an offense: "But it is of this life that we concern ourselves. It is of our actions here, our position among the nations, our reputation as a people, and our characters as individuals that she should think."[48] If they would not accept their responsibility to the race, they would fall short of their Christian duties as men of God. Ending with an appeal to them as Christians, she prodded, "A perfect life on this earth means a more perfect one beyond; a useful existence here, means a more happy one there."[49] Alice's shared vision of an acceptable Black man—one that even God approved of—gave insight into how she envisioned and hoped to shape the race. Good Black men were needed for respectable Black women. She asked them to do their part.

Her invitation to speak at this church meant that she was recognized and respected as a woman in New Orleans who had something to say that should be heard and taken seriously. As a model for morality, she was given a kind of authority that she relied on to make her appeal to young Black men to pursue and build a life that would make God proud. Alice, at the age of twenty, spoke with confidence that would sustain her throughout her life. Regardless of her audience, she would reveal a kind of honesty that she felt would sway the listeners to see a perspective that she hoped would result in advancing their position in society. If the men saved their money, they would strengthen Black communities by buying and owning their own houses, for instance. Further, this was only part of what she argued for. She also told the men to not simply work but to develop their "wonderful brains stored in [their] head."[50] Rather, they should buy books and use the time spent on going to "picnics" to read. She offered to them Booker T. Washington as an example of an exemplary Black man. She ended by reviewing her main points: "Put money into your pockets, books into your homes, contempt for gew-gaws into your hearts."[51] While we hear her voice as a teacher, we also learn how she used this opportunity to present to them the kind of man that she found attractive and would seek to marry (three times).

Such characteristics of respectable Black people were being "preached" in one form or another across the country and Alice's circle of women would lead the charge in providing tools for their generation and the next to move as far from the effects of slavery as possible. In 1895, thirty-six Black women's clubs unified under the leadership of Margaret Murray Washington, who was president of the Tuskegee Women's Club, to form the National Federation of Afro-American Women (NFAAW) at a convention in 1895. Perhaps, not surprisingly, the women were not always welcomed among Whites. Black representation at the Atlanta Exposition of 1895 (known for Booker T. Washington's famous "Cast Down Your Bucket Where You Are" speech) was not allowed in the main exhibition, which occurred later in the year. *TWE* articles show that a great deal of debate ensued surrounding the racial restrictions, clearly an affront to these educated women who were striving to prove themselves worthy of respect. Alice reported that the PWC participated in the exposition because they believed,

The only way to convince our friends on the other side that we could do anything was to show them, and here was an excellent chance to show as individuals and members of a race popularly supposed to be unable to do anything but subsist upon the charity of others. There is no doubt but that this exposition, like the one in Chicago, if not representing the negroes would be censured for it by them, and when a disposition is shown by the commissioners to grant space, the usual kick is made. The upshot of it all was that the club gave its decision not only to countenance the negro building but to make an exhibit there.[52]

Her resolve echoed a stance that would remain prominent in her life, that despite the obstacles, a Black woman must continue to move forward and to use her voice in defense of her stance wherever possible, and, above all else, remain self-sufficient.

A year later, Ida B. Wells-Barnett of Chicago, Victoria Earle Matthews of New York, Margaret Murray Washington (who almost always went by Mrs. Booker T. Washington), and Mary Church Terrell came together in Washington, DC to form one organization, the National Association of Colored Women (NACW) in July 1896. At the convention, tensions between the regions and ambitions for leadership emerged, but they also had much to share as evidenced by their reports. Alice's name appears as a voting member and presenter of a paper titled, "The Afro-American Child and Patriotism."[53] Her presentation demonstrated that there was an intellectual engagement component that was typical of the local meetings where committees gave reports on local, national, and international issues related to women and Blacks. At one point, they passed resolutions on the "legal status of women and girls," which called for each club to "look into the legal status of the women and children in their respective states" and resolved to acknowledge the death of Harriet Beecher Stowe, an "inspired woman."[54] During the Wednesday elections, Mary Church Terrell was elected president[55] and Alice Ruth Moore became recording secretary of the NACW.[56] Alice made connections with these women that would remain significant to her once she left New Orleans and moved to the northeast where she continued her activist work.

By all accounts, the PWC made a significant impact in New Orleans when it opened the Phillis Wheatley Sanitarium and Training School for Negro Nurses on October 31, 1896, with "seven beds and five students" to "relieve the suffering and supply the needy."[57] In a report, chapter president Williams acknowledged that two doctors volunteered to work at the Sanitarium and to help with the training of the eight women, three more than had been reported in the paper, who had registered for training. Another note of success was that they received an appropriation from the city for $240.00 annually. However, giving money could not accurately solve the inhumane problems of discrimination. Williams emphasized, "Our colored doctors are not allowed to practice in our city hospitals not even in the colored wards." Prior to this, the young Alice Moore reported that questions were asked about allowing Black doctors to practice in Charity Hospital; however, they were "urged" to continue to do their work to endow the special ward of the hospital. Alice probes the subtle irony of placing a restriction on Black doctors but accepting the money of "colored" people to help those folks that the doctors could not treat. Given the fact that Charity Hospital was founded to serve the health needs of the poor and "colored" who were not "received" elsewhere, Alice's decision to place the refusal and acceptance in the same sentence illuminates the negotiations of nineteenth-century Southern Black folk, both the professionals and the working class, all of whom found themselves in social need, a fact her witty tone cannot mask. Perhaps not coincidently, the Club's Sanitarium opened the year following her *TWE* article and employed Blacks who helped Blacks. Still reeling from the impact of slavery and in the year of the 1896 *Plessy v. Ferguson* Supreme Court ruling which established separate but equal, PWC members opened this facility to address the vital need for health care among African Americans as well as the need to educate African American female nurses. The New Orleans club members were fully aware of national conversations and needs in Black communities as represented by their local projects. A year prior to the facility's opening, Lulu Johnson, in a different article published in *TWE*, argued that Black women who chose nursing careers became compassionate heroes, doing the work that doctors, family, and friends would not do: "The doctor has written his last prescription; the nurse has given the last dose of medicine. In the still hours of the night[,] the patient realizes her condition. She turns to the nurse for a ray of hope or comfort, and the last look on earth from some loving wife, mother or child is given to the faithful, patient nurse."[58] To support their efforts, PWC members made donations and hosted fundraisers.[59] But it was not enough. Due to lack of funding, the school was taken over by New Orleans University in 1897.[60]

Alice's work in the Black clubwomen's movement is inextricably bound, and remains so, to her exploration of various forms of writing. As an emerging writer, she served as "Newspaper and Current Events" chairperson and as the New Orleans sales agent for *TWE*. Surviving articles provide insight on the PWC's implementation of activities designed to bring awareness to their concerns as Black women interested in bettering the community. Notably, Alice's work with this paper documents her early years as a journalist and activist. Between 1894 and 1895, she appears to be one of three women of the South (Virginia and Texas being the other two states represented) who contributed to the paper on a regular basis. In her work readers find a more personal approach, as if talking on the phone with a girlfriend in comparison to the more formal approach of fellow activist Mary Church Terrell, who reported from Washington, DC. Alice reported on teachers' training and arts programs; questioned Black people's practice of segregating themselves in Catholic churches; admonished the practice of discriminating against Black doctors while taking money from Black donors; praised her alma mater, Straight University, for its accomplishments; and reported the activities of the PWC. Her creative writing style emerges in these articles, and with it, the nuances that would become hallmarks of her activist career—interest in politics, concern with racial climate, and the social status of women. At times, her articles showed a comedic style that is common in her letters to Paul Laurence Dunbar and in her diaries, while probing serious social matters.

Two areas of interest emerge in her columns that remained prominent in her body of work throughout her career. One area is her developing feminist perspective and the second is her love of New Orleans. In one article, she touched on multiple subjects focused solely on the life and experiences of Black New Orleanians, despite the fact that she was writing on behalf of the PWC. Her central interest is not exclusively on the work of the committees but on multiple aspects of the community as one would see or experience them—happening simultaneously in multiple spaces across time. For an audience of Black women, she celebrated the ability of women, as seen in her description of how the PWC memorialized Frederick Douglass: "Of course there had been memorial services and memorial services piled up in honor of the champion of our people, but there had been none like this, where everything, even down to the pumping of the organ and the ushering of the audience, was *done by women*" (italics mine).[61] Even focusing on a revered leader could not overshadow the talents of Black women.

Through her clubwoman's perspective, the experiences of the Black citizens of New Orleans were broadcast to readers around the country. In the same article, she mentioned that the Women's Relief Corps required them to offer a prayer "that our husbands, brothers, fathers and sweethearts may do their duty Tuesday as true citizens and men." She immediately dismissed this attention to men, which overtly placed women as subordinate to them, and began the next sentence by raising awareness of how the "colored women" had the power to affect the political climate. Women did not have the right to vote, but Black women had an impact on leveraging the Black vote, resulting in the "opening of a new public school."

Even at a young age, Alice saw the importance of placing Black women in conversation with important issues, such as politics, class, and education. Notably, her approach was not to pit women against men, but she probed how women could work to support the work of men, each other, and the entire race. What effected one, she showed in the May article, affected all. This is a tactic she would use years later during her suffrage campaign speeches. She went on to note, in the rather long article, that a "committee of men and women," obviously a committee not directly affiliated with the PWC, worked for four years to send a young man to Germany to study music. Her attention to him culminated by announcing his death and the impact it had on his family and the community. Eddie Moore (no known relation) exemplified respectability and he represented the hopes of the Black community to put its best forward: "all members of the race must feel a part" of the loss. The last two paragraphs of the article recorded the rehearsal of a drama and pending weddings scheduled to occur when the school term ended. "Next to politics the most talked of thing is weddings and wedding garb and gossip," she reported. Having a husband was not only greatly encouraged by religious denominations but also by presses that were organs for their beliefs. Societal expectations that women should marry presented challenges to emerging feminist ideas that had influenced the women of the Reconstruction Era and their sisters of the Black clubwomen's circles.

During the first twenty years of her life, she learned from older Black women how to build coalitions that were meant to change the society and advance the social position of Black folks. Most of all, she formed an ideal of what a good Black woman should be. Only experience would augment this thinking, but during the late Victorian age, with other Black women, she envisioned the future of a well-positioned Black race and did the work to make the vision a reality.

2

The New Negro Woman in Alice's Early Literature

The period 1894–6 was most certainly a pivotal time for Alice when her opinions and interests in race, class, and gender received national attention. During those years, not only was she involved with the Phillis Wheatley Club (PWC) and participated in its national affiliations, she also emerged as a talented writer when she released *Violets and Other Tales*. Several pieces, published in various journals, captured the attention of the African American literary elite, including Paul Laurence Dunbar, who had read her poetry in the *Boston Monthly Review* and became enamored by a picture of her in *The Women's Era*. Alice's collection of short fiction, sketches, and poems spoke from her unique Southern vantage point. Adenike Marie Davidson observes that she "was praised for her traditional lyric verses and is said to have made competent attempts at the short story genre."[1] In these, she did not indulge the common aspects of "ideal domesticity" as identified by Claudia Tate in reference to Alice's peers. In contrast, her short stories critique "ideal domesticity." A common ending of her "romances" or male-female relationships leave in question the fate of the woman. As a result, her ability to navigate respectability politics and to set her own definition of self as an individual is a prominent concern in her work. It must be noted that any relationship is usually in question; why they got together or why they are still together haunts the short stories as other lingering questions emerge. Usually death has had some impact on the woman's future or fate, leaving her vulnerable to further exploitation, and leaving in question her ability to uphold respectability standards. To be sure, Alice's two selves merged in her fiction: the young Black activist met the romantic writer.

Among themes of love, class disparities, and exploitation, *Violets and Other Tales* is expressive of the debates women of the era were having. Davidson observes further, "Dunbar-Nelson's collection can be viewed as an early attempt at coalescing both the emerging New Negro and the New Woman."[2] Alice wrote about women who attempted to integrate desire for a romantic relationship and a respectable public image, an acceptable pursuit, with their move toward a professional life, unacceptable after marriage. Black women, like White women, were tasked with the influences of the elitist New Woman. Anastasia Curwood states, "contemporary writers invented an archetype called the New Woman, which referred to a female individual who advocated woman suffrage and sexual freedom (or the emasculation of men, according to detractors)."[3] In an attempt to defend New Women, who were criticized for their attempts to more fully integrate into a decidedly male-centered society, in 1897, Lillian Bell described the New Woman as a woman "whom you wish you knew."[4] She was clever, humorous, interesting, and therefore not prone to staying at home too much. Bell described her further as "silk-lined, nearly always pretty, always a lady, and always good."[5] More importantly, what made her "new" was that she was aware of what made her interesting: "she has opened her eyes and has begun to see the value of the simple, common, everyday truths which lie nearest to her."[6] She was not the woman who neglected her husband and lets her "children grow up like ruffians"; there was nothing new about these women, according to Bell, as they have always existed.[7] Bell notes further that they had a very distinct place in society that would make them unquestionably discernable in social circles:

> They are not poor girls either, who are doing these things. They are not obligated to earn their daily bread. They are the daughters of the rich. They are well travelled, cultured, delicately reared girls. . . . I glory in the new woman in that so often she is rich and beautiful.[8]

Being wealthy meant that "she can support herself, so that in case her riches take wings she need not be forced to drudge at uncongenial employment, or to marry for a home, she will be more particular than ever in the kind of man she marries."[9] Although Black middle-class women strove to exhibit these characteristics, the additional experience of financial independence for the reasons stated proved problematic for some Black women to attain. In the case of Alice and Leila, their mother's own vision for the advancement of her daughters moved them into a growing middle class determined by education and the possibility of financial stability. Alice's work reflects her responses to the New Woman, namely the challenges of respectability as defined by society.

For her part, Alice presented complicated characters who mirrored her own personal attempts to live the lifestyle that Bell described. In fact, Alice, who was often in a state of financial instability, did all she could to present herself to the public as a woman whose finances matched her level of education and her intellect. In Alice, spectators found a woman who was "humorous," "interesting," and "nearly always pretty," at least by her account and some of the doting men in her life. But she was a Black woman, the daughter of a former slave and a man who seemed not to have married her mother; and this presented challenges as racial history's impact on the present status of Black women could not be overlooked. As early feminists, the New Negro Women supported both the idea of women working outside the home, through volunteering in their communities and preparing those who "entered waged labor."[10]

However, some Black women who considered themselves middle class openly admonished the feminist aspects of the New Woman ideology. Seeing New Women as a "fad," an unnamed author of an article titled "The New Woman" dismissed the relevancy of New Women: "There is not the slightest probability that the great mass of women will forget their womanhood."[11] The writer takes on the idea that the home could be disrupted if the woman was not there to tend to the needs of her husband and children. She could not possibly work successfully in the home and outside of it. Alice, however, disagreed.

While African American clubwomen tried to follow some of the prescriptions that Bell asserts, race was a factor they could not overlook. Expanding the idea of the New Woman to include race became important to Black women who were already working outside their homes. Before the New Negro Movement of the twentieth century, in 1895, Margaret Washington, wife of Booker T. Washington, identified the emerging class of educated Black women as New Negro Women. "Like New Women, New Negro Women enacted poised, bourgeois womanhood," Curwood observes.[12] What made them even more distinct was their commitment to "uplifting the race as a whole."[13] In her speech "The New Negro Woman," Washington states, "We are a race of servants, not in the low sense of this word, but in the highest and purest sense, and, in our serving let us keep these beautiful lines of the servant of all women as our guide."[14] In other words, serving those community members in need elevated the women morally and socially.

Alice's fellow clubwomen gave voice to the balance Black women hoped to achieve between race and gender. First, Washington addressed middle-class Black women who felt that service should be done at home. Washington advanced a perspective that placed the community and family ahead of the woman in an effort to preserve the sanctity of the race, thereby uplifting the race to a place of social prominence and respectability. However, marriage was as important to these women as it was to privileged White women, but having an identity that was specifically theirs and contributing to the advancement of the race by helping members of their community was, at times, more important than marriage. Some of these New Negro Women, once widowed or separated from their husbands, never remarried; instead, they committed themselves to education and social activism, proving their efforts to exert more control over their careers and pursuits. Secondly, she established class distinctions—servant class as lowly and the middle class as high and pure. This latter class, then, was responsible for improving the lower class. Thus, movement from the lowly to the pure was possible in one generation, as Alice and Leila hoped to prove.

New Negro Women advanced their voice and made valiant efforts to define themselves, which challenged the limiting notions of true womanhood that women must be pious, submissive, pure, and domestic. Of the cult of true womanhood's four virtues—piety, purity, submissiveness, and domesticity— this emerging class of Black female activists and professionals struggled with the virtue of submission. If submission meant sacrificing a woman's right to define herself by engaging in activities she chose, Black clubwomen were unable to fully comply. A description of the New Woman from the Black woman's perspective had to be inclusive of those women who worked to support themselves and/or their families as they struggled to be "pure" in a society that historically did not acknowledge Black women's bodies as her own. Asserting their right to define the spaces they would occupy in America, these women sought to advance the race use their college degrees to work and marry suitable men. Extending from her personal life, Alice teased out these challenges in her literature.

Alice's first anthology *Violets and Other Tales* (1895) reflects and engages these debates about positions of Black women. As her literary debut, the collection is the first time she presented the concerns of her personal narrative—a history that speaks of the silence associated with Black women's attempts to survive while maintaining a reputation as respectable—an issue that ushered her toward activism in the Black clubwomen's movement. In it we find women grappling with attaining satisfaction through liberation and control of their bodies but also with a sense of themselves that is not deterred by societal critiques and criticism.

Alice's "The Woman," a sketch that highlights a timely question posed at a meeting about the role of women, emerges as a clear statement, by clubwomen, in opposition to forms of gender oppression. It begins, "The literary manager of the club arose" to answer the question: "Mr.—, will you please tell us your opinion upon the question, whether woman's chances for matrimony are increased or decreased when she becomes man's equal as a wage earner?" A debate among the women and men in the room ensues, but the response comes from an unidentified "I." One of the flaws of this collection is that, at times, who is speaking, is not clear. Perhaps this is what Sylvanie Williams meant in her preface of the book when she stated, "There is much in this book that is good; much that is crude; some that is poor: but all give that assurance of something great and noble."[15] Readers may assume that the interjection is that of Alice's who would have attended such meetings where there would have been discussion around questions regarding the hope of professional women to receive equality in the workforce and respect from potential suitors.

The unnamed woman's challenge of pursuing a successful career and marriage is a major theme of the short sketch. While the question is about women's salaries, the response does not address whether women will become men's financial equal; the answer focuses on the ideal woman who is, presumably, a wage earner. Providing a description of the ideal future woman, Alice prophesized the woman who could reach a level of success: "she may preside over conventions, brandish her umbrella at board meetings, tramp the streets soliciting subscriptions, wield the blue pencil in an editorial sanctum, hammer a type-writer, . . . or wield the scalpel in a dissecting room."[16] A woman who has any of these positions is also described as "independent, happy, free and easy."[17] She can travel when she wants and has her meals prepared for her. What is missing, however, from this picture is the "manly embrace."[18] Alice gives the description of the woman's life in nearly five and a half paragraphs, but the actual response lies within the last sentence. The full sentence reads:

> Well, she may preside over conventions, brandish her umbrella at board meetings, tramp the streets soliciting subscriptions, wield the blue pencil in an editorial sanctum, hammer a type-writer, smear her nose with ink from a galley full of pied type, lead infant ideas through the tortuous mazes of c-a-t and r-a-t, plead at the bar, or wield the scalpel in a dissecting room, yet when the right moment comes, she will sink as gracefully into his manly embrace, throw her arms as lovingly around his neck, and cuddle as warmly and sweetly to his bosom as her little sister who has done nothing else but think, dream, and practice for that hour.[19]

Alice's sudden shift from the successful professional woman whose ideal life makes up the bulk of the sketch, to her movement to a man, to a comparison of that man to a little sister suggests the author's reluctance to offer an answer to the important social question about women's quest for acceptance in the workplace. Respectability standards required that a woman marry and then surrender the financial responsibilities to her husband. It was not uncommon for Black clubwomen, especially Alice Moore, to struggle with this expectation. However, there is a subtle implication that a woman's desire to work outside the home does not replace her desire for the love and support of a man. Alice addressed arguments against wage-earning women that maintained a husband's role as a man would be weakened if a woman earned a wage and was not completely available to him. Certainly, it would be a question she grappled with during her courtship and marriage to Dunbar and her last marriage to Robert Nelson.

Exploring social expectations through her writing was a primary goal for young Alice. The clubwomen, as professional women, had a dilemma. On one hand, if they were married, there would be little chance of having to explain away their sexual desires. On the other hand, these women would have been subject to the dominance of their husbands. Wives' roles were significantly influenced and largely defined by their husbands and, in some cases, their fathers, who often wanted them to remain at home. Paula Giddings writes of the activists-wives Ida B. Wells-Barnett, Margaret Murray Washington, and Mary Church Terrell and their experiences balancing a career and family at a time when middle-class married women were expected to stay home. Giddings notes, "All three had to resolve the conflicts between what they wanted for themselves as women and what middle-class society expected of them as women."[20] In other words, theirs was a struggle with trying to attain what activist and cultural critic Audre Lorde calls an erotic life—one that is fulfilling on multiple levels. As Lorde describes it: "a measure between the beginnings of our sense of self and the chaos of our strongest feelings. It is an eternal sense of satisfaction."[21] Indeed, a public fight for equal rights met with resistance in the personal women's lives. Terrell's father did not speak to her for a year when she returned to work, according to Giddings. Booker T. Washington initially did not support his wife's decision to teach. And, once she became a wife and mother, Wells-Barnett retired multiple times from public activism. How did the professional goals of the nineteenth-century feminist who sought social equality balance with the expectations of Victorian era-inspired respectability? Hull observes:

> Dunbar-Nelson is writing in a transitional era—when Victorian ideas maintained force, but when social and legal changes were widening women's lives and increasing their participation in paid labor. Work outside the home was still felt to detract from the true femininity and was seen as temporary/secondary. As a young, informed, progressive black woman, Dunbar-Nelson reflects the contemporary debate, but also her own personal-historical experiences of work and women's roles.[22]

"The Woman" certainly speaks to the fear of women trading feminine desires for companionship with social rights. Beyond the local color and sentimental romances, Alice's early work soothed fears by revealing the desires of the woman to have both companionship and a career, as she also subversively contested patriarchal restrictions.

A compliment to "The Woman" is "A Story of Vengeance." Again, a woman's voice is prominent as she too answers a question: "Why did I never marry?" Surely her dilemma is whether pursuing a career meets the limiting standards of respectability. Prior to posing the question she admits to her friend that she is "nothing but a lonely woman."[23] If "The Woman" provides a broad description of a successful woman, the narrator here is a specific example derived from the composite. After her five-month relationship with a man ends when he leaves her for a former lover, she observes, "Fortune, showered every blessing, save one, on my path."[24] When the lover returns and asks her to take him back, she dismisses him. At the last second, she accepts him, but his pride will not allow him to return to her. The short story reads as another chapter with different characters asking the same question, neither of which suggests a race. Alice presents the dilemma: "I gave up all my most ambitious plans and cherished schemes, because he disliked women whose names were constantly in the mouth of the public."[25] Alice's miserable, but professionally successful, female narrator does not find the man that the narrator of the woman says she should find, one who "respects the independent one and admires her."[26] Sacrifices, it seems, would have to be made for women who chose the New Negro Woman way of life, especially if their only focus was on attaining a career and marrying.

New Negro Women had those ambitions and others in mind. Building on the idea that there were two classes of women, the ones who had attained an education and those who needed stability, Alice's collection shows the diversity of the women and their vulnerabilities. Margaret Murray Washington's 1895 speech to the educated Black female "servants" of the First National Conference of Colored Women of America makes note of the relationship between the women that

> shall divide the negro race of women into that class which has had opportunity to improve themselves mentally, physically, morally, spiritually, and financially, and that class who, because of the cruelty of the master for more than two centuries—the master, who thirty years ago, turned his slave mothers away without giving them a single idea of the beauty of home life, a single idea of the responsibility of womanhood, wifehood, or citizenship—are our inferiors. This latter class is overwhelmed in its numbers, mighty in its strength if only these numbers and this strength can be lifted.[27]

Washington, as did many of her educated peers, believed that certain Southern Black women were deficient in meeting respectability. If the race was to advance, it was up to the women to be at the center of the advancement by helping one another. Alice was cognizant that class distinctions meant the difference between having protection from exploitation and falling prey to it. These were personal issues for her, as the daughter of a father known only to the family, she was a woman who seemed always conscious of using her writing to exorcise the shame associated with her parentage. Alice's fiction consistently showed her attention toward those who were most vulnerable. Specifically, her short stories "In Our Neighborhood" and "Little Miss Sophie" illuminate what became of women who did not have the support of other more fortunate Black women, who could not comply with respectability politics, and who were not New Women or even New Negro Women. Further, her protagonists represent women who falter under the weight of attaining respectability. They were those who could "be forced to drudge at uncongenial employment, or to marry for a home."[28] As middle-class women, their social status also meant that they were expected to practice the ways of genteel respectable ladies. For example, women were expected to speak proper English with clear diction, learn to manage the affairs of the home, and, above all else, never engage in premarital sex. These short stories overtly depict the women the New Negro Women sought to help—those whose values are compromised in a society that does not respect Black women.

"In Our Neighborhood" depicts a family that attempts to rise up the social ladder of New Orleans. A story that anticipates the porch storytelling of Zora Neale Hurston's fiction, this work features women who spy on the Hart family and speak about what they can only know from their obsessive observations of the family's social gatherings and the women's dresses. The Harts show no concern or regard for their neighbors' interest in their lives; if they are aware that they are the topic of conversation, they appear nonplussed as they go on with their plans without extending invitations to their parties or explanations of the purpose of their festivities. By the end of the short story, the father has died and is buried. His death causes the neighbors to ask who will care for the family that obviously depended solely on his salary. Though she has no voice and is seen through the eyes of the neighborhood women and children, Lillian, the eldest child, appears as the focus of attention. Thus, the family's stability may depend on her.

Lillian's matriarch-centered family in a patriarch-centered society is seeking to redefine its social status, and Lillian's role as a young maiden is to help them achieve her mother's goal. Like many of Alice's characters, Lillian is not specifically "raced," but there are clues that she is of African and European ancestry. An observant voice describes her as curling her "auburn (red)" hair with paper. As Caroline Gebhard observes of the author's use of race, "While Dunbar-Nelson often presents racial markers subtly, her purpose is not to erase racial distinctions altogether but to present them in ways that resist racial stereotyping and highlight the oppressive systems in which such distinctions have meaning."[29] Lillian's features closely resemble those of Alice Ruth Moore when she was a child. Other clues mark the daughter as "colored" in New Orleans. Later, a child remarks that she saw Lillian with a "yellow-haired man"; her attention to the color of his hair and the child's mother's piqued curiosity marks the man as White or at least as a foreign presence in their neighborhood.[30] His presence with this family grabs the attention of the nosy neighbors, especially the child, who also overhears him say that he will take care of her.

Mrs. Hart, whose first name we do not know, does not work like the other neighborhood women, such as Mrs. Tuckley identified as "the dress-maker." She relies on the husband whom she seems to have little respect for, but she understands that he plays an integral role in the family's social status. When he enters the home after a day of work and asks for dinner, she points him to a piece of ham and bread in the cupboard. He is not a priority in the plans she has to elevate the family from the status of the neighborhood to the Avenue, where the best entertainment takes place. His voice is also muted and relegated to how people react to his presence. In addition to his wife directing him to the cupboard to feed himself, readers see him briefly standing in front of the mantle during the party and telling a story. Later, his family ignores him when he makes a comment about the success of the party. It would seem that the only time he receives respect is from the young male partygoers who listen to his storytelling. Mr. Hart embodies both absence and presence. His family appears entirely uninterested in him, other than his ability to provide for the family with a job of working-class prestige as evidenced when Mrs. Hart shows pride to the man who comes to the house and asks if her husband works at the mill. His position as supervisor and ability to talk about the machinist work gives her a sense that he possesses something more than the ordinary. But, it is this position that finds him unexpectedly dead, the result of an accident at work. His absence leaves the family's future in peril.

A more defined idea of Mr. Hart—how well he was respected by his peers and what he contributed to their lives—surfaces at his wake. If the people are happier about a wake than they are a wedding, death speaks louder than life for this family. Mr. Hart's sudden demise carries the weight of either catapulting this family into financial obscurity or elevating it. It depends on the results of the coupling that occurs at the parties. To be sure, there is a strong implication that the purpose of the parties is to find a mate for the Creole daughters. Lillian and her sister wear dresses that attract the attention of Mrs. Tuckley who remarks:

> I always did wonder how them Harts do keep up. Why, them girls dress just as fine as any lady on the Avenue and that there Lillian wears real diamond ear-rings. 'Pears mighty, mighty funny to me, and Lord the airs they do put on! Holdin' up their heads like nobody's good enough to speak to.[31]

In a statement of foreshadowing, she remarks further, "speak about anybody, but mark my word, girls that cut up capers like them Hartses' girls never come to any good."[32] Mrs. Tuckley serves as the communal voice by questioning the girls' actions rather than their choices.

Alice makes a subtle statement about women's social position. The racially obscure woman represents the precarious and fragile life experience of Black women who relied entirely, either by choice or by expectation, on a man to provide for them. Mrs. Hart's extreme interests in "putting on airs" to impress people, outside her social circle, may be offensive to her neighbors, but when her husband is gone, who will give her children what they need to survive? On the other hand, Mrs. Hart seems lost in the days of old, when women were taught to think of elevating themselves based on the status of a husband, or in the case of Lillian, a male lover. In fact, it would seem that Mrs. Hart is involved in arranging opportunities for her daughters to meet affluent White men.[33] Joan Martin finds in the early 1800s, "Each mother's aim was to engage an unmarried [white] Creole gentleman as 'Protector' for her daughter."[34] As noted ealier, Alice's mother may have engaged in such a relationship. However, by the 1890s. the emerging feminist thought shied away from dependence on men and shifted toward capabilities of the female self. Mr. Hart's death, then, is a chance for a rebirth for the women to consider how they can redefine themselves and be an example to the junior male Harts, who have no names but are presumed to be the next generation. While it is not clear how much support, if any, Alice's mother received from Alice's father, it is certain that she encouraged her daughters to seek social elevation as they both attended college then pursued teaching careers and married men regarded as respectable by the Black middle class.

Black women's struggles to maintain a sense of moral purity or respectability in the South were expressed in venues beyond fiction. A *Southwestern Christian Advocate* article, published in New Orleans during Alice's days of activism, recorded the concerns the community had about Black women's ability to stay pure and pious. One author advocated support for Black women to have access to admirable employment, such as teaching positions that would "raise her to that degree of independence that would leave her reasonably sure of securing a comfortable living."[35] Some Black girls and young women were still subjected to sexual exploitation by wealthy White men. Consequently, the woman's lack of independence and limited choices, especially in the South where customs prevailed, left her vulnerable to "those who have the advantage of her in wealth, education, and the support of public sentiment: against whom she has no redress."[36] Alice's characters represent the vulnerable African American women and Creole women with African ancestry who were subjected to racial restrictions; consequently, at times, their only recourse for survival was the giving of their bodies at the risk of defying the moral social codes of the day.

"Little Miss Sophie" makes an even stronger statement about the exploitation of Black women of mixed ancestry by the "yellow-haired men" who enter the neighborhood. Since Alice published "Little Miss Sophie," in both her first and second volumes (*The Goodness of St. Rocque and Other Stories*) of literature, we can consider how the story continued to resonate (at least with her) from 1895 to 1899. Miss Sophie is a Creole woman who has had a relationship with a White man, Neale. She is not a woman of means, but her lover is and his standing in this position depends on Miss Sophie. She overhears a conversation that reveals that her former lover has lost one fortune and will lose an inheritance if he does not provide proof of his identity. Kristina Brooks observes, "The fact that it is the white man in the story who has a 'difficulty of identification' typically experienced by the light-skinned African American citizen and illustrated so clearly by the characters of Sister Josepha and Miss Sophie, whose unknown or hidden racial heritage is the source of their tragedies."[37] Miss Sophie is in a difficult, but powerful position of influence over a White man's future as she is in possession of the proof, the ticket to a ring she pawned for money. The poor woman determines that she will take on extra work to retrieve the ring. Consequently, she dies. E. Frances White sees sacrifice and work as inherent in respectability politics: "The politics of respectability was also a discourse within the black community, demanding the end to open expressions of sexuality and shows of 'laziness.'"[38] Miss Sophie's story is an example of this discourse.

Race, class, and gender collide in this short story. Miss Sophie is an unmarried woman who loves a man, but she was only one of his love affairs. According to what she overhears the men say, the unnamed Creole woman took it hard and he "went off and forgot the woman."[39] African ancestry makes her susceptible to being marked as impure and, therefore, disposable. Miss Sophie's "tainted" body means a loss of its social worth, except to use her skills as a seamstress to maintain her meager living in a rented room. Alice contrasts her sewing, a skill expected of ladies if they were to be proper mates, with her lost (in religious and social perspectives) sexual virtue. Dressed in black, she sits on a streetcar, a poor woman, unwanted and unseen. The men's casual discussion of a woman who has been mistreated by one of their circle further illustrates how she has been disregarded and discarded.

It also shows a relationship between Neale's privilege and his actions as they further reveal that he is a careless, irresponsible individual who relies on his family's wealth to sustain him. His privilege does not guarantee his claims as heir. Therefore, Neale must prove himself the proper inheritor of the estate, probably the result of other possible heirs who may be of mixed ancestry that the Southern state would not recognize as genetics alone are insufficient. Miss Sophie's "Creole blood" marks her as "too proud," according to the narrator, to give him the ticket and leave it up to him to retrieve the ring and save his fortune.[40] Her love for him proves to be more certain than his family's riches and the history that marks him as privileged and her as dispensable.

Alice uses the Catholic church in this short story and others as a historical place where people pray for forgiveness as the exploitation by White men of African-descended women was acknowledged through baptism and other ceremonies. Such truths consume "Little Miss Sophie" as they did the everyday practices in New Orleans. It begins with Miss Sophie passed out in "a black heap" in front of the Virgin Mary. Alice's craft as a storyteller emerges in the first paragraph as she contrasts the blackness of the female figure to the presumed purity of a White religious female figure. Of this binary, Brooks states, "Exploring color oppression through a consistent motif of dark/white oppositions, Dunbar-Nelson constructs a covert narrative that registers its political import only on those predisposed by their racial or their local identity to decode a black/white binary in terms of race."[41] Neale's rejection of Sophie has made her an outcast and further exacerbated her marginalization in a society that values women's purity, a virtue hardly associated with Black women. She thinks that she is repenting for her relationship with Neale by praying obsessively, fasting (or starving herself), and living the life of a pauper. In sum, she seeks forgiveness for having been with a man who did not honor his commitment to her, which he promised with betrothal of the gold ring. Giving it back may provide her with an opportunity to redeem herself and to move beyond the solitary life she has endured in the little cottage in the Third Ward. The fact that she fails to return the ring before her untimely death suggests that society has no sympathy for a woman who has not met the standards of respectable living.

But Alice will not forgive Neale either; for his exploitation of the vulnerable, he will know what it means to be an outcast, unable to make claims, and unable to look forward to a stable future for we cannot be so sure that the power that has been left in the hands of Miss Sophie's Creole landlady will be gifted to Neale. A mixed-race woman, like Sophie, the landlady knows what it means to be born into a social order that thrives on the exploitation of Black women's bodies. Miss Sophie has redeemed herself by making her body into a virginal sacrifice, but Neale has not proven worthy. If his social worth is determined by his wealth, then he too may suffer from a form of social death stemming from Sophie's physical death.

Alice uses "Little Miss Sophie" to demonstrate the unreasonable expectations of women. Jordan Stouk concludes, "Placage defines sexuality in terms of race, marking Miss Sophie as tragic mulatta, as sentimental stereotype and sexual object, while also, in this case, throwing white subjectivity into crisis."[42] In their failed relationship, we can see the author's concerns with the contradictions between the treatment of women and the expectations of men. Further, Elizabeth West finds, "Here Dunbar-Nelson underscores turn-of-the-century paradigms of marriage and male-female relationships that oftentimes leave women systematic outcasts, particularly Creole women of color in New Orleans society."[43] If the women of this era were punished for not conforming to living a life of piety, then what also occurs is that a woman is unable to explore the erotic, in the sexual sense and the ways in which it leads to self-affirmation. Indeed, Miss Sophie clearly had emotional feelings for Neale, regardless of how he may have felt about her. She was willing to explore these feelings, despite what society may have expected of her. Doing so placed her in a state of vulnerability because she had to know that she would never find certain security with this man who, unlike her, was protected by the laws of Louisiana. Thus, Alice not only points at Neale but also what he represents as the villain in this scenario. Sophie's willingness to explore her own sexual desires is unequally matched by Neale's power to explore his.

Women in Alice Moore's work face societal challenges to living a fulfilling life, one that they hope to define on their own terms. Her women express a desire to be treated with respect. In an effort to combat how women are perceived, Alice sought to unveil the intimate thoughts of women and to show their diversity. Works set specifically in New Orleans reveal the exploitation of women of color, those who may have wanted to seek careers as an educated professional, if only they were not met with the limits placed on them because of their African ancestry and society's tendency to favor men's desires over women's. Living a fulfilling life where a Black woman's desire for respect then proves especially difficult in the segregated South.

Relationships she forms and explores in her writing develop in her personal life as well. Alice's relationship with Paul Laurence Dunbar began when he sent her a letter of introduction. By 1895, Dunbar had earned notoriety as a poet, mostly revered for his dialect rhymes. When the poet approached Alice, he engaged her as a fellow artist. In his first letter to her, he asked her opinion about the literary forms, presumably dialect, in literature made popular by Joel Chandler Harris and others. He followed by offering to "exchange opinions and work with [her]."[44] It took her about a month to respond to the poet's introduction of himself, giving her enough time to make a rather dramatic entrance into his life as she explained that a house fire had delayed her. This is possible, but her additional response that she "did not care" about the arrival of his letter suggests a coyness that would have been expected of a respectable young lady who had been approached by a man. Coyness may also be found in her response to his query where she maintained that she possessed "Not much liking for those writers that wedge the Negro problem and social equality and long dissertations on the Negro in general into their stories." If she was implying that she stayed away from "social equality" issues, she was either not being truthful with herself or with the famous author.

While Alice focused primarily, although not exclusively, on the lives and treatment of women, she shied away from writing overtly about Black experiences in her earlier work. She wrote to Dunbar, who was known for his depictions of Black life, "Somehow when I start a story I always think of my folk characters as simple human beings, not as types or a race or an idea, and I seem to be on more friendly terms with them."[45] Her response to Dunbar's question regarding her feelings about addressing race in literature, her involvement with Creole communities, her light skin, and her depiction of nontraditional "Negro" life have led scholars to question how she felt about her own racial identity.[46] How she felt about her own identity as a Black person who had "a real love for the mother race" is, at times, reflected in her choice to not write about obviously Black characters. First, several of her characters parody her own physical appearance. When she chose to identify the physical features of her characters, she focused her earlier work on the experiences, primarily romantic love, of Creoles or people with auburn-colored hair and white hands—people who looked like her and probably many of the people she knew in her New Orleans community. Second, as for her interest in Creoles of color (being neither Black or White, but more Black than White legally), Alice concentrated on what she saw as unique and interesting about New Orleans. For her, that was Creole culture. Her attendance at Straight College, as well as her work with the PWC, meant that she was often in the company of those who identified as Creoles and other light-skinned African Americans of the emerging educated middle class. Admittedly, Alice was light enough to pass for White and sometimes did. Hull has speculated that Alice Ruth Moore was Creole, but this is unlikely as she never identified herself as being a member of any of the Creole families. Like Dunbar and so many other writers, she wrote about what she knew best and what she probably thought was of interest to her readers. It was not unusual for writers who set their work in South Louisiana, particularly New Orleans, to focus on Creoles.[47] As one Black writer to another, Paul Laurence Dunbar lauded her work in this area as comparable to that of her contemporaries, encouraging her when she appeared to doubt herself: "Your determination to contest Cable for his laurels is a commendable one. Why shouldn't you tell those pretty creole stories as well as he? You have force, the fire and the artistic touch that is so delicate and yet so strong."[48] Like Alice these writers crafted stories that presented Catholic influences, Voodoo, local dialect of French or patois, Mardi Gras, and other wonders that have made New Orleans popular throughout the world. If her life's experiences, hopes, and desires inspired her work, her literature stands as an expression of her life.

Her perspective as a Black woman added another voice to the experience of being from New Orleans. Regardless of the phenotype of the characters, her literature has a strong social message regarding the treatment and experiences of Black women. Alice was a young writer, with a clear reluctance to provide "a dissertation on the Negro problem" and may not have been honest with herself about how she wanted to define her literary intent and purpose. As a young fiction writer, Alice, a woman who lived in the South, was not likely to have taken many risks by making overt comments about Black life in her work. It was one thing to be an activist and to express one's self in a newspaper whose audience had certain expectations, but it was quite another to seem assertive and brassy in her writing, as she would later become. I argue that her women characters stand as representatives—non or slightly racialized women, exploited women in Black, abused ethnic women—for Black women, the most oppressed group of women in the American South. Ann duCille, in her response to critics of Black women writers who developed light-skinned or nonracial characters, observes, "These writers created virtuous, often light-skinned mulatta heroines whose heroine's sexual purity reigned on the page as a rebuttal to the imagining of black women as morally loose and readily accessible."[49] duCille refers to nineteenth-century novelists such as Pauline Hopkins, Francis E. W. Harper, and Harriet Wilson, all of whom depicted the tragic experiences of light-skinned heroines during and after slavery.

Alice was no different from her peers. Further, Alice mastered the short story form as a way to critique the intersections of race, class, and expectations. According to Thadious M. Davis, "she pushed the short story form to express the vibrancy and the complexity that lay below the colorful figures."[50]

Well on her way to developing a career as an activist and writer, the first twenty-two years of her life in New Orleans set the foundation for what was to come. Her life exposed her to the sexual exploitation of Black women, as well as sexual oppression, and the discrimination of Black people. Additionally, she would come to learn more about sexual violation, which would challenge her ideas of romance and love. Such experiences and observations were the foundation of her transformation as a woman who was part of a movement that was highly influenced by Victorian expectations of respectable living. New Orleans at the dawn of the twentieth century allowed her to see the potential of racial advancement despite Blacks dealings with growing racial hostilities and political disenfranchisement. Her concerns and activities became the basis for the issues that would remain prominent in her activist life and would come to define her as a woman with an emerging and evolving voice.

3

Activism, Love, and Pain

In an age when writing letters to lovers and potential spouses was common, Alice's correspondence with Paul Laurence Dunbar tells us, in her own words, how she attempted to fit into the expectations of a post-reconstruction society. Their correspondence began in 1895 and documents the emotional trials of their courtship, engagement (1897), marriage (1898), and final separation (1902). Within these lines are expressions of love, requests for forgiveness, attempts for attention, and pleas for understanding. We also see Alice's perspective as she strove to establish her place in Black middle-class society at a time when purity and submission were expected of Black women, regardless of their educational backgrounds and individual desires. Hopeful, prideful, and fanciful, she embarked on a journey north to advance herself through education and to use that education to help the race and to further develop her career. Yet she found herself in a tragic situation that could have easily been a subject of one of her short stories. Her life and choices show the effects of the politics of respectability and the moral life she tried to uphold.

Letters narrate her complicated relationship with Dunbar. Referencing fiction, Bülent Cercis Tanritanir and Hasan Boynukara note:

> In letter-writing a female protagonist uses the pen not only to confirm herself, not only to bridge the gap between self and other "but often to rewrite the self, presenting a personal self-definition that refutes, replaces, or complements the identity. Her concerns and activities will necessarily echo one or more aspects of feminism(s)—discovering and questioning her own voice and language." (1997, 14)[1]

Although Tanritanir and Boynukara focus on fictional letter writing, I find this quote serves as an appropriate description of Alice Moore's letters. On a whole, her letters track the hope she had for a loving relationship, the sorrow and shame of being in an abusive relationship, and show her remarkable movement past this tragedy, as she further developed her skills as a writer and started the process of reclaiming her independent and liberated voice.

Alice's fears of having to abandon her budding career as a teacher and writer are prominent in *Violets*. In the year that the twenty-year-old Alice published her anthology, she began her relationship with Dunbar. A son of former slaves, Dunbar was born in 1872 in Dayton, Ohio. Through her correspondence with a respected writer who genuinely liked her literature, Alice expressed her passion for writing—its significance as a form of communication and its ability to record thoughts and to inspire emotions. Alice's letters and Dunbar's responses illuminate her maneuvers to maintain her reputation as a pure lady and her development as a woman and writer at the turn of the century. Ultimately, we learn how Alice navigated respectability politics in her status as Dunbar's love interest and how she defined her complex role as writer, activist, and sexual being.

To a romantic such as Alice, Dunbar's letters must have been most appealing. In the short story "Violets," she writes of a man who reads an old love letter from a woman who has sent him a lock of her "pretty brown hair."[2] Although his wife rejects the idea of such actions as "sentimental trash," therefore turning the onus of romance back on the man, Alice's work centers on women as the objects of affection and the authors of romantic desire. While the bulk of her short stories are sentimental, capturing the emotion of romantic interest, expressing love and admiration in letters was very common during this period. In some ways, Dunbar's access to her literature would have given him an upper hand when it came to knowing the desires of Miss Moore. What Dunbar might have surmised from her literature was if the woman had to choose between her career and marriage, Alice would prefer to marry him as indicated in "The Woman" and "A Story of Vengeance." Three months after his first letter, on June 6, 1895, he ended his letter with "A Song": "My lady-love lives far away / And, oh my heart is sad by day / And, ah my tears fall fast by night . . . My love knows not I love her so." Their correspondence reflects Alice's hesitation to accept his increasing requests for her to reciprocate his feelings.

Like Dunbar, Alice also published love poems or complaints. One is a prayer to God about her lover who has gone away, titled "A Plaint." It appears as an appeal to the Divine to help her deal with her feelings regarding the absence of a lover who has gone "afar." There is a complexity here that she played with that brings forth a mystery, a sense that the woman's voice is in a state of flux. The persona states, "And bitter questionings of love and fate, / But rather give my weary heart thy rest, / And turn the sad, dark memories into sweet." The woman appeals to God for help with her sense of unfulfilled sexual passion here. She states, "Chide not, dear God, if surging thoughts arise." She later states, "I send him forth, and back I'll choke the grief / Rebellious rises in my lonely heart." Certainly she is experiencing "grief," "heartache," and "wistfulness," but how much control she had over the circumstances that brought her to this state of being is unclear. A question lingers here: Why has the lover gone away? Has he been called away because of circumstances beyond his control, or did he leave on his own volition, with no intention of returning? Love is associated with a struggle to maintain control. Silenced here is the man's voice and what he did or did not do to make this woman feel the way she does. He is only acknowledged in the last line, "I crave of thee, / That he shall ne'er forget his hours with me." It would appear, then, that she hopes to wrest control of her body, her feelings, her desires, through her voice and will not allow him the opportunity to obstruct her attempt. In this poem, readers can see how single women of the nineteenth century who struggled to uphold respectable public personas were encouraged to place erotic desires on hold.

"Farewell" is another poem that silences the man's voice and makes him object rather than subject. Her poetic persona addresses him as "sweetheart" and "my love," indicating that she perceives a level of intimacy between the two; yet there is a distance noted here. It appears she is writing this lover a letter, as she addresses him in the first line with "farewell, sweetheart, and again farewell," though in the next line, she states, "Today we part." Written in the present tense, her formal address of him indicates that she is not speaking directly to him. She ends, "In sorrow or in happiness, nor let you / E're me forget." As with "Plaint," this poem is about a separation of the two from the woman's perspective. However, this reads more like a fantasy and follows a theme in *Violets* of unrequited love and unfulfilled desires.

In "Paul to Virginia," she creates a dialogue between a man and a woman[3] that shows the power a woman possesses, much to the frustration of the man. Written and at press before Alice began to correspond with Dunbar, the poem follows the collection's probing of women's attitudes toward romantic love. More specifically, this poem is written from the point of view of a man, unusual for the collection, and speaks of the tension between a man in love with a woman named Virginia and his expression of jealousy:

> I really must confess, my dear,
> I cannot help but love you, . . .
> But then you know it's rather hard,
> To dangle aimless at your skirt
> And watch your every moment so,
> For I am jealous, and you're a flirt.[4]

She repeats the last line in all four stanzas of the poem. Virginia's suitor sees her as a girl who smiles at all the boys, "a half score" who surround her, but treats Paul like "dirt." His desire for her places Virginia on a pedestal above him as he "dangles aimless at [her] skirt." Alice presents a man whose feelings of powerlessness equate to his feeling of love.[5] In fact, at this "Fin

De Siècle" as the poem begins, or "End of the Century" in French, love appears as a struggle between men and women for power. Alice suggests that if a man loves a woman, she must sacrifice her chances to define herself to appease his ego. Ironically, this poem identified a struggle that would occur in her relationship with Dunbar.

In this first year, before their engagement, Dunbar encouraged her writing and appeared very supportive of her work. He graciously thanked her for the poems she sent to him. He also gave her his "honest opinion" of her fiction, including "Little Miss Sophie." On June 13, 1895, he wrote, "Your poem 'Love for a Way' I consider exquisite. It is rich, warm." He goes on to say, "You cannot send me too much of your work; I shall be glad to have anything you can spare, either prose or verse." His June 25th discussion about the progress of his own work, such as "When Malindy Sings," indicates that he respected her as a literary colleague. Dunbar reiterated his interest in reading her work on July 25, 1895: "[W]henever you have a spare poem or story, I should be glad to have it, as I prize your work very much." For the female activist, equal treatment means as much, if not more, than mere flirtation.

Of course, Dunbar was most certainly using this form of correspondence to get closer to young Alice. He asked her multiple times to send a picture. He knew what she looked like from the photograph printed with her collection and in *The Women's Era*. Again, Alice kept him at bay. Flattery is an expected part of courtship, as Alice made clear in her work, for example, "Paul to Virginia." Surely she saw multiple reasons to keep Dunbar close, but not too close. First, Dunbar was an emerging African American writer. In this position, he could help her to make contacts in the literary world, where she sought a position of notoriety. And, of course, he did. He helped her to sell her books and later introduced her to his literary agent, Paul Reynolds. Second, as would any respectable lady, she kept him at an acceptable distance. It is very likely that her delayed responses were strategic. Making him wait for a response could have sent the signal that she was interested in him but that she was not an aggressive woman. Third, Dunbar was known for his drinking habits, which she would come to regret having excused. When she finally did send her photograph, Dunbar gushed with excitement about the woman's beauty.

Dunbar is aggressive in his correspondence with her, but Alice is coy in the attention she showed Dunbar. Although younger than Dunbar, she had experienced love. As she noted in a 1928 dairy entry, "This date always fills me with amusement—October 5, 1892, and how heartbroken I was when Bis Pinchback[6] went away and life was all black. And exactly a month later, November 5, began my romance with Nelson Mitchell."[7] He often asked why she hesitated in responding to his letters and insisted that she write longer ones. In one letter, he asked if he had offended her in some way, to learn why she had not responded to his previous letter.[8] He soon became more aggressive in expressing his feelings for her and in trying to coax a favorable response. In August 1895, he felt "sure" he had offended her, but "For the feelings it [his last letter] expressed, I have no wish to apologize." He went on to ask if she was willing to go on "as if the letter had not been written."

Most of Alice's early letters to Dunbar are not available. Though her voice is not on record, however, the impression she made on him speaks through his recorded responses and interpretations. Alice did not initially give him the attention he sought; indeed, she was occupied by loss of one man and may have had her eyes already set on the next. From miles away, Dunbar persisted, on October 13, 1895, by declaring his love for her based on the photo she had sent him: "I have kept your picture this long because I could not bear to part with it. It seemed to me, your other self and I was better for its presence. I am afraid that you will think I am foolish when I say that this 'counterfeit presentment of yourself has kept me from yielding to temptations.'" Dunbar's statement reveals much about nineteenth-century men's attitudes and the pressures placed on women to comply. Dunbar, the poet, indulged his infatuation with Alice's looks and created a fantasy of her. From his perspective, her looks "were the sudden realization of an ideal," and his honest confession that she kept him from "yielding to temptations," a clear reference to sexual liaisons, speaks to the contradictions of men being allowed to have premarital sex without judgment.

He would eventually make her the "ideal" that kept him pure. He stated, "I am better and purer for having touched hands with you over all these miles." Her status as a woman, presumably a pure and pious woman, meant that a relationship with him would, certainly in his estimation, remove any of his moral shortcomings. There is an implication that Alice is responsible for how he lived his life. His subsequent letters reveal her unwillingness to take on this responsibility. A gendered power play persists between the two. Consequently, Dunbar resorted to manipulating her into responding in kind. His letter of March 6, 1896, shows his attempt to make her jealous by speaking of a woman whom he talks to about Paris. He described her as a woman with "soft brown hair and blue eyes." What Alice could not know is that Dunbar would never waiver from these tactics, even after they were married.

In 1896, Alice made a major life change when she followed her sister, new brother-in-law, and mother to the Boston area, where her brother-in-law had a business. Her ties to the NACW continued to yield leadership opportunities. *The Evening Star*, in its Monday July 27, 1896 edition, reported that she became a vice president of the Frederick Douglass Memorial Pilgrimage Association. At the time, she was listed as residing in West Medford, Massachusetts. Accordingly, "The meetings are to be annual contemporaneous with those of the National Association of Colored women." The women's commitment to activism and uplifting the most honorable of the race led them to meet at the home of Helen Douglass, widow of Douglass, where they defined their objectives to "commemorate his illustrious service to the state by appropriate exercises on Feb. 14 of each year; to encourage the people throughout the various states to make pilgrimages to the Douglass estate, and to co-operate with any movement looking to the now historic Cedar Hill of Anacotia."

In a letter to Alice, Dunbar boldly told her that she needed to follow her sister's lead and get married.[9] Dunbar was certainly not the only man who had caught her attention. Whomever she married, however, had to be a man of means, as was expected of any educated African American woman, especially one who moved in clubwomen's circles. Dunbar was not rich or an educated man, but he was a popular one. Alice would soon have a decision to make about the future of their relationship. Dunbar was known among his peers for his writing talent and his addictions, as well as his relationships with women. For months, Dunbar laid the onus of his sobriety and celibacy on Alice, complicating their move toward exchanging vows. His reasoning: if she remained in his life, he would try to stay true to her. During the three stages of their relationship—courtship, engagement, marriage—she contended with his confessions of temptations and pleadings for her to help him to resist.

In February 1897, Dunbar was scheduled to leave for a reading tour in England where he was to stay for six months. Probably curious to meet the famous man with whom she had been corresponding with for nearly two years before he left the country, Alice risked her reputation as a respectable woman and went to Dunbar on the evening of February 10 before his departure. In a letter to Arthur Schomburg, she gave the details: "When he was about to sail for Europe, Mrs. Victoria Earle Mathews gave a farewell party for him and invited me to come over from Boston to New York. I accepted the invitation, met Paul for the first time the night before his sailing, and became engaged to him that night." She admitted that even though he asked her to marry him in his letters, she "scoffed at the idea of becoming engaged to a man I had never seen. But after seeing him—"[10] Apparently pleased with what she saw and impressed with his letters, the two became secretly engaged—news they kept from Alice's family, though Dunbar's inability to keep a secret resulted in the knowledge being revealed to his friends and mother. From the ship, he wrote to his mother:

> You will be surprised to hear that Alice Ruth Moore ran away . . . and came to bid me good-bye. She took everybody by storm. She was very much ashamed of having run away, but said she could not bear to have me go so far without bidding me good-bye. She is the brightest and sweetest little girl I have ever met, and I hope you will not think it is silly, but Alice and I are engaged. You know this is what I have wanted for two years.[11]

After his return from Europe several months later, he wrote to Alice's mother to ask her permission to marry her daughter. But Dunbar, with Alice's consent, had crossed the line of respectability when he asked for her hand and she accepted; for that reason and others, receiving her mother's approval would prove difficult.

As she dealt with the excitement and stress of their hasty engagement, she also dealt with Dunbar's personality. She would learn that the ideal of a romance clashed with the reality of a relationship. In their case, Dunbar's sexual desires and his male privilege of expressing—through practice and word—his erotic proclivities muted any such strivings Alice may have had. On February 20, 1897, he wrote, "I wish to Heaven you were already mine. You could keep me out of a deal of mischief and share a great many pleasures with me." In response to her query about his ability to control his urges, he asked,

> Will I love you tenderly and faithfully? Darling, darling, can you ask! . . . Already I am living for you and working for you and through the gray days and the long nights I am longing and yearning for you . . . For your sake I will be true and pure. You will help me to be this for you are always in my thoughts.[12]

As they awaited a favorable response from Alice's mother, Patsy Moore, Alice dealt with the anguish stemming from Dunbar's confessions that he experienced constant temptations from women. Hoping to appeal to his moral and spiritual sensibilities, she wrote, "You will be strong for my sake, resisting evil and temptation because you know I am praying for you? You will not let man or woman come between us? You will be strong for my sake, resisting evil and temptation because you know I am praying for you?"[13]

In these letters, readers have to wonder just how Dunbar defined marriage. What Dunbar wanted became the center of their intimacy. It was clear that he saw a marriage to Alice as fulfilling a desire that he had for a Black Madonna, a sexually pure woman. She was to carry the emotional burden of his confessions to "kiss" other women, show understanding and patience, and ready herself to be his wife when the time came. How sharing this with his fiancée might affect her, especially when they were in a long-distance relationship, was not his concern. Only a woman of "angelic" proportions, as he often referred to her, could endure the pressures of such a relationship.

Dunbar and Alice came to agree that she must be instrumental in keeping him from indulging the temptations that he shamelessly flaunted—his desire for women. She acquiesced to this role by promising to pray for him to find the will to refrain from drinking and seeing other women. At this point, Alice's public persona established her as a respectable woman. In this role, she sought to have a respectable relationship. Notably, society did not admonish men for having sexual urges, therefore reducing expectations that they meet respectability standards. However, there were expectations. According to Anastasia Curwood, middle-class African American men or New Negro Men acted responsibly and did their part to uplift the race:

"Men were no longer expected to drink, gamble, dally with other women, and remain emotionally aloof."[14] Further, men would be the sole providers for the family, as women were the "emotional and moral caretakers."[15] Dunbar's letters reflect these expectations as much as they acknowledge his inability or unwillingness to abide by them. Although he and Alice were not married, their letters at this point are signed "Your wife" and "Your husband," suggesting that they were carrying out marital roles, at least in terms of gender expectations.

Soon after their engagement, she struck out on her own and moved to Brooklyn, New York, to continue her education, write, teach, and further her social activism. While there, she worked closely with Victoria Earle Matthews, fellow clubwoman activist and founder of the White Rose Mission.[16] From New Orleans to West Bedford, Massachusetts, and then Brooklyn, New York, Alice continued her correspondence with Dunbar—allowing them to build their relationship through writing.

Alice's independence and dedication to advancing herself and others emerged as two prominent concerns in her letters. While in New York, Alice committed herself to continuing her education as she educated. She worked on her graduate teaching certificate at Columbia University, and she taught at a Brooklyn Public School. Dunbar was not supportive of this work, and in several letters he asked her to quit and marry him. Determined to maintain her independence and build a career that she enjoyed, she ignored his protests. This pattern of her rebuffing his attitude toward her working continued throughout their courtship.

Beyond how she is seen by Dunbar is how Alice saw herself. On one hand, she was very proud of her life as a teacher and mission worker and seemed to very much enjoy her lifestyle. Her sense of self and her intention to preserve her sense of independence and security by working clashed with Dunbar's idea of masculinity, which prompted him to make his active career-minded wife into a domestic depended on him. In one of her letters, she told him that she would prefer not to work. Explaining her position, she stated:

I am far from having extravagant ideas, and no one realizes more than I do the swiftness with which an income like yours can be eaten by bare necessities. I will try to help you to save not spend. I wish I could add some to the income, but the only things I can do are write, teach, and be a stenographer, and keep books and give lessons in some things. I can do fancy work too, but it's slow and doesn't pay, and folks don't take lessons in things much, and you wouldn't want me to be at some other man's elbow taking dictation, would you? And school-boards don't allow married women to teach and editors won't accept my scribbling so I guess I'll have to stay at home and watch over the family exchequer, eh?[17]

Although Eleanor Alexander sees Alice's words as a form of manipulation, I argue that these lines summarize the limits placed on women of this era, and Black women in particular. Alice had been a working woman her entire adult life and, in fact, had two jobs—one at a Brooklyn public school and the other at the White Rose Mission—at the time this letter was written. Notably, Alice gave the list of job skills common among Black middle-class women. Whether she wanted to work or not, what she did make clear is that if society did not allow for a married woman to teach, according to the laws of DC, where Alice planned to move, then the husband was fully expected to assume his role as a provider. But was the financially unstable writer able to accept the responsibility of caring for a wife and his beloved mother?

A second major problem existed between Dunbar and Alice: Alice's mother and sister were not in support of the marriage. Her correspondence with him provides at least two possible reasons why her mother did not respond to his request for consent: one is that she did not receive the letter, and the other, more probable, is that she was not convinced that he was an honorable man. On at least two occasions, Dunbar wrote to ask permission to marry her daughter. Finally, Alice reported that she had learned that her mother had not received the letter and asked Dunbar to write her mother again, by sending the letter to Alice so that she could forward the letter to her mother. Although a written response does not exist in the record, their correspondence suggests that Alice's mother did not subsequently grant Dunbar's request for her daughter's hand. Dunbar had formed a reputation as both an alcoholic and a philanderer. Reports of Dunbar's drunkenness, including at a reading in Philadelphia, had made it back to Alice and her family by way of a family friend. Clearly, Alice's mother was concerned for her daughter, particularly at a time when such displays would have been frowned upon. If Alice's father had been present, the request would have gone to him. Patsy Wright Moore had assumed the role of the missing father and was surely doing her best to ensure that her daughter would have a respectable life with a respectable man. She had already seen her eldest daughter married to a businessman. For a woman who was shrouded in mystery, we can imagine the importance of her attempts to avoid having a daughter enveloped in more shame. Their removal from New Orleans could have—in fact, should have—meant a fresh start to establish a life of respectability.

Dunbar's passion for Alice can be read as romantic emotion that fed the vanity of a naive Southern girl in an era of sexual conservatism. What Alice did not see was Dunbar's alarming but subtle obsession with claiming her as his wife. Beyond the fact that he expressed his love for her only a few weeks after they began to correspond, Dunbar sent a series of letters expressing his fear that he would lose Alice as a result of her mother's unwillingness to give her consent. Despite the fact that she told him she would not leave him, Dunbar seemed almost consumed with his obsession to make Alice his wife. And this obsession would manifest itself in violent ways.

Dunbar understood the power his position as a man afforded him in their relationship. Unable to control her mother, he made strategic moves to mark Alice as his. On November 16, 1897, while in Brooklyn, New York, he sent her a telegram stating, "Come to sallys[18] am sick." Three days later, Dunbar sent her a letter that, while a bit vague, is the beginning of a confession that he had sexually, through "brute" force, violated her. He wrote:

> My feelings this morning have been a strange admixture of remorse and exultation. I know I have done wrong, very wrong. My course has been weak and brutal. I have dishonored you and I cannot forgive myself for it. I have no plea to make, no excuse. I can only say that I cannot be happy again until you are my wife.[19]

He proceeded in the next paragraph to confess that he was drunk and had spent a great deal of money. If one does not linger much over the first few lines as quoted above, it would be possible to think the major problem is his lack of sobriety. In his note, Metcalf states, "in a drunken state, [he] had intercourse with Alice and injured her internally."[20] But, I agree with Alexander that there is much more here. Dunbar's confession, veiled as an apology, speaks of his feelings and proves that he was thinking primarily of himself. Dunbar left little doubt of his intent that night, as he proceeded to center himself and expressed his desires for how she could make him happy—by becoming his wife. This, notably, followed his statement that he had "dishonored her." These words, within a society that highly valued *pure* women, illuminated Dunbar's understanding of his power in this situation and her lack of choices. Seemingly unaware of the psychological impact that rape could have on the woman he claimed to love, he continued by defining the meaning of the sexual violation to him: "Dear, while I feel myself a scoundrel, do you know that I feel infinitely nearer to you?" He went on to limit her choices by admitting that he had told their mutual friend Sally, and "she only advises me to hasten the wedding." Sally's response, if we believe Dunbar, only proved how much women and men valued the virtue of purity measured by virginity. Above all else, the social, public performance of the violated body must supersede any emotions—feelings of pain, reluctance, anger, self-pity—associated with the heart or mind.

Silence represents a gap that is filled by Dunbar's pleadings for her to respond. He proceeds to assure her that he will refrain from drinking and that he wanted to marry her. Dunbar stated, "I have tried to compromise with love and share her dominion with liquor. From now on, there must be no compromise. Love must rule."[21] He wrote to her again on November 20, 1897, that he was feeling "like a young knight" and had "drawn a half-month's salary." This, it seemed, was what he needed to feel secure. Love is mentioned only twice in this letter, compared to nine times in the previous letter. Dunbar's mood and his admittance to dealing with depression related to guilt for his drunken behavior effects the decisions he made—how he spent money, how he felt about himself, how he interacted with Alice. Not hearing from her since the night he assaulted her, he finally asked in a November 22 letter, "For Heaven sake write and tell me when you are coming?" If he kept her response to him, it is not in the collection of letters. Whatever details she provided about what happened that night must be inferred from his response. "Your letter has almost killed me," he responded in a second letter he wrote on November 22, 1897. Without denying her truth, he wrote, "when I looked the horrible fact straight in the face and could feel neither honor nor shame, how the pain is back again, but dull, constant, insistent." Responding to an accusation of the pain he caused, he accepted this as true by stating, "Do you mean that I in my bestial lust have so hurt and injured you." Alice must have expressed her pain and perhaps a fear of being near him: "I am not sorry that you will not let me come to you." Between these lines is a confession of a violent act that was enacted on a woman by a man she loved.

Subsequent correspondence suggests that Dunbar was not simply drunk when he raped Alice, but that he had enough time to calculate a strategy. His letter of December 14, 1897, confirms this line of thinking: "I am so glad to hear that you are better. It is bad that you had ever to be sick. It would be better had I taken your decision as final the night we walked Brooklyn bridge together and life stretched away before so bleak and bare." There is a strong suggestion here that she had decided not to marry Dunbar before the assault took place or at least to put off marrying him indefinitely. A year later, Alice confirmed that she ended their engagement: "Do you remember that night we walked over the bridge and I said I would not marry you? You were hurt to tears."[22] There is no doubt, then, that Dunbar willfully rejected her right to say no to him. Dunbar's insistence that she marry him, as early as Thanksgiving, further suggests that he acted strategically. He followed this November 19, 1897, letter with a number of responses in December that weakened his stance that his judgment was impaired by alcohol: his confession the next morning that he had been with someone before her, his revelation that he was too drunk "for flow," his recalling what she had said to him on the Brooklyn Bridge.[23] It would appear that his memory of that night and the following morning was quite sharp.

Alice projected silence as he continued to write letters of self-deprecation. She was not only healing from her injuries but also contemplating how she would move forward. She was by this time a public figure with growing popularity as well as an activist dedicated to the race. What further sacrifices would she have to make to maintain public respectability? On November 19, 1897, he declared his intention to marry her and asked her to "consent to a civil marriage" on Thanksgiving. He went on to make her responsible for curing his weakness by stating, "When I feel like taking a drink, I will sit down and write to you first, and maybe the thought of the best little woman in the world will make me strong." There is no doubt that Dunbar suffered from a drug and alcohol addiction that hindered them from having a healthy relationship. His placing the burden of his alcoholism on Alice follows his earlier proclamations that he could remain celibate if she would pray for him and support him in other ways. Their relationship, even in its darkest moment, reflected the expectations of the woman and not the man. Remaining oblivious to her pain, he asked her to tell him when she was coming to DC.[24]

While scholars such as Alexander and Kevin Kelly Gaines have noted that the letters reveal that this sexual violation occurred, there is scant analysis of the meaning of such a traumatic event on the woman who endured it. Through a brutal act of violation, Dunbar marked her body as his, and Alice's best response must have been to keep her public persona intact, despite her personal feelings. A lack of a diary for this period makes it impossible to know her feelings. Curwood provides context: "At the turn of the twentieth century, . . . African American public culture presented female chastity and morality as the cornerstones of a respectable middle-class marriage."[25] Dunbar's position as a man in this era challenged Alice's power as a woman, that is, her ability to define her "self" as a young woman in a society that did not value her decisions about her body. Defining rape has changed over time, but, at its core, it is a violation of a woman's "personhood":

> Once it was acknowledged a crime, rape was still considered not a violation of women's personhood (which throughout most of women's history has not been acknowledged) but a damage to male property, a kind of robbery, and thus primarily a threat to the established socioeconomic order and a class issue. Accordingly, while sexual assault first ranked as a physical violation— and continued to do so among the lower classes—the late eighteenth century reinterpreted rape as a theft of (a poor) woman's only capital: her chastity.[26]

Dunbar indulged his knowledge that his act of defiling an unmarried woman's body allowed him to define her social worth, a fact that he was acutely aware of. Alice, meanwhile, endured a great amount of shame as well as physical pain that impacted her daily life. There is no indication in these letters that she consented to having sex with a man she had chosen to leave. Their correspondence confirms that this was not only an act of nonconsensual penetration but much more. She informed him that he had caused significant physical injuries that left her unable to teach for a period of time. He responded, "Do you mean to say that I in my bestial lust have hurt and injured you—my God—my God."[27] Even worse, she soon discovered that she had contracted a sexually transmitted disease, possibly syphillis. Dunbar responded, "I too am suffering bodily now but from nothing so serious that ordinary treatment may not be expected to effect a cure."[28] Dunbar's unsympathetic attitude toward her degrading, traumatizing condition shrugged off the embarrassment she felt in having to seek treatment for a sexually transmitted disease.

Alice's condition was a sort of shameful confession that she had had sex before marriage. Her body could not confess that she had not consented to her partner but had been taken by brute force. To be sure, maintaining a reputation as a "pure" lady was extremely important to her, as evidenced by the scheme she concocted to explain what had occurred to her doctor. Dunbar told her to tell her doctor she had been abused by him. Feeling too embarrassed to be defined as a violated woman, she asked him to write to the doctor that they were secretly married. He agreed to but did not follow through for months afterward, expressing his own shame for his actions. Alice's desire for love and a career had resulted in what would become an abusive relationship with a highly revered and exceptionally talented Black man. What we learn here is that women's, especially middle-class women's, desire to be in a loving relationship was challenged by a society that questioned their purity status and sexual choices.

Embedded in her request to contact her doctor is her confession about how she felt. We must recall that Alice had been working to uplift the position of Black women, whom she had deemed vulnerable to sexual oppression. She had written about the exploitation of women in her fiction, such as "Little Miss Sophie" and "In Our Neighborhood," and been active in local and national organizations dedicated to empowering Black women. At the time of the assault, she was engaged in mission work. As an educated Black woman and churchgoer, she had stood on the hope that she could maintain her own purity and piety; but if it had been threatened, Dunbar would have defended her.

Whether or not she was able to share her pain and shame with anyone is not known, but it is likely that Victoria Matthews and others close to her noticed the visual injuries she described. Given her mother's and sister's rejection of Dunbar's marriage proposal, and their own family history, it is unlikely that she told either of them. After the violation, how she felt about her worth as a woman who valued her reputation depended largely on how Dunbar felt about her. Along with his November 27, 1897 letter, he sent her a ring to entice her to marry him. Prior to his behavior, which he described as "criminally careless and bru[tish]," she had not been willing to marry him without the consent of her mother. But things had changed.

His response to her anger was to request her hand in marriage, again and again. "You have indeed discovered the real Dunbar himself and given him higher aims in life. But your mission is not yet done. You are to keep him upon the high plane to which you have raised him."[29] In a letter he wrote to her the next day, he called her a "spotless angel"; in some ways this labeling of her may have been a successful attempt to entice her to see herself as worthy.[30] Following his requests to marry her and his willingness to have her confess his violation of her to her doctor, she seemed to soften her anger. In a December 6, 1897, letter, approximately three weeks after the rape, he thanked her for going back to signing her letters as his wife. She eventually made him "happy" because she was "better and wants to marry him."[31]

In a world where sexually active single women, including sexually violated women, were marked as lascivious, Alice acquiesced to Dunbar's advances. In her study of rape in Black women's literature, Sabine Sielke finds that marriage could save a sexually violated woman: "Rape could be made right. In accordance with Saxon law . . . the raped virgin could retroactively consent to her rape and extricate her attacker from his death sentence by agreeing to marry him. As marriage thus 'recasts rape,' it becomes 'a misunderstanding corrected, or rape rightly understood.'"[32] Dunbar confirms this idea of the woman serving in a similar role by telling her that she had a "mission" to save him. Marriage could be a rebirth from a form of social death, brought on by a sexual violation. While marriage is a public act, violations of this kind are often private and reside in silent spaces. Hope resides in public. Sielke also notes, "What emerges from this (re)birth is a sense of personhood coterminous with sexual violation, which eventually gives rise to notions of black women's supposed invulnerability, 'an ability,' as Michael Awkward underlines, 'not to conquer oppression but to negotiate it successfully.'"[33] Perhaps Alice could be sadly redeemed, like Little Miss Sophie—without having to experience physical death.

Irrespective of her violation, she was building a life in New York. Teaching for Alice was consistent. It brought her a sense of pride among her race and provided her with financial independence. As she dealt with the trauma and shame, she also endured his pleadings for her to leave her teaching position and move to Washington, DC. On November 29, 1897, he wrote, "I have no doubt though, that you will soon be up though I sincerely hope that you will never go back to teaching." On December 1, he wrote, "Dear, please don't go back to school anymore. Please marry me as soon as you are well enough." She finally was willing to marry him if they could "marry quietly in NY this month [January] and live apart for a short while." Her plan was to continue the work she had begun in New York because she "owes friends in the schools to complete my courses and get my three certificates," a reference to her teacher certification program at Columbia University. She went on to acknowledge that he was not in support of her work, but "it will simplify matters a great deal." In his response, he did not address her interest in continuing her education or in them staying apart.

Dunbar continued to discuss marriage and Alice was more open to him, but the circumstances made their correspondence tense and uneasy. He said he wanted to marry her if his mother could attend.[34] In a previous letter, he asked her to tell Sallie that they were married in New Jersey the night he raped her. In this letter he expressed his shame at seeing her for the first time after their night in New York.[35] This stressful and tense back and forth between a man and a woman is emblematic of the time period. What people thought of how Black men and women conducted themselves dictated the decisions they made. If laws prevented married women from teaching, Alice had no choice in the matter. If people perceived a working woman as a deficient wife, then Dunbar felt justified in expecting her to stay at home and to focus on him and his needs. If Alice wanted to fulfill her desire of being a working wife, even for unpaid service outside the home, she would have to marry a progressive man who would respect her choice. Unfortunately, the abuse of her body made that seem impossible. Marrying Dunbar was her only choice under the circumstances.

Only marriage could save the reputation of the Black teacher and her poet fiancé. On January 1, 1898, she wrote:

> I hope you are being strong and true. . . . Do not run too much counter to Washington society, please. It will make it hard for me when I come, and I want our home to have the highest position, the respect and admiration of all the powers that be. We owe it to ourselves to create and maintain an unquestioned, looked-up to social position. Don't you think so? And so much depends upon your attitude.

Seeing his behavior as a reflection of her, she pled with him to uphold standards that would endear them to rather than alienate them from Black Washingtonians. Accepting a future with him, her vision was to enjoy a perfect life as a wife, at least in public. It would be Dunbar's job to make the suffering have meaning and significance for the good of their relationship, a union that could be a model to Black people seeking to show themselves as moral beings and to those who believed that Black people were not capable of living respectable lives.

Nevertheless, regardless of the situation, Alice would always find a way to maintain some control over the direst circumstances. Her letter of January 15, 1898, directly expressed her expectations of Dunbar and what she was willing to do as his wife. She began by informing him that she was "studying about mothers of famous men, about lovely homes, about wifehood and all that it means, about the best way to keep you in your life's work" to prepare for their pending nuptials. Her goal was to "be an inspiration to you, a comforter and real helpmate." Clearly, if they were to have a model marriage, then he must keep his composure, if not for her, then for others. Based on a sermon she said she had heard that day, she gave a religious context for the kind of man she hoped he would become:

> Reflect everytime you do a wrong or abuse your own nature, you hurt not yourself alone, it is like a ripple in the water, ever widening, ever increasing, touching infinitude as it were. You hurt the whole human race, for you weaken your children, and through them humanity. You have no right to drag down the standard of humanity. You have a right to do as you wish to yourself if you intend to die at once and childless, but otherwise you do a wrong against nature and humanity and they will be revenged.

In other words, even if he was willing to act in a way that was harmful to her and him, he must at least make decisions that would not just negatively affect Black folks, but the entire human race. Curwood provides the context for Alice's attempt to control the way in which she would be viewed by society: "In addition [to presenting female chastity as a cornerstone of respectable middle-class marriage], marital partners were often assumed to be teammates working to promote the progress of the race."[36] In the age of Booker T. Washington and W. E. B. Du Bois, African Americans hoped that all their men could be leaders that the world would applaud. Alice was not just looking for a leader, she desired a man she could trust—a man who would help her to produce "nobler, purer, and farther advanced" children.[37] Though he was a renowned poet, Alice knew from firsthand experience that Dunbar had fallen short of the desirable Black male model that would stand out among men. If she was to be his wife, she had to do what she could to preserve the sanctity of the union. And she did.

Alice still had not seen Dunbar since the night he raped her. Surely, she struggled with trusting him to commit to monogamy; notably, in his attempt to assure her that he had been with someone shortly before her, leaving him without "much flow," he also admitted that he had betrayed her trust as her fiancé. More importantly, she must have feared that he would harm her again. Her letters reveal that she still struggled physically as a result of that night. She felt the burden was hers to make him into a respectable man, or the New Negro Man discussed by Curwood, who could provide her with a safe environment. Alice's suffering became symbolic, in her mind, of the sacrifices of women to appease men. She finally resolved that what had happened to her was within the will of God and that her suffering was not in vain:

> My long suffering of those last two months, dear, was a veritable Godsend. My love came out of it like a Phoenix from the flames, strengthened, purified, beautified. Temptuous passion, mad desire impatient for pleasures have gone and I am as a wife to you now, true-hearted, constant, a little more prudent, ambitious for you and desirous that we both get and maintain the proper position before the eyes of the world.[38]

Alice provided a powerful statement that strongly reflected the sentiment toward sexual suppression of the era. Donna Aza Weir-Soley's analyses of essays by religious Black women of the late nineteenth century, such as Jarena Lee and Rebecca Cox Jackson, argue that their work both empowered "black women as speakers and writers" and "demonstrate[d] the limitations placed on black women's sexual expression."[39] She notes further that those religious women, such as Maria Stewart, who proclaimed the importance of "piety, morality and virtue" for Black women expressed "Judeo-Christian negation of female sexuality and the racist and sexist narratives of carnal licentiousness that so unfairly painted black women as inherently 'fallen' when subjected to the ideals of the cult of true womanhood."[40] Alice's way of dealing with her rape was to see it through the lens of Christian teachings and their influence on how women were perceived. Being sexually violated, then, meant the appropriate end to her sexual desires, resulting in an acceptable, "purified" version of her old self. Any interest in living an erotic life had been eclipsed, perceived as wrong.

Sexual desires were suppressed for the purpose of advancing the ideal Black family. What Alice had felt for Dunbar before was unacceptable for a wife who was meant to be prudent and work for the advancement of the man toward his "proper position" before the world. Experiencing trauma forced Alice to revise her way of thinking and to see herself as having a greater purpose. She was no longer her own person—if she ever was in a Victorian-influenced society—as she claimed to submit to the will of God. A woman who worked for women's rights and for the protection of women became the woman who saw herself through the eyes of her abuser. Though she wrote to him of her "purification," healing was clearly a process that did not yet allow her to fully trust him to honor her body as "respectable." She did not go near him, even though he asked her to return so he could "cuddle her" if she came to visit for Christmas.

As she dealt with her troubled relationship with Dunbar, Alice continued her work with the White Rose Home for Colored Working Girls. Managed by her friend and fellow clubwoman Mrs. Victoria Earle Matthews, the Home was noted in the *New York Times* as "endeavoring in the midst of vice, immorality, and unfair competition to protect and place negro women in honest work."[41] The article spotlighted the needs that the mission addressed in providing housing and training for "negro girls," of most concern those who were brought to New York from the South after having been sold into slavery; such girls would sign a contract in the South agreeing to work from one to two months without pay upon arrival in New York. As part of their passage, it was understood that they would work at a "disorderly house." Once housed, the girls were obligated to give their money and other belongings to the agent and the housing agency for storage of those goods, which were confiscated upon the girls' arrival. Compounding their difficulties was the fact that jobs for "unskilled workers," which had once gone to African Americans, now began to go to newly arrived European immigrants.[42] Moving to New York was expensive and risky, notes Steve Kramer: "With the inability to earn good wages and the strong prejudice against them, black workers had to lease substandard housing, often at higher rents than other groups, and home ownership was rare."[43] In sum, such girls, in their haste to escape the discrimination and horrors of the South in search for freedom and opportunities in the North, often found themselves victimized by another form of racism and slavery.

Sadiya Hartman provides more context for the treatment of Black women and girls during late nineteenth century. She finds that "In 1883, the age of consent was ten."[44] But what did this mean for "colored girls" who "were always presumed to be immoral."[45] Consent was not required for those who chose the immoral. As more Black women moved from the South to the North, measures would be put in place to protect them from being taken into prostitution by men who waited for naive Black Southern girls at ship docks and train stations. Unfortunately, for those who wanted to enjoy the pleasures of sex, they "risked harassment, arrest, and confinement."[46] Hartman goes on, "All colored women were vulnerable to being seized at random by the police; those who worked late hours, or returned home after the saloon closed or the lights were extinguished at the dance hall, might be arrested and charged with soliciting. If she had a sexually transmitted disease or children outside of wedlock or mixed-children, her conviction was nearly guaranteed."[47] In other words, freedom did not guarantee a right to safety.

Aware of the dangers, Alice and Matthews formed a needed partnership. Matthews, a light-skinned woman who had been born into slavery shortly before the Civil War, had probably been fathered by the plantation's owner. She, like Alice and too many other African American women from the South, knew well the meaning of sexual exploitation of Black girls and women. Such unscrupulous practices were responsible for "the women's first going astray," or, in other words, losing their chance to successfully meet the standards of respectable living by preserving their bodies for a lover of their choice.

To address the exploitation of "colored" women, who were not welcomed in missions reserved for White women, Matthews, with the support of Alice and other African American women, provided lodging and training. She wanted to "secure a good-sized house," with the upper portion being used "as a temporary lodging house for women and girls coming from the South or other parts to New York in search of work." The mission would look after them until they made an "association of a proper and wholesome nature" and would help prepare them properly for work with churchgoing families.[48] For Matthews and her colleagues, this would be the first step in giving the women the tools to survive—through residential protection and training for employment. Women empowered women.

Alice's letters to Dunbar document that the mission also helped African American boys. They taught "race history" by introducing the children to African American history and to poets such as Phillis Wheatley—and Paul Laurence Dunbar.[49] Relying on donations, she shared, "I had $50.00 contributed for my boy's class in manual training at the mission and I start them tomorrow night."[50] In addition to the check, she wrote that they had received a kindergarten table from a teacher's store in New York. Teaching the boys required her training in New Orleans and her tall stature. With pride in her ability not to lose control of the class of teenage boys, she boasted to Dunbar that she had some authority over male counterparts:

Boys are toughest; average age 14, but met their counterparts in NO. An unusually violent break on the part of a stalwart young man of 15 I reached over another boy and grabbed him by the collar and dragged him to the center floor. Lectured him in sentences of four or five words, punctuated them with fervent shakes with the one hand, while my knuckles made dents in his medulla oblongata.[51]

She may have seen her influence over their bad behavior as a way of preventing them from thinking of women as weak and vulnerable. Thus, she made "dents" in a boy's head and boasted of her act to the man who had physically violated her just two months earlier. Dunbar may have known this side of her. References to bruises and other injuries he inflicted on her body may have been inflicted to stop her from resisting his attack.

Working to improve the lives of others was surely a distraction from her own problems. Additionally, her work in the mission meant that she offered services to those who were without proper support. One of the more touching situations that she shared with Dunbar was when she visited the home of two children, one of whom she knew from her mission's kindergarten class and the other from the manual training course, who were clearly starving. When Alice and her friend Delores went to investigate the children's home, which was located in a neighborhood serviced by the mission, they found children overwhelmed by hunger, abuse, filth, and sadness. She described the mother as being "white, German" and the father as being a "dirty, filthy Negro" who "scurries out" when they come. The family was living in "two rooms" that were "squalid, miserable, filthy, to the last degree, and reeking with odors that made one's stomach instinctively turn over."[52] From what she gathered, the father was abusive and neglectful, opting to find food for himself while leaving the four children cold and hungry. Whether the man was dealing with depression or if he was simply uncaring, he was clearly defeated by his circumstances as the unemployed father of biracial children. Probably empathizing with children of a racial background similar to her own, Alice showed the derelict father no sympathy but did pool her meager funds with those of her colleague to buy castile soap for a child riddled with chicken pox, Vaseline, a loaf of bread, a package of meat, and cakes for the nursing baby. These provisions could provide only temporary relief as Alice also informed Dunbar that the family was two weeks behind in their rent and facing eminent eviction. She ended by saying that theirs was not a unique situation and that she choked on her own dinner while thinking about those who were without theirs.

Her decision to share this incident is a rare find in the existing letters. Set apart by her education, she cast herself as a heroine able to give the family what her Black male counterpart seemed incapable of doing or unwilling to do. As a heroine, she corrected the wrong of having been raised without her own father and feeling the support of a "hero." Her work with the mission always allowed her to assume a position of power, where she could save starving children, illuminate the shiftlessness of men, and chastise teenage boys, all in the name of effecting change in some way. In the rare instances where letters documenting her mission work have survived, we find a shift of tone from a socially vulnerable fiancée to that of a capable mature woman.

She was sharing her experiences with a successful writer. Dunbar's response was to think of ways to incorporate these experiences into her writing, as she eventually did in her 'Steenth Street stories, a collection of touching short stories that focus on poverty from the perspective of children. In these, as in some of her earlier work, readers find the rawness of her lived experience and how it informed her purpose as a Black woman near the turn of the century, which far outreached what she could convey in fiction. Both Alice and Dunbar were separated from abject poverty by a very thin line: the reputation they earned as writers, and in Alice's case, her teaching salary. They would never be far removed from the economic challenges that they illuminated in their fiction.

Writing became a tool to both empower her and to give her an opportunity to perform. As a tool of empowerment, she could cast herself as a person with an uncompromising position of authority. Of her experiences with a colleague, she informed him:

> Face was better so went to school today to tease our new "nigger" head of department crazy. She is short and sensitive about it so I've taken to wearing my high collars just for the pleasure of looking over them at her in a lofty, disdainful manner. She tries very hard to let me know how inferior I am and I meet her with what [illegible] calls a magnificent outburst of contemptuous silence.[53]

In the first line, she reminded him of the impact his physical abuse had on her life, specifically on her ability to work—an act that places her in the view and, subsequent, scrutiny of her friends and enemies. Then she quickly moves to her treatment of another Black person. By giving attention to her height in contrast to the female boss, she finds an opportunity to empower herself at a moment in which she is still suffering the effects of having been beaten in the face by Dunbar. One has to wonder if the abuse she suffered at his hands— the feeling of vulnerability, of powerlessness, of inadequacy—was transferred onto Maritcha Lyons,[54] the Black female head of department. She was an authority figure whom Alice did not respect, probably because her friend, Victoria E. Matthews, had engaged in "an angry dispute" over her hiring. The dispute resulted in the "resignation of several prominent members," including

Lyons, from the White Rose Mission.[55] Or was it that Alice identified with the woman and used Lyons as a way to deal with her own hurt feelings?

Although Alexander argues that Alice was a "racist" because she called Lyons a "nigger," this argument dismisses her work and her love for "the mother race." She did feel that the woman treated her as an "inferior," and she may have held animosity because the woman, and not Alice, had been appointed to the distinguished position as assistant principal. Furthermore, there is no doubting that class differences and/or regional identity were at play here. Alice was a leader who preferred to be in charge, but she was also a woman of questionable parentage from the South. Lyons was from New York and had been reared in a two-parent home. As a local woman with an established teaching career, she certainly had an advantage. The tension between the two may very well have been a case of petty jealousy.

Alice rarely ever used this word to describe other African Americans, but when she did, she usually referred to a Black person or people that she thought of as less than respectable. In one reference to Dunbar about Black Christians' method of worship, she stated, "[H]aven't I seen the niggers shout all the way up the aisle and back again!"—clearly describing behavior that she saw as disreputable.[56] Undoubtedly, this is a reference to forms of worship in Black churches that involved shouting, dancing, and singing. A young woman from the conservative Christian South, she must have preferred quieter forms of worship, ones that were more "respectable" for an advanced race. Notably, however, she would find much of the expressions of Black culture as unique and worthy of imitation by the time of the Harlem Renaissance. In another reference, she tells him to stay in "first-class white hostelries." "Then you will be away from the—well niggers."[57] Another reference to class. In this instance, she wants him not to lodge in a place where he would engage in drinking and other behavior viewed by middle-class African Americans as shameful and where Dunbar would very likely get into trouble.

To be sure, both Alice and Paul used the word only at rare times in the letters and those times, ironically, show a level of comfort and familiarity that counter other moments of tension. In a telling statement, when Dunbar expressed his feelings about concerns regarding his reputation and the possibility of her marrying another man, he declared, "For the Boston fools who are mad because you won't marry Stewart or Forbes, I don't care a damn and the rest of the niggers if let alone will come home draggin their tails behind them."[58] If we are to believe that her use of the word is a form of racism, then we must believe this of both Dunbar and Alice. It is possible that both of them, as children of formerly enslaved people, shared internalized ideas of personal racial inferiority, pushing them to seek unreasonable measurements and standards that were established by their White peers.

Fame and education placed them at an advantage. As noted in Chapter 1, the Black clubwomen at the executive level and in the New Orleans branch saw themselves as different from uneducated Black folks. In one of her essays,

Audre Lorde addresses the problem of Black women's perspectives on difference when it leads to negative outcomes, such as oppression: "As women, we must root out internalized patterns of oppression within ourselves if we are to move beyond the most superficial aspects of social change. Now we must recognize differences among women who are our equals, neither inferior nor superior, and devise ways to use each other's difference to enrich our visions and our joint struggles."[59] I am not arguing that their attempts for respectability led to their seeing themselves as superior members of the race, but Alice certainly was aware of the problems within the community as they tried to make advancements. In some ways she rejected any idea that she did see herself as better or superior. To be sure, as she stated in her essay "Brass Ankles Speaks," she felt as though her light skin often led to judgments about her feelings regarding other Black people. Many of the leaders of the Black clubwomen's movement were light-skinned and found themselves with more access to education and other resources than darker-skinned Blacks. When reading personal correspondence, readers must consider not only the historical context but the personal nuances that lead to the writers' expressions.

Alice and Dunbar's relationship certainly left a lot to be desired. Plagued from the early months of their relationship by Dunbar's need to share his temptations with his fiancée, she acted quickly when, several months after the rape, Dunbar sent her a scathing letter, in which he explained that he had made an arrangement with an old flame that had been misconstrued by the ex and that she was sharing it with others. In sum, he confessed to Alice that he had given an ex-girlfriend, Maud Shannon, taffy and offered to pay her wages and expenses for two weeks to come down and make his mother's dress, but he emphasized that she meant nothing to him. He closed by asking Alice what he should do. Alice would not be Dunbar's public fool. In an age when reputation and perception were valued more than the actual truth (if Dunbar was actually telling the truth), Alice solved the problem by sending a mysterious telegraph: "Come at once. Make no delay, matter of Life and Death," a statement that was reminiscent of his "come to sallys am sick" telegram. When he arrived, she met him with a minister who was prepared to officiate a wedding ceremony on March 6, 1898. More important to her than her mother's consent was not losing Dunbar to another woman, an act that would leave her socially embarrassed and, more importantly, unable to redeem herself from the rape. Indeed, this was a matter of (social) life and death. Their rash act would remain a shadow over their union, as neither was prepared for marriage.

Dunbar never seemed much concerned with his public reputation before their marriage, but he became obsessed with it after they married. Over a period of a month, he wrote to her to move to Washington, DC, to keep people from spreading gossip about why he had suddenly left and married a woman who remained in New York. While Dunbar may have said yes to the marriage, a union that he pushed for very soon after beginning his correspondence with her, the elopement would become a weapon he used to place her decision-making and his love for her into question.

If the two were in a war for power, Alice won this battle for she would not take the chance of losing the man to another woman. His letter of March 8, 1898, written after they eloped and he returned to DC, gave an almost scene-by-scene replay of what had occurred the day they married. Hastily responding to an urgent telegraph from Alice, he returned feeling as if they had acted like a "pair of criminals or two plebeians with the fear of disgrace hanging over them." His only responsibility in marrying Alice was that, if he had not, he would have seemed "selfish or uncaring." In effect, he characterized their marriage as criminal and undesirable. Gone is the romantic poet persona that had authored letters for two years; now he is a sterner, compassionless Dunbar. In his role as reluctant husband, he berated her for not trusting him, telling her they should have "waited longer"; since she did not, he presumes to take charge of repairing the damage by issuing performance instructions for putting on "the most dignified face possible. Just as soon as you wind up your affairs you must come to me and take your place in my home." He ends with a statement of irony: "I love you and can love you no less than I have ever done, but see now that unless I temper my love with common sense, it will lead us both into innumerable follies."[60] On the one hand, Dunbar was correct in asserting that common sense had been set aside by both of them in marrying. His inability to properly manage his life, which was plagued by an addiction to alcohol and chronic health problems, as well as his responsibility for his influential mother, would now be further complicated by caring for a wife who had an independent spirit and who had been abused by him. Notably, his financial situation had changed little since he met and proposed to her, except that he had become more popular, through his steady stream of publications and public readings. DC's restriction on allowing married women to teach was certainly a deterrent to a woman who enjoyed her career and was proud of her accomplishments. Teaching was part of her activism. She would have to learn who she was without this aspect of her identity.

On the other hand, Alice often walked the line of social boundaries, occasionally crossing over them in discreet ways, and this would only increase as she grew older. Her decision to take control of their relationship by surprising him with a marriage ceremony sent a signal to the temptresses he boasted of, but also to Dunbar himself, that she was not going to be left behind to bear the brunt of being an unmarried woman with an STD. Victorian-influenced middle-class society dictated that proper ladies and gentlemen planned weddings, invited people, and made announcements— all with the permission of the bride's family. She knew the risk she was taking by marrying without her mother's blessing. Shadowed by a brutal rape, placing Alice's reputation as a lady in peril, Alice and Dunbar's union was never traditional or the stuff that fairy tales were made of. Dunbar had long ago led the couple into a folly. His last proclamation in the letter, "be guided by me," unfortunately was what Alice had done.

What occurred next was Dunbar's attempt to "guide" his wife and her attempts to live with his name but not with him. Likely fearing being under Dunbar's roof and motivated by her reluctance to relinquish her freedom in New York, she replied on March 13 with hope. By answering that time might show that she was right, she tried to distract him from pressing her about a moving date, telling him the doctor predicted that they were going to have twins. Dunbar continued to press her, resorting to wooing her with expressions of love again: "My whole heart is yearning toward you. I want my wife with me. I do not want to ask you to obey. I prefer to have you use your own judgment and come because you see things as I see them." Marriage to Dunbar may have addressed the respectability issue, but it conflicted with Alice's career aspirations. Clearly Dunbar knew that telling an independent woman to come to him immediately would not work. It is also worth emphasizing the fact that Alice was the youngest sister reared in a family of women. She had no experience taking direction from a man who was not her boss or in a professional position of authority. Dunbar softened his tone and redirected his approach by asking her for her advice about bedroom furniture. This letter is somewhat deceiving, as he shifted from one approach to another. He attempted to make her rethink her plans: "[D]o you think that just marrying me and living away from me means my safety. . . . I am the same man surrounded by just the same dangers. . . . I wish you were with me to reinforce my strength." She may have changed his title from fiancé to husband, but she must still contend with the same concerns that led her to hastily plan their elopement. Showing little regard for their marriage vows, Dunbar's tactic was to use his temptations and her absence as a threat.

Probably because she was now married to him, Alice seemed nonplussed by his threat. Still resistant to packing her bags, she replied with more reasons why she had no immediate plans to leave New York. On March 14, she told him that she did not have a decent wardrobe with which to entertain the Black middle class of DC and therefore had to stay in New York to earn more money for her purchases. Although she did not say it in her March 14 letter, her resistance was surely connected to shame and fear of her mother's and sister's response to her having married Dunbar despite their pointed reservations. On March 16, she told him that she planned to stay a month or two longer to tend to her responsibilities, namely the mission.

Finding his wife steadfast in her reluctance to move to his home in DC, Dunbar must have realized at this point that he needed to use yet another approach to lure her to him. He responded by telling her that she would have time to buy new items before seeing people. Notably he changed his tactic, by March 18, from blaming her as the source of causing a problem to thanking her for her initiative: "You were a seer who not only saw the dangers of the future but provided a way to avert them." Unimpressed,

Alice persisted in providing several reasons for not leaving, including her work with the mission and her budding teaching career. It appeared that the latter reason was one of the main reasons why she did not want to leave. By this time, she had been moved from her post at Public School no. 83, an integrated school, where she did not get along with Maritcha Lyons, to take a position at a Jewish school in Brooklyn. According to the very light-skinned Alice, she was a test case for this position, and finding a suitable replacement would not be easy. Alice was proud that she had been chosen to teach at this school, it would seem, because she was teaching at the closest facility that might be deemed "White," even though Jews faced discrimination during this period. For this Southern Black woman, having an integrated experience was an accomplishment that she could not have enjoyed in the segregated South or in segregated Washington, DC.

As a teacher and in a different city, Alice could maintain a well-established identity that was separate from the one that she would have to assume as Dunbar's full-time wife. Once she moved to DC, not only would she not be able to teach but she would also have to share her husband and home with Dunbar's mother. Dunbar was asking for all the power; she would have to rely on him for emotional and financial support, and he had not proven himself fit to assume either of those roles. Although she would be the neighbor of activist Mary Church Terrell, whose family owned the house Dunbar was renting, she was not likely to be as active with the local or national Black women's clubs as she had been as a single woman. Dunbar had been resistant to her earning her teaching certificate at Columbia, as well as to her teaching positions, both at the mission and in the public school system.

Nevertheless, she remained firm in her resolve to care for herself, being careful to resist asking him for money unless it was absolutely necessary for her survival. This was a curious practice, considering that they had openly shared information about each other's income and had referred to each as husband and wife long before they were actually married. Shortly before they were married, she asked him for a loan to cover money she said was stolen from her. Dunbar responded with compassion in his letter, but it is not clear whether he sent her the amount, as there are no further references to it in the letters. Relinquishing her independence was difficult; asking for help was almost analogous to shame. After they eloped, she asked him for a loan to cover expenses associated with moving to DC that she promised to return when she received her last check. "But I'll need that money so I want to give you my warrant, which can be collected and paid you when it is due. You see I vowed to myself that I wouldn't ask you for a cent until I went home, and I'm not doing it."[61] Alice's marriage, as she outlined in this letter, had unleashed a burdensome load of anxieties that she did not anticipate. She listed them as anxieties about finances, health problems, concern about her mother and sister's opinion, and "fearsome regret for having hampered him possibly." Not an ideal set of circumstances for a woman whom even Dunbar had called a New Woman when they met by mail.[62]

If she remained independent-minded, he remained true to his nature of threatening his wife with sexual infidelities. On March 19, 1898, he remarked, "[N]o woman can be a substitute for your sweetness, but if you don't soon come, I will not be responsible for what I do." While earlier she was to bear the responsibility of keeping him true simply because he loved her, this was no longer the case. This line continued in subsequent letters. He informed her that he would not broach the subject of her coming again, "[b]ut I shall hold myself responsible for nothing that happens in an enforced separation of three months from my wife."[63] Finally, Alice was no longer able to contain her feelings about the letters he had been sending her regarding their marriage. His emotional blackmail pushed her to respond sharply. She told him he had "wounded [her] three times" since their marriage by expressing regrets. In a bold move, she resolved, "Let it be annulled then." In this line, she showed understanding of her own power—though limited. If the marriage was annulled, she would have the cover of a few weeks of having been lawfully married to him as she resumed her active life in New York. At this point, she was still dealing with the fact that she had received no reply from her mother or sister to the letter she and Dunbar had sent to them and was still worrying about the lack of a marriage certificate. If he would not accept the annulment, she would move at a specified date. Responding in a fit of indignation, she clarified that she was moving for only one reason: because he was "throwing a lot of blame and reproach" at her. And, she did not want him to "wash my face always with—you forced the marriage. If it had not been for you—thus and so." Significantly, she did not say she was going to join him because of her love for him or that she could not live without him; her decision had more to do with resignation to the politics of respectability.

Alice's commitment to moving to DC did not mean that she was willing to give in to his emotional manipulations. Notably, her letters became more resistant to his control. On March 26, she questioned his extravagant spending and went on to share with him what she thought of Dunbar the husband: "I don't like your conception of husbandly ones. You climb up on a pedestal and say things that are not becoming to your style of beauty, nor temper." Critiquing his position as both a husband and as a man, she described him as standing above her in a position of power, a position that he did not deserve because of his treatment of her. Whatever he thought of himself, she claimed sexual agency. In response to his threats of infidelity, she boldly reminded him of her desirability: "If you make love to another girl, I'll retaliate by letting someone here who is very much in love with me kiss me—and that would be simply dreadful." To some degree, she placed herself as an equal to him—capable of the same thoughts and actions. It was her choice not to cross the boundary. Dunbar was on notice that her position as wife had empowered her and that her sense of herself as a desirable woman with an independent spirit had not been extinguished by his abuse.

Yet she still had to deal with the expectations of her family, informed largely by the secret of her paternity. After receiving a tepid letter from her sister and mother granting their blessings, she committed to resigning from her position on April 1, as she foresaw no familial support other than Dunbar's. She first described the letter she received from her sister as "non-committal and disappointing."[64] Her mood changed to upbeat and optimistic when she received their blessings on March 29. Following her family's visit with her at the Matthews' house, where she was a boarder, she was then ready to receive her husband when he came to get her nearly a week later. Their life together began with hope that they would be the Black Brownings, a couple who would shame the critics and impress the elite.

4

Love and Writing

Alice's marriage to Dunbar was both private and public. Dunbar had a stellar reputation as the literary voice of Black people, but he also earned a reputation for drinking and public abuse of his wife. As children of the formerly enslaved, they were part of a historical and social narrative that led to the pressure to succeed. Marriage among middle-class Blacks had its secrets and complications. Neither Dunbar nor Alice had come from homes where they were able to observe marriage. According to Tony Gentry, one of Dunbar's biographers, Dunbar's parents worked hard to make ends meet but fought often.[1] They separated when he was three. By the time the Dunbars married, ideal romance had dissipated, but there was certainly a great deal of high emotion. For Alice, the marriage needed at least to meet the standards of a social ideal. Surely it was her hope that she would redeem the past that involved the secret of her absent father. Only one generation removed from institutionalized sexual exploitation associated with slavery, many middle-class Black women of this era viewed marriage as a way to claim respectability. In Alice's case, she sought ways to empower herself through the reclamation of her sexually violated body and by further establishing herself as a productive writer. If her work mirrors her life as a wife, we find a woman longing to be made whole and to experience an erotic but respectable life.

For Alice, a strong sense of shame and emotional isolation led her to separate from her husband not long after they began living together. Unable to live long in a space that housed both their insecurities and Dunbar's mother, Alice and Dunbar dealt with a long separation that was caused by their emotional, physical, and verbal fights. A letter written by Alice to Dunbar after they were living together opens with a somber tone; although the exact reason for their separation is not discussed, it is obvious that she did not want others to know that she had left him. Private fears must be kept from public scrutiny. Beyond the tone of the letter is Alice's feeling of loneliness and vulnerability, as she informed him that she was keeping secret the real reason why she was traveling northward to see her family. Unfortunately, her desire to guard this information made her feel uncomfortable asking fellow clubwoman Victoria Matthews and her husband for a loan, once she discovered that William Matthews was unavailable to cash her check before the bank closed.

Although the letter does not have a date, references in the previous letters strongly suggest that she is referring to the last check that she had received from her teaching position in New York. Her lack of access to her earnings unless she had a man's assistance illuminates how dependent women were on men to conduct even the most basic business transactions. Alice's letter suggests that she felt compelled to leave because of how Dunbar treated her:

> When you wish me back, dear, tell me, and I will come.
>
> I am not angry, only hurt, hurt terribly. It is of no use for me to say I am sorry that I have come into your life and wrecked it so—I have done it, and I alone am to blame. If I could atone I would.

Persistent and consistent in this marriage were Alice's feelings and Dunbar's resentment about their unplanned, hasty marriage—a ceremony she initiated. Regardless of how he may have characterized her, she did not allow herself to remain a passive victim. Leaving him, despite her uncertain access to her own money and her concerns about her ability to provide for herself, was a bold step and a statement asserting how she expected to be treated by him. As time passed, she continued to make him aware of her expectations.

After leaving New York, she made it back to West Medford, Massachusetts, where she stayed at her sister's home; for about a month and half, Alice and Dunbar went back to writing intimate letters to one another that revealed, among other issues, the source of tension between the two. It began with their tendency to fight, according to Dunbar: "I do hope there won't be any little spats or bickerings. I have been thinking it all over, and I am going to try to be too big to quarrel over petty things with you. I must strengthen your love by loving kindness."[2] Alice's responses acknowledged that he wanted her back, but she also reminded him of their problems—perhaps from his perspective there was her habit of "irritat[ing] you and mak[ing] you despise me, and caus[ing] you to magnify my human weaknesses into unpardonable sins."[3] She concluded that she was of no use to him: "I suppose I am utterly unfit, and it's no use. I am beginning to think you don't love me now, for how can you love a woman who persistently does the wrong thing, and destroys your ideals and hurts your work?" At times, she wavered in her resolve and called herself a "Stupid clumsy brown head," which appeared, at least in part, to be a pet name that he had for her, revealing her willingness to take on the role that he had prescribed for her. Whether she actually believed that she provoked his abuse or whether this was her way of motivating him to take responsibility for his behavior by sharing some of the blame is unclear. Given the fact that she had endured premarital rape, and, nearly two years of emotional and later physical abuse, as I will discuss, she may have been resistant to the treatment but vulnerable to how it made her feel nevertheless. Dunbar responded in a letter that her screaming had given him the reputation of being a wifebeater, a reputation that he had earned for more than any noises people heard coming from their house.

Regardless of his abuse, she desperately tried to establish a respectful loving relationship with her husband. As the children of formerly enslaved parents who had married in a controversial way, their union was haunted by a past that seemed to hinder their ability to bond with one another. In a letter dated after their six-month anniversary, she laid out her requests for promises she wanted him to make:

> Promise me that you'll let past be past, for as long as you brood and harp upon the things that were, just so long will there be inharmony and unhappiness. Promise me that you will try to control your tongue and your temper. Love that is strong as death cannot long survive under a constant fire of insults.[4]

Through her own words, we learn of the abusive environment she had lived in for approximately five months, an environment that she initially tried to avoid by staying in New York. Further, she revealed other issues that she wanted him to deal with, namely a tendency to "throw bits of her personal history into her face," a barrier that impeded her ability to know him on an intimate, personal level. In all of their written correspondence, there appear only two things that she could be referencing. One is the issue of the rape, and the other is the issue of her parentage. According to Gentry, Dunbar's parents often quarreled, and this likely led to their separation, but Dunbar's father remained in his son's life. His parents' marriage, as well as the public knowledge of it and the relationship he had with his father, established Dunbar as unquestionably the product of a respectable union and as unquestionably Black. Not even in this letter does Alice give details of what her husband may have been referencing, but it certainly must have appealed to one of her most deep-seated vulnerabilities, as Alice never directly wrote of her family history, particularly not her paternal side. It is likely that this personal history had to do with her parental background, considering that a reference to the sexual assault would have implicated him as well. Whatever Dunbar knew about her "personal history," he undoubtedly used it to humiliate her and, probably, to call her standing as a respectable woman of a "proper" marital union into question. In addition, she had to contend with his mother's presence and influence over her youngest son: she told him to promise that he would not let his mother rule the house because there "cannot be two heads." While details of his mother's intervention are not given, she was a constant presence in his life and cared for him until his death.

In one of, if not the, most passionate letters written by Alice to Dunbar, she expressed her acute sense of loneliness, resulting in her "long[ing] to be really and truly be a part of your inner life, and for you to be a part of mine." She saw the obstacle to this as "a wall built up of scorn and laughter and false dignity."[5] Finally, she ended by asking him to show respect for her and her love for New Orleans. No written response appears in her archive. Despite the fighting, she hoped that they could remain married. Trusting that her love would be sufficient, Alice gave in and resolved that she could change him: "When I come to you, my darling, even though you may wish to brood and scold and punish me, this great love of mine . . . will disarm you."[6] Considering that he was in the habit of responding to her letters within a week, Dunbar appears to have reserved his response to her letter for her return, suggesting that he resented her comments about his behavior toward her and her request to limit his mother's influence on their marriage. Although she mentioned in the next letter, which was written from New York, that she had been reoffered her old position as teacher, she had, in a manner of speaking, lost her ability to negotiate her independence by telling him that her love for him was greater than his abusive behavior toward her. However, this reference also reminded him that she understood her worth and her ability to care for herself if needed. No matter what, she could always teach. This was the last letter she wrote before her return to DC.

As indicated in their letters, Alice lived in a house where she was being abused. Eleanor Alexander remarks, "Just when her husband became a wife beater is uncertain."[7] Yet, from the letter he wrote to her about screaming in their room and the reputation he was gaining for being a violent person within the first six months of their marriage, it is clear that the verbal and physical abuse began quite early and was an extension of the violent behavior he had exhibited before they married. Alexander points to evidence that the physical abuse was regular and well known to those who were friends of the Dunbars.

Alice must have confided at least some of her experiences to her mother. In a rare letter from her mother, upon her daughter's return, she sent her parental love and support. Since Alice spent so much of her life living with her mother, this letter stands as a rarity, highlighting the glaring necessity of the mother's desire to provide guidance and comfort to her daughter from across the miles. She told her youngest daughter:

> My Dear Bay I was so sorry that you had to leave so soon[.] I hope you had a nice time here. I wanted to see more of you[.] Many thanks for your gift[.] I hope when you come again I hope you will [illegible] [illegible] sun schine [sic] in your home Alice is so happy and now I have nothing to

worry me[.] I know that you are as kind as you can be so may God bless
you[.] My Dear Bay take good care of your self.[8]

While she did not clarify how much she knew of what was taking place in
the marital home of the Dunbars, a reference here to her daughter finding
"sunshine" and that she is "kind" and must "take good care of her self"
suggests that she knew that her daughter and son-in-law were not getting
along and that Alice needed comforting and reassurance. Patricia Moore
reminds her daughter that she is welcomed in her home, even though she is
staying with her daughter and son-in-law. The closeness of the three women
meant that each woman would always have the support of the other.

At one point during their brief marriage, Dunbar received orders from his
doctor to recover from a respiratory illness in a dry region. Dunbar was often
sick as indicated in his letters; of course, some of his health problems were
as a result of his addiction to alcohol. The two went to Denver, Colorado,
during the fall and winter months of 1898–9.[9] Dunbar admitted to slapping
Alice while there and concluded that she "didn't seem to mind."[10] There is
a bit of irony here; if she didn't seem to mind, then why would he slap her?
Perhaps her response to the abuse was not what he expected or hoped for.
Nevertheless, it continued. Other rumors floated of violent public outbreaks
occurring when they returned to Washington. Dunbar's depression and
related addictions certainly contributed to his behavior, but Alice would feel
somewhat responsible.

Her life with him amounted to an emotional battle that may have been
best represented in her poem "Rainy Day."[11] Published in *Advertiser* on
September 18, 1898, it projects a somber mood: "Life may be drear, and
hope seem far away." However, it shifts to a tone of optimism: "But ever
through the mist some bird will sing / And through the dullest, rainy world
of gray, / Some bright-hued flower, its flash of promising bring."[12] Other
than letters, her poetry and fiction certainly reflect her emotional struggles
and hope for change. Alice knew well that life, as in love, was complicated
and unpredictable. Perhaps motivated by her commitment to respectability,
or maybe by her love and commitment to Dunbar, she was steadfast in her
resolve to remain Mrs. Paul Laurence Dunbar.

Not all of their letters dealt with matters of a troubled marriage. In fact,
it would seem that the two enjoyed physical intimacy, which they referenced
quite often in their letters as husband and wife. Or at least they enjoyed
talking about it. Often signed as "Little wifie" and "Hubbins," letters written
to one another when Dunbar was on tour also signaled their intimacy with
"baby-talk," a language that they used to communicate with one another
in private. A way to romantically charm or emotionally disarm the other,
this language served to capture moments when the writer was trying to
connect across the distance and remind the other of times when they both
were happy, even when they were dealing with tension that caused concerns.

One such example is an inquiry Alice wrote about the lack of a letter from Dunbar: "Ittle brown head been wondering what for it doesn't get any little letter. Wonders likewise if it ever will get one anymore."[13] Most likely written in a moment where she feared his silence was a sign that he was not being "true" or "good," she placed the onus of answering for his activities on him. Notably, there were multiple times, including in this letter, when she asked him to alleviate her concerns by telling her that he loved her. Dunbar followed with a letter informing her that he wanted to see her so they could "snuggle, snuggle, snuggle."[14] As an abused woman, Alice could never trust that Dunbar felt satisfied with her as his wife.

Two years after the rape, she reclaimed her body and redefined herself in their marriage as a sexually free being. Despite the fact that their first known physical encounter had not been consensual and resulted in Alice being badly bruised, her "Miss V" longed for "Sir P." In a revealing, highly private statement, she wrote, "Dear, how I want you. Miss V rose up early this morning before I was awake and demanded Sir P. I tried to comfort her with a nice drink of hot water, but she wept and asked for him with tears in her eyes."[15] If we recall that she wrote to him before their marriage, "Temptuous passion, mad desire impatient for pleasures have gone," it is clear that a new Alice had formed, and this Alice rejected suppression of her desires. Remarkably, Alice seems to have risen above the sexual oppression that limited such brazen expressions, thought of as sinful among women, especially an African American woman of her background, during the Victorian age, and seized upon a level of sexual freedom with Dunbar that she was not afraid to share in writing—even though one never knows who could have actually read their letters. In some respects, this letter acts as a form of resistance to the prohibitions set on women's expression of sexual desires. As if winking to an audience of readers, she acknowledged her temerity: "How is Sir P? Tomorrow will be two weeks since he and Miss V had a visit together and she has been making some solicitous inquiries as to his health. Oh, isn't this a naughty letter? It is the wickedest yet. I'd better tear it up for fear someone will see it."[16] Of course, she did not destroy it but sent it to Dunbar and saved it through two more marriages, even until her death.

Exploring the private moments of their life revealed through her frank references to her desires and his inability to satisfy those desires—because of his absence and because of illness—underlines the challenges of their marriage. On the one hand, he had the sole charge of caring for a family of three, which necessitated frequent traveling. On the other hand, he was often physically unavailable due to poor health exacerbated by addictions. What this letter also reveals is that there seemed to be a problem between her and Dunbar, possibly bouts of impotence, which prompted her to ask about Sir P's health (rather than Dunbar's health) after noting that "the visits" were seldom before his departure. There was also hope that these "visits" would bring them children, but, likely as a result of her having contracted a STD from Dunbar before they married, her desire to have children never came to fruition.

Alice's other challenge was living with Maltida Dunbar, who was a major part of their marriage that Alice had no choice but to deal with daily, whether Dunbar was present or not. "Ma," as she was called, was regarded by Dunbar as his best friend, and one of his regrets about eloping was that she had not been there. She was an aging woman who suffered from constant ailments, and Dunbar's prolonged absences from home on reading tours meant that Alice was "Ma's" primary caretaker, although the couple had hired a woman to assist Alice. Letters written to her by Dunbar during his trips always ended with him asking her to give his love to Ma, and it was not uncommon for him to give a bit more attention to expressing his affection for his mother than he gave to his wife, the addressee. Now without her beloved teaching career, her position as his wife consisted primarily of caring for his mother, writing, and managing his business affairs—for example, answering his letters, responding to requests, and providing advice. This life, full of long dull days that depended largely on the excitement of a letter from Dunbar, was a far cry from the active life she had enjoyed prior to her marriage to him as it does not seem that she was active with the club women when she was in DC. This major lifestyle shift also points to another probable reason why she left him for over a month to live with her family and to visit her former colleagues among the women's activists in New York.

Nevertheless, marriage left her with time to dedicate to writing for the first time in her life. Alice's marriage to Dunbar inspired her to write in new forms and genres. Not only did he encourage her to write, but her lack of a salary for the first time in her adult life and the drama that was her life as Mrs. Dunbar gave her enough ideas to set on paper for years to come. At times she would struggle to write and even more often to publish. We find an emphasis on longings. Whether they are for standing in society, for a loving relationship, or for economic stability, these longings make apparent her vulnerability as a woman and as a writer. To satisfy their tug, there is an apparent attempt by the protagonist to make herself whole.

Without question, the most mundane days of her life were when she was Dunbar's wife. For the first time in her adult life she was not working. It is no wonder that she wrote the novella titled *Confessions of a Lazy Woman*.[17] It features a middle-class, married, childless woman who spends her days talking with her housekeeper, reluctantly entertaining guests, and visiting others. Alice confided to Dunbar, who was also a novelist, her frustration with the writing project, saying, "I have done a little, very little work on the 'Confessions' bringing it up, so far 12,000 words. I am much disgusted at it now."[18] Taking advice from Dunbar about making a certain word limit, she recorded the tedious work of building her novel:

I brought "Confessions" up to 14,000 words last night, among other things I arrived at the conclusions that the graduating habit is a national characteristic just as is drinking ice water with meals and having tin-types taken with freak scenery for back-grounds.[19]

Later she wrote him,

I have brought Confessions up to 25,000. . . . I did over 17,000 words in one week. . . . I began copying to-day and I shall revise and arrange it, because it is not written consecutively. In the arranging and revision I expect to add from 3000 to 8000 words, which will make it long enough. Now when it is finished, what am I going to do with it?[20]

She sent it off at 30,000 words to Doubleday, but the work was never published.[21] Interestingly, she spoke of writing the novella as if she were taking medicine. Crafting the novella was a part of a measured daily routine that she regularly followed. Her struggle with meeting the demands of constructing a novel as a young writer is painfully obvious in this unpublished work. Their literary agent Paul Reynolds would write to her on July 27, 1901, after she completed the draft, that he was unable to find a publisher for the work for three reasons: first, it was "too short" as "most publishers like a book of 100,000 words" to make a profit; second, the genre of writing in the form of a diary; third, it lacked action.[22] On the latter point, Reynolds's expertise proved indisputably accurate.

Confessions is a long, underdeveloped short novel set in an unnamed Southern city where carnival is celebrated. Pauline Young, in her letters to potential publishers, described the value of the manuscript: it is

106 typewritten pages, touches on a variety of subjects—most of which are timely—patriotism, feminism, leisure, barbarism, the beauty of naturel [*sic*]. The diary, begun in January of one year, ends in December of the following year: and is a record of the thoughts, actions, and reactions of the narrator, who describes herself as a Lazy Woman, but who demonstrates that she is otherwise.[23]

However, it lacks any form of conflict, resulting in the absence of resolution or intrigue and this is probably why it was not published. The unnamed wife is married to a man named Ned, who appears to have a great deal of time to socialize with his wife and their friends, though he is reluctant to engage with the latter. Fenella, her younger housekeeper who is also her orphaned cousin, is described as "sage and worldly wise and appears aged, and this impressing of her extreme youthfulness makes [the narrator] seem younger."[24] Although the narrator hopes that Fenella will never marry, the young woman does. The fictitious writer's biggest complaints are that she has to accept calls from people who annoy her in various ways and that she spends time with her rather easygoing husband, except on the rare occasions when he complains. Her laziness is made obvious on the first page, where she confesses, first, that she is lazy and, second, that she began her diary twenty-five days after the new year began: "When we are tired of the rest of the world, we go into a retreat, which is furnished as we want it, not as fashion and the upholsterers dictate. There, Ned smokes and grumbles if he wants to, and I pretend to read, though lately I have not gone beyond the magazines." In fact, it is the story of a wife who has decided, "In a rash moment last year, . . . to keep a diary beginning with the new year."[25] Yet in this form we also see that Alice is exploring her purpose. What does it mean to confess to being "lazy"? Is she resisting or critiquing the idea that if a woman does not have a paying job, she may find herself contributing very little to society? For Alice, this may indeed have been the case. Critiquing marriage is a major theme that emerges in this novella, as she dealt with the tension that existed in her own marriage and that appears in this novella as well. In some ways, her struggle to find the words to write a novel written from the point of view of a married woman represented her position as a woman in a marriage where she had already expressed to her husband her desire to "truly [be] a part of your inner life, and for you to be a part of mine." Lacking in her life is closeness with her husband and a career outside the home.

Confessions is an obvious attempt to conjure a fantasy marriage as a means of escaping her own troubled marriage. While the woman and Ned have a "retreat" that symbolizes closeness and intimacy, there seems to have been no such place, either figuratively or literally, for the Dunbars. Interestingly, Alice used the form of confession through diary-keeping as a means to say very little about marriage other than to point to minor irritations and complaints about anything that might distract the two from being together. In her letters to Dunbar, she had asked him not to do anything to run afoul of the people of Washington before she moved there. She had hoped that their marriage would indeed be one that others would talk about as a form of envy. What they ended up talking about, of course, was not what she had hoped.

Given the fictitious *Confessions*, we are left to wonder why there is no diary of this period of her life in her archive. She and her sister, Leila, kept diaries throughout their lives, but the "lazy woman" confesses, "They were also in the habit of burning diaries at the end of the year."[26] There she probably gave voice to the details that would not allow her to fulfill the desire of her fantasy: "We have a nice little game of cards and a bit of a supper afterwards downstairs, all to ourselves, and go to bed serene and happy." Thanks to Dunbar's travel schedule, the presence of his mother, and the abuse, Alice and Dunbar rarely enjoyed the experience described by the Lazy Woman, although they are known to have played cards with other members of the Black elite. This novella, therefore, works more as an allegory for Alice's longing for a married life.

Prior to her attempt to complete *Confessions*, she successfully published a second collection of short stories, *The Goodness of St. Rocque* (1899). Alice never mastered novel writing, but she grew as a gifted short-story writer who could give captivating details of a setting and pose a provocative question in just a few pages. Named for the saint and a diverse section in New Orleans, the collection is clearly set in this area as it focuses on the population of the people of the area, including Black folks, Creoles, Germans, and other European immigrants. Unlike her first collection, *St. Rocque* is a production of more developed short stories, showing the maturity of the author. Although three of the stories, "Carnival Jangle," "Little Miss Sophie," and "Titee," are reprints from the first collection with some variations, *St. Rocque*, unlike *Violets*, does not have overtly strong themes of women's pursuit for equality. In fact, *St. Rocque*'s romantic stories speak more decidedly of relationships and women's treatment by men in those relationships; as in her earlier work, she remained focused on important social concerns regarding the position of women in society. In many of the short stories she published during this period, she explored the theme of fragility and vulnerability as social issues that complicate and, in some cases, disrupt the pursuit for respectability. These may have emerged out of her own sense of uncertainty, as she had left her home state in pursuit of a better life in the North and found herself married to an abusive man. Furthermore, the turn of the century was near. What would be the next step for the country as it addressed unfinished, burgeoning matters—race relations, women's rights, gaps between the poor and the rich? All of these concerns emerge in her literature. Women's desires, among them a search for their place and purpose, figure prominently in her work, where the focus is on women's lives.

Alice relied more on a critique of women's precarious societal position in her story "Sister Josepha," which is one of Alice's most intriguing short stories featuring a woman. One of her most well-known stories, the short story features a young, racially ambiguous orphan, "a child without an identity," whose apprehension about a couple, specifically the man, who wants to adopt her leads her to declare her wish to remain with the nuns who have been caring for her.[27] By the age of eighteen, she has a sexual awakening that compels her to regret the decision and long for freedom. However, her fear that her lack of identity will harm her forces her to remain with the sisters. Kristina Brooks sees her as "particularly vulnerable, given her ambiguous identity."[28] Identity here involves not only her family background but also her unnamed or silenced racial (possibly mixed-race) identity.

Camille represents the uncertainty related to women's social and political positions as the twentieth century neared. When the child is first brought to the sisters, she can speak only in French and prefers the comfort of sucking her thumb. At some point, the child had an identity. Someone gave birth to her and communicated with her in a language that she has come to understand as her own. Whether the family has purposely abandoned her or whether they were separated by no fault of their own is not known. What Camille knows is that she has been abandoned and has not been given a story that will help place her in a community. Consequently, she is given another language. And when she blurts out that she would prefer to remain with the sisters, she is given a name: Sister Josepha.

However, being among the sisters, a community of women, still does not provide her with a home. She feels socially and sexually stifled among the women and their religion. It becomes clear that the young woman is there out of necessity. Between them and the monastery itself, she does not feel as though she belongs. Instead she feels trapped and longs for freedom and love. The longer she stays, the more difficult it is for her to leave. In all practicality, it would be possible for her to leave the convent and to find a community that will accept her, as she has done among the sisters in the convent, but she remains confined by what she does not know.

To some degree, Camille is aware that she has an identity associated with her beauty. When she is a child, the sisters take note of how she receives attention for her looks, especially from the Monsignor. Implied, but not stated, is the idea that the sisters bring the couple to adopt her because they want to remove her from the community. Though she "cannot divine the meaning of the pronounced leers on the man's face," she knows to stay away from him. To the nuns, she is a temptress to the man of God, or perhaps the women are simply jealous. Whatever the reason, her position as part of their community is threatening to the other members. As a form of protection, she shaves her head, but her beauty remains prominent. If she is not one of them, she cannot be among them. Her declaration that she wants to take the vow of chastity puts them at ease but also seals her fate.

Alice makes a strong statement regarding how a woman's inability to define herself or determine her own purpose without hindrance can lead to forms of social and emotional confinement. Camille finds herself at a very young age without a voice and a language: "No name but Camille, that was true, no nationality, for she could never tell from or whence she came."[29] She only has questions: "Who am I? Who am I?"[30] Her desire to pursue the feelings she has for the young man she sees only alerts her to social restrictions that are magnified by her position as a nun. She is not encouraged to move beyond this status when she becomes a "bride of Christ," but rather she languishes in a state of longing. Simply put, she has a set order for her life and expectations that are given to her. Camille as Sister Josepha is pious, pure, submissive, and, based on the duties she performs at the convent, domestic. Brooks observes, "She must consequently quash her individuality under cover of the veil if she wishes to avoid the institutionalized sexual victimization of placage."[31] Independence is only an option if she chooses to seek it. However, it must be noted that Camille does make a conscious choice, albeit a safe choice, to become Sister Josepha. Her choice, then, is one step in asserting some control over her life.

Unlike Camille, Manuela of "The Goodness of St. Rocque" sets a goal to satisfy her desire to capture the undivided attention of a young man. Manuela, a brown-skinned Creole, determines that Theophile will be hers and not Clara's, her blonde, blue-eyed Creole rival for Theophile's affection. Fearing the loss of her love interest to Clara, Manuela makes the decision to seek a woman who gives her a charm and instructions that will sway Theophile in her direction. Rather than languish in a state of longing, Manuela, whose name means "God is with us," takes control of her situation to ensure the desired outcome.

All of the characters are part of the New Orleans Catholic Creole community of St. Rocque. They go to Mass often, say novenas, and light candles to the saints. Yet Catholicism alone may prove ineffective when trying to reach a goal. Alice subverts the idea of a woman being in service and submission to a man: "Theophile was Manuela's own especial property, and Theophile had proven false."[32] Catholicism could not make him behave, but a charm could. Notably, the charm is given by a woman who knows that Clara has made a novena for Theophile—in Catholicism a novena is a series of prayers, possibly on the rosary, spoken for a specific purpose over a period of nine days and usually addressed to a saint. If the saints are kind to the blond-haired girl, the brown girl will need something stronger to counter their kindness. Her charm will win Theophile back, but she must light a candle and say a prayer of thanks at St. Rocque's, the Creole's Catholic church.

The Wizened One is knowledgeable in conjuring. Although Alice was Christian (though not Catholic), the traditions of conjuring are so ingrained in New Orleans culture that it is a wonder she did not write many more stories about Voodoo and conjuring. She would have had some sense of traditional West African religious practices, which were common though not discussed in public in New Orleans culture. Her mother, according to Akasha Hull, was a practitioner of Obeah.[33] Although I find no references to this particular religion in the archives, it is likely that the formerly enslaved woman engaged in some form of traditional African practices. Alice's mother, Patricia Moore, was an enslaved woman who would have probably passed down knowledge of African religious practices to her daughter. In "The Goodness of St. Rocque," Alice does not name the religious practice of the Wizened One; as with Catholicism, the practitioners may know little about the origins of the traditions they are following. However, it should not go unnoticed that Alice has the brown girl seek the assistance of the Wizened One so that she can overpower the blonde girl.

This is not simply a story about a love-sick girl who wishes to marry the man she desires. It is a story about a young woman's decision to have what she wants. It is a story about pursuit of the erotic and resistance of the cult of womanhood, symbolized by Clara, who acts as a barrier to that possession. Donna Aza Weir-Soley provides insight into the struggle for agency in this era:

> Nineteenth-century black women writers formulated a dual strategy for addressing this issue: they internalized the moral standards of Judeo-Christian theology to support the maintenance of this separation, while simultaneously claiming that due to their condition of sexual servitude, black women were incapable of living up to the Victorian standards of sexual purity that the cult of true womanhood demanded.[34]

If Manuela's purity is to be legitimized through the sanctity of marriage, then she will choose to whom she will be married. Reacting to her own lack of choices, Alice consented to marrying Dunbar despite a rape but possibly to not live under a shroud of mystery as her mother had. In this fictional case, however, she creates a romance in which the young woman does not simply consent. Simultaneously, she rejects the idea of women submitting by having the man submit to his lover, whether he knows it or not. Manuela finds spiritual liberation by "empowering spirituality."[35] Probing the meaning of coupling or marrying from a woman's perspective is a major theme in Alice's work. While she may have purified herself through marriage to Dunbar, Alice initially chose not to marry him. However, there is no evidence that she was opposed to marriage or even to a woman marrying the one she loves.

Other women in Alice's fiction do not find liberation and empowerment through choice in love as does Manuela, and we learn from them that marriage or coupling can be stifling, confining. Though Alice was married at the time when she published this collection, only two of the stories, "Msieu Fortier's Violin" and "Tony's Wife," feature couples, one legally married and one not legally. In these, she explores the meaning of marriage as representative of respectability. Both these stories make statements about the treatment of wives.

First, "Msieu's Violin" is about a talented violinist who loses his job with the orchestra, and as a result he, his wife, and his cat suffer from the impact of his lost income. After selling the violin, he retrieves the prized instrument from the buyer, who also allows him to keep the money. This short story is about a man and his violin; unlike Alice's short stories about relationships in which the woman appears prominently, Fortier's wife is relatively silent. Fortier thinks, "He told all his troubles to her [the cat]; it was no use to talk to Ma'am Jeanne, she was too deaf to understand."[36] His dismissal of his wife as unable to offer any support about his worries renders her silent, absent, and deaf. Yet the stream-of-consciousness narrator says that she waits up every night for him to return home from the orchestra. Since the narrator relays the events through the point of view of Fortier, Alice suggests that it is he who silences her. What does it mean to be "too deaf to understand?" At the end of the short story, when he asks for the violin back, he tells the man that his wife has "mope[d] and look[ed] bad too" since he sold the violin. Clearly, she can hear well enough to know that the violin music is no longer part of her household. Fortier does not recognize his wife as a partner in their relationship. He is in charge of the household, and she merely lives there.

Alice presents another woman who is without a voice in her "marriage." "Tony's Wife" has a misleading title. An abusive Italian man and a German woman who are not married but live together operate a store on Prytania Street in New Orleans. Once he becomes ill, the "wife," who is rumored to be named Mary (a play on marry), begs him to legally marry her as her "brother-in-law," John, awaits Tony's death and his fortune. Tony, who admittedly hates his "wife," sticks to his resolve that she will not inherit his fortune and, therefore, refuses to marry her. Once he is dead, John takes possession of the man's estate and she finds herself homeless and penniless. Alice poses an important question in "Tony's Wife" about the importance of identities and women's rights. More personally, she also makes a statement about the feeling of dependence on a man whose treatment lacks respectability. Like Alice in her letters to Dunbar during their separation, she begs her abusive common-law husband (which has no legal meaning in Louisiana) to move beyond coupling and to give her the respect of marriage. This is the second story in the collection where a woman's sense of her own identity is limited by the confined space she occupies, the other being "Sister Josephina." For at least one generation, the children and others in the neighborhood know the woman only as "Tony's wife," the person who sits behind the counter and knits lace. She answers to Tony's orders and tolerates his physical abuse. "When she displeased him, he beat her, and knocked her frail form to the floor." Her bruised body, described by the narrator as "frail," becomes a narrative of vulnerability that makes the children feel sorry for her and think "poor Mrs. Tony."

Alice focuses on the woman's hands, which give her the ability to create work that people see and admire and which allow her to forge an identity apart from Tony and the store. Just as Alice's ability to write gave her an independent identity, so "Mary's" ability to craft lace makes her an individual, though the lace, a symbol of femininity, is also expressive of her delicate position in Tony's life and in society as an unmarried woman. Because of the lace, people see her and not just as a bruised woman. Furthermore, she has contact with people who want to emulate the beauty that she creates with the "incessant twist."[37] This knitting allows her to make a space of her own in the space that is his. At times, she is engrossed in the knitting and only ventures from it when someone calls her to fetch an item for sale or to do housework. When she is cast out of the patriarchal space of the house, it is possible for her to make a living with her creative abilities. Years later, in the second stanza of her poem, "I Sit and I Sew," Alice wrote, "I sit and sew—my heart aches with desire." Although published in 1920, the poem very well represents the theme of desire—for respect, stability, and love—found not only in this short story but in Alice's life and other works.

Hopeful that her desires for social respectability and financial stability will be met, "Mary" remains silent and endures abuse. Her lack of a voice, combined with her eventual begging of the man to make her his wife legally, minimizes her worth even more in a society that limits women's access to full citizenship. There is an important statement here about the significance of voice for women in a society that restricts women's rights. Many questions emerge: How did the woman come to be with a man who is not her legal husband? Why does she stay with the man considering his treatment of her? One answer might be finances. We know that nineteenth-century women who were sexually active before marriage would have stood little chance of being respected by other men. She may have found herself stifled by the Victorian virtue of purity, like "poor Miss Sophie" and, to some extent, Camille. Identifying a common theme in the experiences of Miss Sophie, Camille, and Mary, Elizabeth West posits that Alice "suggests that failed romance is connected less to chance or individual failure, and more to a social and economic system that leaves women the more vulnerable party in romantic encounters."[38] We hear the confidence of Tony's voice in this short story. He refuses to marry her because he says she only wants his money, but marriage to her would mean more than inheritance. If they marry, she would also have a moral standing in the church as his widow and not as his concubine. Tony has the power to influence the German woman's legal, religious, and social standing. It is a power that he uses to further abuse and silence her.

Kristina Brooks sees this story as making a statement about ethnic purity and racial pride, a position that Tony feels he holds as an Italian and that his wife does not as German. Brooks asserts, "The foundation for Tony's abusive domination, though, is his sense of ethnic superiority."[39] A woman who was herself in an abusive relationship and the daughter of a man who seems not to have married her mother, Alice understood "Tony's Wife" intimately. Secrecy surrounding the writer's parental background was a source of tension that Dunbar possibly drew from to shame his wife. His sense of purity as a man of two parents identified him as Black, giving him a claim on Blackness that was not so easily given his wife.

Respectability politics' intersection with identity and a search for wholeness continued to dominate Alice Dunbar's literature. During her marriage, she also wrote and sold "Stones of the Village," a short story featuring Victor Grabert, a Creole reared in a small town under the care of his prejudiced West Indian grandmother. Learning from his grandmother through public reprimand not to play with his yellow and brown "nigger" neighbors, he finds himself at the age of fourteen isolated from his community. In a fit of compassion for her grandson's long suffering, she sends him to board with her only friend in New Orleans. Having been sent there to make a man out of himself, he lands a job with a bookseller who assumes from his light skin color that he is White. Victor's position allows him to indulge his appetite for knowledge, and he becomes a voracious reader of philosophy, history, and French literature, a habit that brings him comfort, until the bookseller dies and the store is sold. Shortly thereafter, Victor learns from a lawyer that the man has left him a sum of money to attend Tulane College, a segregated school for White men. Indulging this request means the end to the few relationships that could inadvertently expose his African ancestry. After rising up through the social ranks to attain a judgeship and marry a member of an influential White family, he dies silent never having shared the secret about his racial identity.

Plagued by his inability to speak his frustrations and fears, this man illuminates the meaning of silence. We meet him at the age of fourteen, when his grandmother has already determined that silence about his parentage will determine his social identity. She is a mysterious woman who may have Caribbean ancestry—where exactly is not clear, but considering the history of Louisiana and the language she uses, she is probably from Haiti. At some point, she has informed Victor that he is parentless; his mother died when he was a baby, and his father is simply not present. Where his other relations are located is not known, and asking his grandmother, a woman who seems content with their isolation from both the White and the Black communities, is not an option he feels comfortable exploring. Silence, a relative of secrecy, is often present in ruptures of respectability. Victor learns from her to communicate with the world through suspicion and silence. By the time he goes to New Orleans and is offered the opportunity to attend Tulane, "No one had asked any questions, and he had volunteered no information concerning himself."[40] But silence is haunting.

The New Orleans that Alice knew and experienced was a central location for race-mixing and activism, but there was not always a balance between the two. He has power of the law, which enables him to effect change in how people are classified, what they have access to, and how they are able to contribute to society. In "People of Color in Louisiana," her historical study of the African presence in New Orleans and the people's contributions to the development of the territory into a state,[41] she probes the meaning of law in examining the history and treatment. "The person of color was now, in Louisiana, a part of its social system, a creature to be legislated for and against."[42] Victor has the potential to disrupt the legislation that is the history of the state and to push or resist being legislated against. However, he fears this power, knowing that his possession of it also means that he can become an enemy of the institution. It is only when dealing with the court and in the face of the decisions that he can make that he reacts emotionally. First, when a well-dressed Black man is insulted by a court recorder, a person who does not have a professional position analogous to him, Victor reacts by firing his own assistant, a Black man, and hiring an Irish man. His reasoning:

he does not want anyone to suspect that he and the man are of the same race. Second, when a Black man is removed from a restaurant, Victor has an angry reaction but excuses himself in front of his colleague for fear that his colleague might detect his African ancestry. Last, when he is asked in court by a man who knows the woman with whom he boarded in New Orleans if he would remove his own son from an integrated school, he knows that silence is not absolute protection. Victor wants desperately to speak against the racism that has influenced his grandmother's decision to mark him as different from the yellow and brown "niggers," who retaliated by throwing stones at him. Jordan Stouck observes, "In a performance of whiteness that undermines supposedly naturalized concepts of race and cultural identification, Victor reveals the cost of maintaining identity fictions."[43] Victor feels that his "blood is tainted in two ways";[44] we can only guess what the two ways are.

In addition to illuminating the pain among mixed-race, light-skinned Southerners, Alice probed the relationships among masculinity, race, and power. Her marriage gave her an opportunity to engage masculine perspectives as she was able, for the first time in her life, to observe a man and talk with him on a regular basis. Therefore, she probed the lives of men. Mr. Fortier, in her *St. Rocque* collection, is similar to Victor, as he resides in an isolated world while his wife seems unaware of his feelings of despair. Victor feels guilty about how he has gained his power, and this guilt makes him socially unable to use it at a time when people of New Orleans, including a Black woman and an attorney, appeal to him to help correct the wrongs that he knows from personal experience do exist. Only a man can be in a position to make these changes, as Tulane was a college for men—men held the right to vote, and men held positions as judges. If a man did not change the laws, then the laws simply would not be changed. Alice's short story, then, sees the limits resulting from the intersections of race and gender. Ironically, even though she sold the story, she remarks to Dunbar that she was unhappy with the amount of money her male agent, Reynolds, would receive for its acceptance.[45] Although she took on the role of being Dunbar's wife and her mother-in-law's caretaker, she continued to use her writing to analyze gendered positions of power and the reality of race relations in America. Victor's death—"The secret died with him, for Pavageau's lips were ever sealed"—represents the social death that is bound to occur when Black people hesitate to protest legalized racism, especially in the South.[46]

The story of Victor's secret, protected by silence, is not simply about racial identity and its intersection with class and privilege. It is also a story about the silence surrounding the origins of a man who may exist as a consequence of sexual violation. It is not known who his parents are. Did his mother have a loving relationship with his father? His grandmother's insistence that he know nothing of his parents suggests her navigation of the politics of silence, because the consequences of sexual violation emerge every time the question is asked and the answer is denied. Such silence furthers his separation from

Black people, leaving him without a home and place. This is where his troubles begin, and his need both to establish this for himself as a husband and father, to make his own family history, is what leads to his untimely death and, along with it, the failure of his hope for a purpose that extends past simple survival and social status.

Deeply entrenched in him is his desire to speak out about racism and its relationship with interracial prejudice—an issue that Alice knew personally. In a letter to Dunbar, she wrote about his expressing negativity about her "personal history," which she did not explicitly name in the letter. Later, in "Brass Ankles Speaks," written between 1928 and 1931, she wrote of how she was mistreated by those who thought she was different because of her light skin, declaring, "It is not so much that they dislike the darker brethren, but the darker brethren DO NOT LIKE THEM."[47] She provided absolutely no reason for why her own skin color was light enough to pass, resulting in her being called "half white nigger" and "yaller nigger" by those Blacks darker than she. Her focus was on the discrimination and labeling, as well as the division that led her to feel that she was part of the Black community but somehow not accepted as a full member of it. Like Miss Sophie and Tony's wife, Patricia Moore might have sought some level of financial security through a relationship with Alice's father but would also have given away both her virtue and her chance at marriage to a Black man. The result was rearing daughters without a paternal presence in a society that valued clear paternal ties. As Elizabeth West observes, "The conspicuous absence of clearly distinguishable black characters paves the way for [Alice's] conspicuous critique of the self-proclaimed white male hero" who leaves the woman vulnerable.[48] Such a critique of the White male hero is not simply fictional but is certainly derived from her biography. Heroes have a purpose to serve the needy in some capacity. Like Victor, Alice was unable to escape the mark of light skin and auburn hair that divided her from her maternal race and possibly even her husband. Like other White men in her stories and possibly in her life (Dunbar may be included here), Victor, a man who passes as White in appearance and deed, fails to achieve hero status.

Her writing was certainly inspired by her own experiences—both lived and observed—and family instability resonated as a major theme in her work. It is no wonder that so much of her literary focus is on the misunderstood, forgotten, marginalized, and unseen. During her marriage to Dunbar, she continued to work on a number of manuscripts between 1899 and 1910, a period overlapping with her marriage to Dunbar and extending into her second marriage to Henry Callis. *The Annals of 'Steenth Street* was clearly inspired by her work with the mission, "located around 87th between Second and Third Avenues, underneath the El with the East River in view."[49] Following the advice of Dunbar to write about her mission work, she crafted these short stories to reflect her service as a teacher and social worker at the White Rose Mission.

What is most notable about these stories is her attention to the destitute people of a neighborhood of European immigrants, including Irish and German (as she described in a letter to Paul Laurence Dunbar), and her interest in the impact that a lack of resources has on children. As Caroline Gebhard asserts, Alice "mutes racial markers" in these stories.[50] We see here not only her own experiences as an observer of poor immigrants and African Americans but also her own commitment to children, which began when she was in New Orleans, continued through her work as an educator, and was strengthened by her experience as an aunt to her three nieces and her nephew in Delaware. Part of the mission of Black club women was to help poor uneducated Blacks, as Mrs. Booker T. Washington stated. In the 'Steenth Street stories, what we often find in Alice's literature, especially these short stories, is not a judgment of the poor through the lens of respectability but rather a desire to reveal their humanity. For the most part, these short stories illuminate the lives of people in need, especially parents' love of their children and the children's love of their parents; the stories place these experiences in contrast to the rich, who appear as self-centered and selfish villains. All of the tales show how precarious a family's attempts to survive can be when the specter of financial instability looms near. They also allow Alice to revisit a time when she felt she had a clear purpose in her own life—to improve the lives of the vulnerable.

Among the stories inspired by her work is "The Revenge of James Brown," published in the *American Episcopal Church Review* in 1929. In the absence of a father, who prefers to receive sustenance at a place that only services men, James Brown, a proud child of the neighborhood, rebels against the mission that has been opened in his neighborhood by forming a gang. When his mother spanks him and makes him go to the mission to obtain help for the destitute family, James goes once but then stays away to find a job.

Building on her ability to capture local color, Alice provided a backdrop that pit the rich against the poor. Seen through the eyes of the people in the community, the "outsiders" are wealthy folks: "Aristocracy in silk-lined gowns was walking in and out among the babies and dirty little folks swarming on the curbstones."[51] Though these "aristocrats" were there to open a mission, "'Steenth Street felt itself disgraced and intruded upon."[52] She used dialect to express the child's feeling of "disgrace": "I wonder who dey s'pose is a going' ter be foolin roun'here wid dey bible talk?" His reference to the Pure at Heart Mission, poised to help the lowly and the "dirty," comes from a child who sees himself as neither lowly nor dirty.

In the next paragraphs, Alice outlines the purpose of the Mission with particular emphasis on the women proprietors. She cast the leader as "a nervous, energetic woman with a white, sorrow-drawn face, and voice of caressing monotonous sweetness."[53] Without question, Alice relied on her own experiences as a woman who worked in a Mission with the sole purpose of providing "Soul-saving, child-training and mother-helping" services. These three objectives accurately reflect the aims of the settlement work done by the women's clubs and her own interactions with wealthy White donors, whom they had to solicit for funds. Though "The Revenge of James Brown" was published in 1929, Hull believes it was written nearly a decade before, but probably not long after Alice was in a position to observe the children she described and the wealthy women she criticized in these short stories. At this point, she seemed to have been questioning the level of respect and consideration given to the people of the communities they entered and served. By giving the children a voice, she reinstated an identity that the club women and the donors had silenced as they worked to improve the community members' lives. Questions emerge: Were the standard expectations fair and humane? Who benefitted?

"'Steenth Street was noted as the resort of every kind of wickedness."[54] In this, the Pure at Heart Mission does not represent just the rich versus the poor but also good versus evil. What is not evident, however, is who defines evil? The passive voice used in this statement leaves readers to wonder by whom the Street was "noted" as "the resort of every kind of wickedness." Jimmy, a thirteen-year-old block captain, "was proud of the reputation of his community."[55] Yet Jimmy is relatively harmless and hardly appears an imp of Satan. This is made painfully clear when he is "spanked, ignominiously, unreservedly" by his mother for refusing to go to the mission to ask for aid, though his siblings are hungry and sick. He'd rather fight members of his "gang" than deal with his mother.

His revenge is to get a job, so he can assert his manhood and gain a feeling of independence from his mother and the father he cannot rely on for support. Alice focuses on the boy's perspective on the mission and his mother, which allowed her to shed light on the complexity of a community. While she shows the need for the mission, she also shows the people's desire to do for themselves and not to rely on others to provide for them. Interestingly, debates about the working poor and their "reliance" on handouts continue to persist.

A second story about the children of the neighborhood is "The Downfall of Abe Powers." Abe, one of the gang referenced in "The Revenge of James Brown," is the son of an alcoholic woman; along with other neighborhood boys, he avoids fighting and mayhem in the days leading up to Christmas to earn a gift from Mrs. Monroe, a mission worker. Abe is successful, somewhat. Unlike those in the other stories in the collection, the mother in this story is the center of her child's troubles. True to Alice's pattern, there is no father present in the home or any male hero, leaving Abe to assert his manhood in the neighborhood by bullying the other boys, much like James Brown, who is not mentioned in this short story. One has to wonder what has become of James: has he succumbed to the pressures of the vile streets, has he successfully moved beyond gang life, or has Abe separated from him and formed his own independent gang? Is he still alive? Whatever the reason for James's absence, Abe is no better off than James was. He, like James, must fend for himself when his parents are incapable of providing for him.

In an era when Prohibition was at the forefront of American politics and religious concerns (alcohol was outlawed between 1920 and 1933), the alcoholic mother emerges as a source of evil in her son's life. Abe Powers is able to shy away from fighting for two weeks and is proud of his achievement. His mother's alcohol addiction makes him reliant on the Pure at Heart Mission, which will give him a gift if he changes his "bad" behavior, even if his reform is temporary and carried out to satisfy a desire for a gift. On the other hand, he is a child, and his desire for the Christmas gift reveals his emotional and financial fragility and his need to be acknowledged as worthy, even though he is too embarrassed to admit it to his peers. His mother's drunkenness humiliates him and threatens to ruin his chances of achieving the goal he has set for himself of being good and receiving an award for his goodness.

Abe's act of lashing out against the pastor illuminates the clash between the religious and secular, begging the question of who is right and who is wrong. The pastor's visit brings upon the child the shame that he felt in the street of seeing his mother publicly drunk. He knows well the lessons to be learned from drunkenness. The pastor does not question Abe about how he is doing or offer any aid; instead he simply tells the boy of his mother's indiscretions and reminds him not to follow her lead. Ashamed, tired, and in need of love and support, Abe responds in anger and jeopardizes his chances of receiving the Christmas gift.

A child with an uncertain future, Abe must find redemption during the season of birth and renewal. In an effort to be "Pure at Heart," Abe writes a letter to Mrs. Marion, confessing his sins and apologizing. His childish scrawl, replete with misspelled words and run-on sentences, only further highlights the boy's need for support and the meaning of the small gift. It also reflects his longing for understanding, which he receives. Mrs. Marion's acts of giving the child the gift and later providing a lesson on proper behavior are acts of love that he desperately needed from someone, especially a woman whom the boys seem to respect. In this short story, Alice humanizes the poor and needy as well as celebrates the sincerity of a community servant.

A third story, "Miss Tilman's Protogée" (1899), is the story of a wealthy woman who assumes that a poor child needs a proper home, that home being hers. She goes so far as to take the little girl, Hattie, from her home to try to convince her that she should leave her parents and brother to live with her and enjoy the toys and other items she is willing to purchase for her.

Hattie's physical state is what draws Miss Tilman's attention:

Hattie was deformed. Her eyes were dim and near-sighted, and one of her legs was twisted painfully. But she did not like to be pitied or petted, and she was happiest when it was taken for granted that she was like other children.[56]

How Hattie sees herself and her own life shows her ability to define her own social condition. "Poor" and "disabled" are not words that enter into her psyche as a way to determine her state of being. "She had her brother John, who always took prizes at school, and her kitten, and she was happy." In the very next sentence, Alice writes, "They were poor, but she always had enough to eat, and her mother and father, rough generally to all the world, were singularly gentle to her."[57] By ending one sentence with the word "happy" and beginning the next with an emphasis on the family unit as "poor," Alice emphasizes that the girl's social condition is based on her own perception and is not subject to reinterpretation by a person like Miss Tilman, who is not part of the child's family.

However, Miss Tilman has no respect for the child's agency; instead she is intent on exploiting the child to define her own happiness. Similar to James Brown, Hattie does not see herself as a victim of circumstances. Drawing from her work as a social worker with the White Rose Mission, Alice pits the child's welfare against the selfish desires of a wealthy woman. Miss Tilman insists that Hattie, a little girl who has a limp and is the daughter of poor, working parents, must want to live with her. But Hattie's answer to Miss Tilman's question: "Don't you want to come and live with me?" reveals that she has no interest in leaving her family. She says that she will go only if her brother, Johnny, can come too. On second thought, she informs Miss Tilman that she wants to stay "wid her mothu." Miss Tilman's lack of interest in Hattie's brother and Hattie's response shows that she considers the members of the child's family and the life that little Hattie has as unacceptable in comparison to the life she wants to give to the girl.

Miss Tilman wants Hattie to form part of the iconography of her own life. As she tries to tempt the child to choose to live with her and to abandon her own mother, enticing her with toys, she clearly sees the child as a possession. She tells the social worker, "She'd look lovely in a dear white apron with her hair smooth sitting at my feet in the study."[58] Her picturesque description places the child in a position of servitude that relegates her to the floor level. Furthermore, the child who adores her family would find herself alone, far from the center of the family's loving unit, a protective space that she has become accustomed to occupying. In Miss Tilman's home she would be treated as "different," an experience that she does not want to have, preferring instead to be treated as any other child. But Miss Tilman does not see her as any other child; if she did, Hattie would be of no interest to Miss Tilman, who "had a charitable soul."[59] It was part of her "artistic spirit to note the supposed contrast between herself, and those 'dear people' as she was wont to call them."[60]

Her obsession with making the child hers despite the little girl's rebuffs and lack of interest highlights the meaning of the statement Alice uses to describe Miss Tilman: "[She did not] understand many things. Indeed, it is doubtful if she ever could."[61] Obsession clouds her ability to benefit from her own observations. When she makes her way to the child's home and finds her alone but content with a little dollhouse, dolls, and other playthings, she is repulsed by what is not there rather than pleased with what is. It is clear that although Hattie's parents cannot stay home to watch her, they are capable of providing their children with a furnished and loving home. Yet Miss Tilman cannot or will not understand: "The idea of the workingman paying for a decent home for his family had as yet not occurred to her."[62] Instead, she chooses to convince herself that the child is not properly cared for by her parents, who return home to find her missing; she has been taken to the toy store by Miss Tilman without the parents' consent.

Miss Tilman's presumptive attitude about the needs of the child, based solely on her own self-interests, marks her as "needy." Once they return to the child's home and find upset parents, it still does not occur to her that what the child most cherishes is the love of her family. Miss Tilman leaves, feeling that she has dealt with people who are ignorant, but the unsympathetic observant narrator makes sure to emphasize that the ignorance is Miss Tilman's alone. Her obsession with having the child as her own, a child who is not up for adoption and is lovingly cared for by her parents, reverts attention to Miss Tilman. Her lack of respect for the family unit leads to a question about her own family. Given her title of "Miss," it is safe to assume that she is not married and does not have her own children. To fill her days, she sings in the choir and finds charitable projects. Her interest in the child points to her desire to have someone in her life, a family of her own. While Alice appears critical of wealthy people presuming to dictate all aspects of the lives of people in financial need, she also explores the motives of female philanthropists. Miss Tilman's wealth cannot fill the hole of unmet desires in her life.

By giving voice to society's neglected and misunderstood poor children and immigrants, the *'Steenth Street* stories make prominent the theme of vulnerability that is also prevalent in *Violets* and *The Goodness of St. Rocque*. In the earlier stories, Alice took her cue from the New Negro Woman movement to critique the treatment of women and to show how the idea of the New Woman offers no protection to women of color and ethnic women in the South from sexual exploitation. Women must find ways to circumvent a society that does not support their desire to move from economic uncertainty to independent financial security. *'Steenth Street* reminds us that some of these women are mothers. If there are no male heroes to save the women in the earlier collections of short stories, there are rarely any on 'Steenth Street. The feelings of shame, loneliness, oppression, and vulnerability are seen through the perspective of children marked as "other" and "different." Alice's own experiences as the wife of an abusive man and the daughter of a woman who had no legal husband—experiences that left her with a sense of shame and vulnerability—are central to the work she produced.

Enduring abuse from Dunbar was not the only experience she had with violence and injustice. Newspapers would report that she had been assaulted by a police officer on September 17, 1901, which occurred at the Capitol at the time of President McKinley's body lying in state. During a stampede, Alice was struck on the left temple by Officer William Kemp. The commissioners found that the matter could only be decided by a jury. Although Dunbar was present and supportive of her complaint, they were Negroes, and both would be dismissed.[63]

Life with Dunbar may have exacerbated Alice's empathy for those who fought desperately against feelings of shame, weakness, and vulnerability. Despite her efforts to be a wife to Dunbar and to maintain the ideal of the respectable middle-class African American couple, their love for one another was not enough to keep the two together. Abuse continued during their marriage. He would often beat her, something that was public knowledge to their friends and to her family, who had moved in with them. As vile as these acts were, society would not intervene in a man's right to deal with his wife as he pleased. She wrote to Dunbar's earliest biographer regarding why she left him in spring 1902: "He came home one night in a beastly condition. I went to him to help him to bed—and he behaved as your informant said, disgracefully." Consequently, she claimed to have "been ill for weeks with peritonitis brought on by his kicks." Dunbar's view of her, which he shared with others immediately after the incident, caused her to leave him. Ultimately, she left him not because of the physical abuse but because of "the slander."[64] Exactly what he said remains as obscure as her father's identity. In the end, respectability clearly determined what she would tolerate and what she would not. Slander may very well have been an attack on her sexual morals, whether it has to do with her family or her as an individual. Evelyn Brooks-Higgobatham provides context: "respectability offered these women a perceived weapon in defense of their sexual identities."[65] Retaining her identity as a married woman, they never divorced, and she remained his wife in the eyes of those who respected Dunbar's work. Striking a balance between public expectations and private experiences, she kept his name but would not keep him.

Black elite circles knew of their "marital troubles," and some were involved in one way or another. Dunbar's close friend, Sallie Brown, wrote a letter to Alice asking her to return to her "brother" Paul whom she described as "suicidal." He, according to Brown, admitted that he had "acted as a scoundrel." Alice had heard this before as early as his response to her rape. She remained unmoved by his latest attempt for reconciliation. For her part, Alice's friend Victoria Earle Matthews was highly disturbed by how Dunbar had included her in their troubles. She wrote a passionate letter denying any "malicious" lies told by Alice's husband and "men of the world." She began in her letter dated April 4, 1902, that she had "heard that . . . your husband claims that his brutal treatment of you was based upon something I had said to him against you." The rest of the three-page letter refuted any claims that she would have shared any of her "confidences" with Dunbar. Yet, in her outrage about Dunbar implicating her in his abuse of his wife, she did not hesitate to berate her friend for believing Dunbar, who "lies in every thing." She told her, "Your experience ought to have prepared you for such an outrageous lie."[66] Matthews may have been referring to the premarital abuse. To clarify her position as her close friend, Matthews closed by extending Alice sympathy as she told her she saw Alice as a "suffering wife regardless of her attitude toward [her]."[67] In defense of herself, she cast this as a gender debate. Dunbar, as far as Matthews was concerned, was using her name and impugning her reputation to justify abusing his wife. Her letter is an attempt to reject Dunbar's use of her in this way to harm another woman. Matthews's letter is an example of how the abuse of one woman effected other Black women in their lives.

If Dunbar could use a woman to justify abuse, then he would use one to try to convince his wife to return to him. During their separation, Dunbar expressed sympathy for his abandoned sister-in-law[68] as he tried to convince his estranged wife to return to him. Relaying what he heard from a female acquaintance, he wrote:

> She spoke of Leila's coming up unexpectantly to see [her husband] and of his resentment and she sent love and sympathy to the deserted wife! My God, how I felt, Alice, there must be some plane upon which we can come together. I have been a coward and a bastard but I love you.[69]

It was probably Alice's closeness to her sister that fueled her resolve to concentrate on her own family and to remain separated from Dunbar, regardless of the fact that her departure would surely become the talk of Black social circles. But, as Matthews made clear, she was already the subject of public discussion. A return to the letters shows the beginning of major financial problems for Alice after she left Dunbar. Her most valuable assets were her talent, her education, and her last name, which she used to make the money that meagerly provided necessities for her mother, sister, three nieces, and nephew, in the absence of their father.

In the light of the politics of respectability—or even more blatantly put, the history of sex, both consensual and nonconsensual—among African Americans, Alice struggled to critique the experiences of her early life, as she came to know them in her work as a writer, activist, and wife. She was a woman who proved her love for the "mother race" with hopes that what she did for the race would mean a better life for herself as well. As a Black woman committed to work to uplift the race by providing services to protect Black women from exploitation, using the power of writing to bring light to the history of sexual exploitation in the South and revealing the humanity of America's marginalized communities, she found herself limited when it came to dealing in real life with a man of her own race. For Alice, maintaining the status of a pure lady would take on various meanings, and she would spend a lifetime finding ways to confront the various violations of women, including herself, in both her public and private life. As she rebuilt her career and defined herself, she would learn to make her experiences as Dunbar's wife into an asset and to move past the pain and shame.

5

Loving Alice after Paul

Without Dunbar, Alice moved with her fractured family to Wilmington, Delaware, in 1902, where she and her sister began teaching at Howard School and she became the co-parent of her sister's children. Settled in a new home at 1008 French Street, they found a community among other Black people in the growing city. On French Street, Alice not only became a respected member of the Black community as the published writer and famous wife (later widow, in 1906) of Paul Laurence Dunbar but also became romantically involved with three different people—an older man, her female principal, and a younger man (her second husband)—before she settled down with her third and last husband, Robert "Bobo" Nelson.

In Wilmington, where she would spend the bulk of her life, she built coalitions across the city's racial, ethnic, and religious communities and further developed her national network among the Black elite on the east coast. When she moved to Wilmington, the city, similar to so many American cities, was trying to find its identity. Wilmington, Delaware, was quite different from the metropolitan city of Washington, DC. The city was small and segregated with a growing Black community that depended heavily on Howard School. It was founded as a "farmers town, a place of trade, and for the service of ships and mills" but eventually became home to the mill industry, processing commodities such as cotton.[1] As an early slaveholding state, there was a presence of people of African descent and a history of oppressing those people. Nearly thirty years after the Civil War ended, the formerly enslaved and other newcomers to the state were trying to find their place and establish their path toward equality. Slow progress was measured when the state joined with philanthropic groups to open schools for Black children. In 1891, Delaware State University opened to educate "colored citizens." Political gains were made locally through optimistic Black Wilmington citizens when Tomas E. Postles, a small businessman, was elected to the City Council in 1901 and then reelected in 1905. However, a man named George White was lynched in 1903.[2] There were no safe places for Black people in the United States during this era, but she would not cower to fear of death. It was the perfect place for Alice to grow her activist profile.

Along with their mother, she and her sister, Leila, made a life for themselves as lifelong supporters of each other. Although each had their own lives and Alice often complained about her sister's trivial annoyances, they worked together and lived together. Most of the records show that Alice's organizational activities did not involve her sister, at least not as an officer. This may have been because her priority was to her children. However, the women entertained at their house and, of course, they worked together. What Leila knew of her sister's sexual life, we will never know, but it is likely that she had some idea of her sister's intimate relationships.

Four years after she moved to Wilmington, Dunbar died at home in Dayton, Ohio. Alice had not complied with Dunbar's requests to visit him; the fact that he was often ill meant his illness was not an indicator to her that he would soon die. Having asked his friend to let her know if Dunbar's condition worsened, she was not aware that the friend himself had died and therefore did not learn immediately of Dunbar's death and burial until she read of it in the papers. It was a devastating experience. Thus, their relationship ended by death and not with any romantic moments of closure. Whatever feelings she harbored against him for his "slander" and abuses would not be reconciled between the two.

With the interdependent support of her mother and sister, Alice moved on with her life in Wilmington. She could always rely on her education to survive and her archives show how she recommitted herself to her career and made a space for herself among the Black Wilmington community. A complex dialogue between Alice's personal documents and her fiction becomes even more apparent as she transformed from the wife of Paul Laurence Dunbar to his estranged wife and then to his respected widow. Interweaving fact with fiction, almost as a call and response, her writings—the published, unpublished, meant-to-be-published, and personal—provide insight into the person that she was as well as the person that she hoped to be. All told, her desires and unmet goals strain against the boundaries that restricted her because of her race and gender in the early twentieth century. During this period, as she developed her public activist career, she also renegotiated respectability politics by discreetly crossing private boundaries. We find Alice as pursuing what Sharon Holland calls an "erotic life—a desiring life" that also involves "the messy terrain of racist practice."[3]

At some point before the death of Dunbar, Alice began an emotional relationship with Major Christian Abraham Fleetwood, who went by C. A. Fleetwood. The Dunbars and Fleetwoods were euchre-playing friends who frequented each other's homes. While on one of his tours, Alice wrote to Dunbar of how his card partner and "the Major as usual came out ahead" in a game they played in April 1901. Apparently, the Fleetwoods were among the Dunbars' social group in the Black community that offered comfort and support to her when Dunbar was traveling. Fleetwood was well respected in the community. In 1869, Fleetwood married a prominent woman, Sara Iredell, a Black descendant of Vice President Aaron Burr, who, like Alice, was college-educated and active with the uplift of women, as when she cofounded the Colored Women's League in 1892. The Dunbars and Fleetwoods probably met within the Black elite Washington circles that Alice inhabited during her marriage to Dunbar. However, letters written to Alice from Fleetwood show that they became closer after the death of Dunbar and the death of Sara in 1908.

Fleetwood was a man with an honorable reputation, and by this point in Alice's life it is clear that she was not attracted to men who did not hold positions of prominence. For her, respectability was not exclusive to Black women's public behavior but also had to do with who they would choose as mates. Maintaining middle-class status was important to Alice; therefore, her partners must have the respect of society, and they must have access to people within and beyond her circle. Fleetwood fit the bill. Born on July 21, 1840, to free parents, he later traveled to West Africa, attended Ashmun Institute in Pennsylvania (now Lincoln University), and then built a career in journalism. He joined the Union Army, receiving the rank of Major, and earned a Medal of Honor for his valiant achievement of carrying the Union flag through Confederate lines when fellow soldiers were struck down during battle.[4]

As noted by Hull, his relationship with Alice, like most of her relationships, "was conducted principally by mail."[5] From these letters, we can glean something of his character. His private self emerges as a man who valued the relationship that developed between him and Alice and made attempts, at times, to reassure her about his feelings. Yet the distance certainly provided him with a kind of independence that he maintained as a widower. He tried to explain his unwillingness to remarry after the death of his wife, and in the absence of a response from Alice, it is clear that she wanted more of a commitment from the older man. Of the letters, Hull states, "His letters—which rarely ran to less than eight pages—often take on a scolding, paternalistic tone, albeit in gentle, well-turned words. All in all, he seems a bit insufferable; but the fact that Alice maintained close contact with him reveals something about her personality and needs and about the forms of black male-female relationships of the time."[6] Paternalistic, perhaps, but Alice benefited from this relationship with the older man. To be sure, nowhere in the archive of Alice's life does she fail to develop intimate relationships with any man or woman who could not support her beyond romance. Fleetwood was no exception.

In a letter dated February 14, 1906, Fleetwood revealed himself to be one of Alice's trusted confidants, as he spoke to her reaction to learning of

Dunbar's death. Fleetwood's letter indicates that she confided in him her feelings about how she had been treated by his friends and family. He began, "You dearest and best of girls." Then he offered words of comfort: "The thought that you had not been notified before the end came never dawned upon my mind. My mind ran only whether you had reached them in time, as I was sure you would go."[7] His response to her exposes her raw emotions, perhaps a mix of sadness about his loss, anger for not knowing, and guilt for not being present at the end.

Later in the letter, he set out to offer words of reassurance. He asked, "Do you feel to blame yourself that you did not go back to him when he asked it? How could you?"[8] After attempting to relieve her of any guilt she might have felt about not being by Dunbar's side at the time of his death, Fleetwood attempted to reassure her that she was a good wife. In a stunning statement, he boldly concluded, "Paul should never have married," he went on, "It was nothing in you that was at fault[,] the same would have occurred with any other woman." Whatever he knew of the relationship, and it was quite possible that he observed abusive character during the marriage, he held a strong opinion about Dunbar that he felt comfortable sharing with the widow.

By 1909, Alice's relationship with Fleetwood had shifted significantly. Regardless of his advanced age and social status, privately Fleetwood was not afraid to show his emotions and vulnerabilities. Thirty-five years older than Alice, he found himself in the position of asking her to explain the distance between them, and he was not referring to the geographical distance. This letter began "Dear Alice" rather than the more familiar "Dearest little girl." In the first sentence, he attempted to establish that she is a priority to him:

You may possibly recall that quite some time ago, I wrote that there were but three people [Alice, his sister, and his daughter] in this wide world . . . [closer] to my heart than you; Subsequently, following the death of my sister, I used the expression that outside of these walls there was no one as dear to me as you.[9]

He revealed that his wife was aware of his love for Alice.[10] Expressing his commitment, he wrote, "No interloper has yet intervened."[11] Further down, he made his intentions clear. Fleetwood wanted to know why, "last year," he noticed a "swift, intangible, [b]ut clearly marked change" in Alice in her letters and "personal treatment."[12] According to Fleetwood, when he addressed his concern with her she dismissed him as "blubbering."[13] His attempt to draw her emotionally closer to him by sharing his love and pain did not bring him the results he sought.

Fleetwood's letters were often long and pointedly detailed. He went on for six more pages, explaining why he felt rebuffed by Alice as he also assured her that his decision not to marry had nothing to do with her. In doing so, he expressed pride in his late wife's ability to associate with the "superior race."[14] While assuring Alice that she was within the age range (thirty to sixty years old) for marriage, he gave three rather vague reasons for not marrying: one was that "it seems like an insult to the memory of the one who left me," a reference to his belated wife. He then discussed his own desires; he makes a quick reference to his physical needs and priorities: "Passion is now with me of course secondary, I need the companionship of the mind more than that of the body."[15] The third reason was that he felt he should not marry unless his daughter was married. Though Fleetwood offered what she wanted— respect and a commitment to her—his commitment did not come in the form of a marriage, a social and legal status that Alice strongly valued. About a year after this letter was written, she would find a younger man of promise who was willing to make the commitment that Fleetwood would not.

After Alice's marriage to a younger man and before her marriage to her third husband, Fleetwood's letters of 1911 were less about the interior of their relationship and more about the gifts or money that he provided. Alice was neither wealthy nor impoverished at the time she worked at the White Rose Mission, as is recorded in her letters of the period; she lived paycheck to paycheck. After she left Dunbar, she remained in desperate need of money, but only those closest to her (such as her lovers and family members) knew just how often her literature spoke to the extent of her need. She was a proud woman who was skilled at "keeping up appearances." However, she had shouldered part of the responsibility of caring for her sister's four children and her mother in the house that they shared when they moved to Wilmington. Surely Fleetwood's "gifts," therefore, were appreciated. Perhaps not unexpectedly, there always seemed a strong emotion attached to each. In a letter of July 13, 1911, he opened with a declaration that he had sent her a package, probably a dress, and encouraged her to send it back if an exchange was needed. His references to his last visit to Miss Kruse and Edith relay that he was firmly involved in her life and that she had welcomed him back. These references also indicate how small the Black elite circle was. This shorter letter, of only two pages, also ends warmly: "I wish you could see and take in the perfection of this most lovely morning, you could then appreciate my wish that your future life might be as clear and bright and everything else beautiful and deservarable [sic]."[16] In September of that year, he wrote a stern letter in which he described her "simple, unassisted ego" in regard to a loan that she owed. To whom she owed is unclear, but he sent her money to cover the debt with requirements of repayment.

Fleetwood, who died three years later, seemed loyal and committed to her, regardless of the state of their relationship in any given year. For Alice, however, marriage would not be the only way she satisfied her desires for companionship. Alice loved Paul, admired Fleetwood, and she was attracted to women. Siobhan Somerville in her study of race and sexuality argues, "[T]he simultaneous efforts to shore up and bifurcate categories of race and sexuality in the late nineteenth and early twentieth centuries were deeply intertwined."[17] Alice's life and literature allow us to consider the deep meaning of this statement. As an African American woman of this era who at times passed for White, she chose to live the life of a Black woman but enjoyed occasional privileges as a White woman. Should passing be considered the indulgence or exploration of a social desire? If yes, her documented same-sex relationships are worthy of note as well, for her middle-class Black peers might be willing to accept racial passing but not necessarily her attraction to women. Passing was a performance that had multiple meanings.

Writing, for Alice, was, at times, a form of testimony as much as it was an opportunity to resist the treatment of women in a society that had prescribed expectations for women. Marriage provided order. One heterosexual partner's expectations of the other ensured that societal norms were being implemented and upheld. But what of those who wanted to move outside heteronormative boundaries? Somerville's definition of sexuality provides context for understanding the bind for a Black woman of this era who was married to a man but had same-sex desires as well:

> [It] means much more than sexual practice per se. One's sexual identity, while at times linked directly to one's sexual activities, more often describes a complex ideological position, into which one is interpellated based partly on the culture's mapping of bodies and desires and partly on one's response to that interpellation. Thus there is no strict relationship between one's sexual desire or behavior and one's sexual identity, although the two are closely intertwined.[18]

At times, Alice's literature reflected her attempt to represent same-sex desires as a mapping of bodies and desires. There are several early examples. Her short story, "Natalie,"[19] for instance focuses on a relationship between two girls—Natalie and Olivia. Although the reason why Olivia ends her relationship with Natalie is in response to Olivia's mother's insistence that Natalie's ethnic and social background is inferior, there may be more to their attraction to one another. The editors of A Century of Lesbian, Gay, and Bisexual African American Fiction, which features this short story, acknowledge that "Natalie" teases a tension between respectability and same-sex desire: "Notwithstanding the fact that the Harlem Renaissance enjoys a popular reputation as a period of extreme sexual permissiveness and gay-themed artistic expression, homosexuality retained an outlaw status that few blacks embraced at the time and, given the extreme racial subordination of the period, that fewer would have championed alongside matters of race and class."[20] "Natalie" is an example of a work of fiction that simultaneously resists the "outlaw status" while acknowledging the diversity of audiences who recognize that there is an interconnectedness between race/ethnicity and sexuality. There are other examples in her corpus.

According to Hull, *A Modern Undine* was written between 1898 and 1903. During this time in her life, she was married but separated from Paul Laurence Dunbar. In September of 1898, she wrote a letter to him expressing the emotional rift she felt being his wife: "I am afraid we are not confidential friends." She goes on, "when I go into myself and become uncommunicative you are hurt." A story that makes use of beliefs in water spirits, *A Modern Undine* combines much of what was significant in the author's life, including her sexual identity, her feminist leanings, her ties to New Orleans, her love of nature, her career as an English teacher, her spiritual beliefs, and her tendency to hurt others when she "goes into herself." Ultimately, it probes the question between Alice and Dunbar that she poses in the letter: "Can't we try to reveal ourselves each to the other without fearing the consequences?"

A Modern Undine is the story of Marion, a twenty-five-year-old Southern woman, who, from the narrative descriptions is likely White, meets a Northern gentleman, George Howard.[21] After a month of staying in Marion's hometown, he proposes. Feeling that she will be an old maid at the age of twenty-five, according to Southern expectations, she accepts his proposal and moves to his hometown, which is located twenty miles from New York. Although Howard hopes that she will make herself at home as a socialite in Lawrenceville, his wife feels uncomfortable with socializing and instead busies herself with the affairs of their lonely household. About four years into their marriage, Howard runs across a poor girl, Grace Weaver, and becomes obsessed with helping her, through a series of acts that he keeps from his wife. Soon she accidentally learns that he has been visiting the nineteen-year-old woman at her home. Assuming that he is having an affair, Marion remains silent about her discovery but punishes her husband by holding a grudge against him that persists after the birth of their son, who is born with abnormally shaped legs. Howard does not learn the truth of her feelings and her knowledge regarding his relationship with the Weaver family until the day that he comes home intent on fleeing the city to avoid charges of embezzlement. After a heart-to-heart discussion, Howard leaves his son and wife behind to fend for themselves. Having no support in her absent husband's hometown, Marion moves back to her Southern childhood seaside home, but their baby soon dies.

The title of the novella, *A Modern Undine*, suggests that Alice, an English teacher, based the novella on folklore of the undine, a water sprite. In other words, she is a binary being with two identities who has an identity in one world and is trying to develop an identity in another world, but she is an outsider. A popular novel during this period was *Undine*, written in German by Friedrich Heinrich Karl de la Motte Fouqué in 1811 and translated into English in 1818. In his reimagining of the undine, Fouqué presents a knight who marries Undine. On their wedding night, she reveals her true identity and tells him that if he consents to stay married to her, she will have a soul; if not, she will return to her kingdom in the sea. Feeling enamored by her, he remains married, and they have moments of happiness and uncertainty when they return to his previous life. After a series of events, Undine leaves, and the knight marries another woman. Fulfilling the promise of the legend, Undine returns and "weeps him to death."

Marion exudes the characteristics of an undine made even more complex by the time period. Kristel M. Mapel Bloomberg posits that Alice makes references to elements of Fouqué's work. In one, Emmie, Marion's perky and sociable sister, refers to George Howard as a knight. In a second one, Marion and Howard, during their first conversation near the water, discuss souls.[22] Yet Marion is not an undine identical to Fouqué's character. Marion's reserved demeanor and absolute lack of interest in her husband beg the question of what motivates her behavior, which differs significantly from that of Fouqué's *Undine*. Given the time this was written, we must consider what the undine itself may have represented to Alice Dunbar.

There is much about the short story that is drawn from her life and her love of nature. Inspired by her background, New Orleans is a likely setting for this novella that focuses on water as natural element. Marion, a name referring to the sea in Latin, is a peculiar and curious character. When we first meet her, she is sitting outside her family home, staring at the body of water that borders the land. Alice thus immediately places Marion in relation to water, a pattern that she follows throughout the novella. While there, Marion is approached by a male partygoer: "It was in the still quiet of a summer night that Marion met Howard. The sea surged at her feet in a low monotone of life and death."[23] His enchantment shows itself in behavior that he finds somewhat embarrassing. Although he thinks her a "straight-laced, high-bred young lady of the last century type," he follows her out to the sea garden and remains there, talking to her despite the fact that she shows little interest in him. In fact, she is "withdrawn into herself."[24] Yet, seemingly intoxicated by the Edenic "scenery," he persists: "The noisy stillness of the deep-hearted night had caught his soul. Unconsciously, too, the woman by his side was inflaming his imagination."[25] Refusing to allow her mood toward him to deter his curiosity, Howard continues to visit. Her reaction to his presence and response to her environment are instructive. However, Howard does not learn from them: "Although Howard had been disconcerted and not a bit puzzled by Miss Ross's sudden coldness, he was nonetheless persistent in his attentions to her."[26] Appearing as seductive, alluring, but cold, Marion is mysterious. Surely her quietness, read as coldness, is a characteristic of her relationship to the deep regions of the sea where she has presumably originated. While Fouqué's Undine was interested in finding a husband she could submit to, Marion shows that she is not pursuing marriage.

Despite expectations and in many ways similar to Alice, Marion never submits to the conformity represented by marriage. When Howard asks her to marry him, a distraction from her sea gazing, she shows an uncharacteristic mix of emotions. She laughs "nervously," then "looked at him in her peculiarly abstract way as if trying to generalize his emotion," and then "a dimple flashed in her cheek." Her reaction appears as a natural response to such a rash act. Notably, she asks about his intentions, showing a hint of interest for the first time. Howard expresses his love for Marion as the reason for his proposal, but she is not impressed:

> "You take it for granted that I love you," she said. There were signs of a timid half-surrender in her manner, and Howard followed them eagerly.
> "Of course I do. You must love me. You will, if you do not already. My own love is so overpowering that it must compel a return. Marion, you will say yes, I know you will eventually, but say so now, won't you?"[27]

Howard appears to be perfect, even to Marion's younger sister Emmie. He is a wealthy businessman from New England and, we presume, a respectable family. New England values were highly respected in Alice's era. Rejecting him would be foolish. Yet she resists. Marion does not say yes to his declaration of love, but after a considerable pause she says yes to the proposal. Within this silent pause is the absence of her consent to marriage and the submission that it entails. Howard admits that her "yes" of that day is not necessarily the "yes" he is looking for, as he also notes that she "half-surrendered" to his proclamations of love. She shows very little interest in marrying anyone, let alone Howard.

Yet, he is not impressive to the woman he has become infatuated with at the water. However, there is considerable pressure for her to marry, and Howard seems to take advantage of that. Previously, when he asked her to reveal her age, masking it as a compliment about her youth ("[you're] not much more than twenty"), she confessed to being twenty-five and then went on to share the meaning of it:

> "One is an old maid in the South at twenty-five," she continued, "but I have been one all my life. I dance, everyone grants me that much, and I suppose I have my share of partners; after that, I must be quiet and orderly and mind my p's and q's."[28]

Marion submits to expectations. Her acknowledgment that she is to act a certain way is accompanied by a sense of reluctance. Bloomberg posits, "Like the water-sprite Undine, who exists in the liminal position between sea and land, humanity and animality, mortality and immortality, turn-of-the-century femin(ine)ist authors of color like Alice Dunbar-Nelson also exist in a 'no-woman's land' between white and black, Victorianism and modernism, the nineteenth and twentieth centuries, the Angel of the House and the New Woman."[29] It is plausible that Marion, like her creator, fears being labeled a "lesbian" if she remains unmarried. Marion is certainly a woman attempting to define herself, if not privately then at least publicly, at the turn of the twentieth century. Although she is afraid of being labeled an old maid and consents to marrying Howard, she does not embrace him in affectionate ways. She seems to resolve that she will obey the rules that a woman should marry a man but will not submit to him.

Marion's disinterest in Howard, as told by a woman who loved both men and women, cannot be overlooked. To be sure, Marion's lack of affection for Howard is unlike any of Alice's other works featuring a married couple. Showing no desire for her husband, her behavior inspires a series of queries: Is it marriage that does not interest her? Is it marriage with Howard? Or is it marriage with any man? There is no reason for us to believe that she holds no interest in men, but there is reason to believe that she is not attracted to Howard. One of the most glaring examples is her response to his touch on their wedding night. After the rushed festivities of the day, he gives her "a kiss that was reverential and holy," and he notices "the quick compressions of her lips as his own touched them."[30] Even the revelation that she is pregnant almost reads as a virginal act: "[S]he remembered trying to go up the stairs before the darkness and roaring of the sea closed over her head."[31] Interestingly, the room she is trying to reach is the bedroom, a place where a child might be conceived. Marion's sexual identity proves complicated.

Marion, like Alice, is close to her mother and sister. Unlike Alice, Marion does not seek male or female companionship outside her mother and sister. She has an awareness of herself that she has accepted. In turn, her own acceptance means that she does not seek acceptance from others. This novel may well act as Matt Richardson observes as "trespassing on the imagined gender and sexuality normativity of the spaces of Black self-making—telling their histories with a queer difference."[32] When she confesses to Howard: "I don't know why, but from a child, people have always taken for granted that I don't care for pleasures and the joys of life like other young people, for I am really not so very old."[33] Hers is a confession regarding the perception of others and how she chooses to fit into that perception. Unlike her "gay and bright" sister, she feels the town would go into "shock" if she should "break into a laugh louder than a whisper."[34] Her revelation leaves readers to wonder: Why is she pretending to be the person that she is? And, what, exactly, gives her "pleasure" and "joy"? Armed with the experience of being married to an emotionally complicated famous man, Alice would search for and find what gave her joy.

Between 1902 and 1915, armed with the name of Dunbar and physically free of his grasp, Alice, like Marion, began to redefine her life. Scholar Ann duCille observes that Alice's literary contemporaries, Nella Larsen, Jesse Fauset, and Zora Neale Hurston, revised the work of their predecessors by developing Black women characters who "begin to become actively sexual beings, implicitly questioning their positioning as objects of male desire and contemplating, if not fully exploring, their sexual selves."[35] *A Modern Undine* is certainly an example of this shift. duCille goes on to posit, "[H]eroines cease to be singularly and uniformly heroic, good, pure, blameless—victims of patriarchal privilege and racial oppression."[36] Emerging from an abusive relationship in which she began to reclaim her body from sexual oppression and violation, Alice constructed herself much like the Black women that duCille describes. Yet she is no character, except in the pages of her personal records and her biography-influenced fiction. At the turn of the century, redefinition for Alice meant that she was free to make decisions that could enhance the quality of her life and were not dictated by Dunbar.

Following her final separation from Dunbar in 1902, Alice, in addition to *A Modern Undine*, wrote two stories about marriage in which the women appear complex and the men appear untrustworthy, if not devious. According to Hull's note, "The Decision" was written between 1902 and 1909. Surely influenced by her own circumstances, in which she struggled daily to pay bills and uphold the façade of a stable middle-class lifestyle, Alice emphasized the distinction between classes—the working class and millionaires—in the story. Furthermore, it grapples with how a woman's private desires are met with the hope of marriage with a man who values and respects his wife.

"The Decision" focuses on a fiction writer, Marion Forman, who elopes with a man, Burt Cortland, but later leaves him. Clearly inspired by her feelings regarding her first marriage, Alice writes of the couple's love and abuse from the perspective of the woman: "For four years she led a life that was a fitful dream of torment, disguise, terror, love, longing for release."[37] Expanding on feelings that both complement and expand the torment and longing, she states further:

> She alternately loved and hated, feared and trusted, caressed and spurned him; and he alternately loved her with the wildest, most insane devotion and lashed her with the most scathing scorn that his ready tongue was capable of.[38]

Added to his verbal abuse, spurred by drunkenness, is physical abuse that is well known to their friends and neighbors. Marion leaves when an unspoken act causes the strained chains to burst and forces her to emancipate herself from the man. Though she returns to her mother and finds herself living in a state of near poverty, she inherits money, which she is willing to share with her estranged husband. However, considering what he really wants, Burt sends word that he is only interested in her return and not the money. Perhaps mirroring the public perception of Alice's marriage ending unexpectedly, "The Decision" ends abruptly with the woman coming to a decision that is not shared.

Since Alice relied so heavily on her own life to write this story, readers who know her will know the ending. Ignoring his letters to her, Alice did not return to Dunbar, and no amount of money or prestige afforded her by his name or even pity for his declining health would allow her to live again with him. In other words, she chose herself over public opinion. "A Decision" speaks of her decision to leave him, from her perspective, and in this way Alice used fiction to empower her life's well-documented story long before she died and left an archive of personal papers—letters, a diary, and other personal and private documents—for curious readers. What we learn is that by the time she left Dunbar, she pitied other married women, wondering "how they could conceal their sorrows so successfully, for hers were suspected by all her friends,"[39] as Marion states. Queried about divorce in case she might want to marry again, "'I wouldn't trust the kingliest man that ever trod the world,' she breathed through tense teeth."[40] And perhaps Alice did not truly trust men either, at first.

6

Love and Education

After Dunbar's death in 1906, she was free to explore other relationships that would satisfy unreconciled and understated needs. Her relationship with Major C. A. Fleetwood was but one of several during a period of about five years, between 1906 and 1911. One such relationship was with Edwina Kruse, the principal of Howard School where Alice and her sister taught. Fleetwood could not have known that she was likely the reason why his dear Alice seemed distant. While it is not clear when their relationship began, what is clear from Edwina Kruse's letters is that the older woman (by twenty-seven years) was in love with Alice and had taken on the position of providing for her and her family when Alice took a leave of absence from Howard in 1907 to attend Cornell. An absence of Alice's letters to Kruse does not allow for a full understanding of their relationship. In this space of absence, we are not made aware of the depth of feeling Alice had for Kruse. The elder woman's letters to Alice during the year of her departure captured not only her love for Alice but also the relationships that Alice formed with men at Cornell, including an interracial relationship and the beginning of the relationship with the younger man who would become her second husband, Henry A. Callis.

Edwina Kruse was born of mixed ancestry in Puerto Rico in 1848. When she was a child, her family moved to the United States. Following Kruse's death on June 23, 1930, Alice honored her by writing a novel based on her old friend's/lover's life. Very little is known about her life making it difficult to conclude how much of the novel is based on fact. *This Lofty Oak* begins in Puerto Rico, where Fredericka's (Kruse's fictional persona) mother, a woman of Spanish, indigenous, and possibly African descent (her mother had brown skin), married a German man, Fredericka's father. Alice casts Kruse as a feisty little girl whose love of her Latin roots is severely discouraged by her stern father, Frederich. After receiving a job in New York, he moves the family into a German New York community and further indoctrinates them into German culture through their communal affiliations. Kruse's mother becomes despondent and saddened by this, resulting in her untimely death. As a result, Kruse is sent away to a boarding school run by Germans. Her father's sudden death leaves her destitute, and she is unable to continue her education, but she has learned enough to find jobs in education. After studying education at a small New England school and then taking a job at a rural school, she eventually makes her way to Wilton (Wilmington), where she becomes the longtime transformational principal of a fictional Howard.

Remaining consistently discreet about their relationship, Alice only appears in composite characters, such as a cousin of Fredericka, who stands up to the new principal and directs a play. Romances with men are avoided and presented as inappropriate. At one point, a young boy tries to sexually assault Fredericka and she makes a physical maneuver to protect herself. Another attempt at sexual assault occurs at the end of the school day in her one-room classroom. Only one time in the novel does she fall in love with a man, and that man is the married father of the child she is caring for. As a result, she leaves the family's home and later learns of the man's death. Adhering to respectability politics, to be sure, Alice created a character in Freddy who works consciously to "protect" herself and the girls in her charge from bringing shame upon themselves or being shamed by lascivious villainous men who cannot control their libidos. Purity is essential and upholding the sanctity of marriage is a major aspect of clean living. "Black queer people," as Evelyn Hammonds maintains, "are dangerous to the collective, for we are a reminder of the accusation of sexual deviance and gender aberrance that we have fought so long to deny, decry, and defend against."[1]

Therefore, there is no space given to explore same-sex relationships in the novel. When studying for her teacher's certification, Fredericka develops a relationship with a classmate named Edith that the narrator refers to as a "slightly unhealthy friendship of another girl." This relationship goes unexplored and underdeveloped in the novel. Just why it is "unhealthy" is a matter of the reader's conjecture.

Fredericka, Kruse's literary persona, is a woman whose greatest love is her position as the powerful, influential principal of Godwin School and her position as a respected community leader. Influenced by public historical records, her own observations, and, quite possibly, interviews of Kruse and her friends, Alice developed a character who outwits villainous men and foolish women. Fredericka's strongest asset is her ability to garner power through acquisition of respect to get what she wants in her efforts to build a stronger community with Godwin at the center. Unfortunately, despite the author's best efforts and those of her niece, Pauline, the novel was never published.

Nevertheless, her legacy as an educational leader of a school that still stands in Wilmington remains prominent. Kruse looked White, had a

European father, but claimed to be colored. She lived with and worked with Black women. With a claim in two worlds, Kruse's light skin resulting from her mixed-race ancestry made her an attractive prospect to lead a small school named Howard, after General Oliver Otis Howard, superintendent of the Freedmen's Bureau, where she was initially hired to serve as one of two teachers under a White principal. The state's history of educating African Americans or rather not educating them made Howard necessary. State funds were not allocated for the education of African American children until 1881 and Howard had to constantly prove that it was providing a quality education despite the lack of funding it received from the state. Soon after the school opened, she started her thirty-year career as principal and built the school—for decades, the only one in the state for African American children—into an accredited and respected institution until she was replaced by a younger man. According to Howard teacher, Kruse's longtime friend and housemate Anna Broadnax, on September 20, 1869, the school was opened at 124th and Orange Streets in Wilmington, Delaware, as a result of "the city council of Wilmington accept[ing] General Oliver O. Howard's proposition to furnish an equal amount of money towards its construction" and provided them with funds. A newspaper article captured the moment by reporting that the school which was one of four private schools, each designated a room erected "for the education of children without regard for color . . . The lower room was densely packed by colored people and a few white citizens." Two White teachers worked with two Black girls to instruct the elementary department. Part of that time she dedicated to building the curriculum, recruiting well-qualified teachers, and soliciting the support of philanthropists and community members in boarding students and teachers. Howard became a "regular four-year high school" in 1904.

"The years 1902–1909 . . . we were closer than sisters . . .," Alice wrote in her diary on June 23, 1930. When the women met is unclear, but a handwritten poem in Alice's papers, dated May 18, 1907, reveals Kruse's attraction to Alice:

"Parted"
Beyond the cornfields and the wood
Nestling beneath the hill
In the old days a cottage stood
Beside a ruined mill

And often on the edge of dark
I lingered in the lane
Until a candles welcome spark
Shone in the window pane.

Long spears / have gone, tonight once more
Beside the foot-worn stile

In the old lane as oft-before
I wait, and dream awhile.

Above the pines one lonely star
Shines like her casement lit
But far away—alas! Too far
For her to open it.

Fond Dream! My longing eyes beguiled,—
Yet must I turn again
And like a little lonely child
Stretch out my arms in vain!

The moon is but a clouded disc
Only the star shines bright
To me it seems God's asterisk
Upon the page of night.

O love of happy days long past
My task is nearly done
Faithful to thee, till life at last
Be ended,—and begun!

Reginald Shepard sees the components of "other" in a poem as poetry itself: "Poetry's otherness enacts an escape from or a transformation of racial and sexual otherness: it embodies an otherness of inclusion rather than exclusion, of possibility rather than constraint. Poetry presents the possibility of an otherness that is liberating rather than constricting: it offers the prospect of an alienation from alienation."[2] This poem certainly embodies inclusion as it is an invitation for inclusion. By comparing her feelings to the wonder of nature, the poem is a clear expression of erotic attraction for Alice. "Parted" speaks of the writer's separation from and longing for her lover. Written in rhyme, signed poem demonstrates her devotion to her departed lover, even though there is distance between them. There is also a sense here that the love between the two is "hidden," like the old cottage, and that the writer is helplessly waiting for the "light"—a sign of consent—from the occupant to invite her in from the lane. A sense of longing is present.

This poem is the earliest unambiguous evidence in the archive not only of their relationship but also of Alice's sexual attraction to women. Other references are slight and provoke curiosity. During her marriage to Dunbar, she made an unexplained reference in a letter to him about one of her female friends who stayed over. On December 3, 1897, she wrote, "Later she went home for news and returned about eleven o'clock to stay all night. Now don't buck your eyes. It was all straight." Why does she feel he might question the "straightness" of this visit? As if to taunt him, she stated further, "She told me to tell you that she enjoyed sleeping in your bed immensely." In this slight but provocative reference, Alice introduced a queer context into her narrative of the night's interactions and, perhaps, a queer context for this time in her life.

Why did Alice choose to go to Wilmington to teach at Howard, a city where she and her family had no relatives, when her national connections could have secured her and her sister teaching positions at any of the other schools for Black children in the country? Why not return to New York? Alice's membership with the national club women probably provided an opportunity for the women to meet while she lived in New York, if not before. Kruse traveled to various cities and meetings and she was well known among Black educators, such as NACW leader Mary Church Terrell, an acquaintance of the Dunbars, who came to Howard School to speak in 1895. Responding to a reference in Alice's diary to a same-sex relationship among two club women, Hull identifies what she terms a "lesbian network" within the club network.[3] Specifically, in her August 1, 1928, diary entry, Alice referenced two women who "want to make whoopee" but leave when "Bobo" Nelson, her third husband, comes home. Frequent travels along the northeast coast could and did allow for discreet intimacies to form among the women. In other words, Alice was among other Black women who defied respectability through exploration of the erotic. Moving within the boundaries of respectability meant balancing discretion with desire.

Writing to Alice while she was at Cornell, Alice would have been quite interested in the contents of the letter. As the woman who was also the head of the English division, her confidante, and her intimate friend, Kruse recorded the work of the school during the 1907–8 school year and the special nature of the women's relationship. "Parted" hints to the relationship that had blossomed by the time she was at Cornell. Kruse and Alice's letters are more direct after the intimacy between the two became deep enough for Kruse to take financial responsibility for Alice. Yet the details of their relationship remained unnoticeable by outside observers of the two, as Kruse clearly valued and honored respectability politics. Her letters reveal that she loved Alice Dunbar as she did no other woman. As Alice's principal, she was in a position of power and allowed Alice to go on leave for a year. Alice relied exclusively on her to support her educational expenses and trusted her to do what she could for her struggling family. What her family members knew of the relationship is unknown. According to Hull, when she met Alice's niece, Pauline Young, to excavate the archives, Hull informed her of another same-sex relationship that she had discovered while editing the diary. Young seemed "surprised."[4] During this phase of their relationship, Young was a child and probably saw her principal as simply a family friend.

Clarifying her role, Kruse wrote, "I am not too good to you, I wish I could be better. You may rely on your board every month. . . . You know I told you, and I meant it, that you are not to be in need of anything."[5] In contrast to her relationship with Dunbar, Alice seemed comfortable taking money from

Kruse, and the elder woman was very happy to assist. Kruse an entrepreneur, who owned property and a catering business, was in good financial shape and was known for being generous with her students. In addition to receiving income for her work at Howard, she shared a home with at least two other women—probably boarders—for years. She was also certain to keep Alice apprised of the Moore family's financial struggles and her attempts to help a family she thought of as proud, by giving them food she bought in bulk but pretended that she had bought exclusively for herself: "I try and do all I can to help her [Patsy Moore] because I love you so much, and told you I would look after them, but I have to be careful because she is very proud."[6]

As the days passed, Kruse became more overt about her feelings, revealing the private moments of their relationship. In at least one letter, she discussed the level of physical intimacy between the two:

> Little girl, I wish I could spend Saturday and Sunday with you. I wish you could come home Thanksgiving: How busy a holiday will you have and will the fare be reduced for you know Cornell plays Penn in Philadelphia on Thanksgiving [?] I just believe I'll get dressed and get on the train and walk into your room at 214 Stewart Avenue—before Christmas. I do want you so—Alice, my own.[7]

The next day, she expressed a similar sentiment: "I want you to know dear, that every thought of my life is for you, every think of my heart is yours and yours alone. I just can not ever let any one else have you."[8] Showing a hint of jealousy, she told Alice not to fall in love with a doctor. He will soon learn that her "skin [marked out] cheek has been kissed by the tropical sun."[9] The tropical sun is an obvious reference to Kruse's national origin. She went on to further illuminate their developing bond of intimacy: "[T]rust me with all your pleasures, hopes, and desires. I'll look after you and your folks here."[10] Making reference to the possibility of barriers to their relationship, she asked questions that are reminiscent of the love letters between Dunbar and Alice:

> Are you flirting with anyone there? You must be true to me—little girl! You did say however, that you only go home when you are blue. I do not want you to blue [sic] so you must stay and act "silly." With all the reading and studying you have to do I should think you need to be "silly" if you can. I do not care how good a time you have, if you only do not have those old women there kissing you and putting their arms around you. I would never do it again if I know that someone there did it. (Underline are in original.)[11]

There is a suggestion here that Kruse's concerns were more with other women and not with men. She had casually mentioned that a man who was annoying Alice might be attracted to her, but she did not seem threatened by him.

Their professional and personal relationship was, to say the least, complicated. Audre Lorde provides fitting commentary for the women's exchanges: "I . . . believe that the love expressed between women is particular and powerful because we have had to love ourselves in order to live; love has been our means of survival."[12] Kruse helped Alice to survive, literally and spiritually. An older woman, Kruse supported Alice when she was unable to find the validation that she sought from her abusive husband, Dunbar. And although Alice made efforts to see herself not as a victim but as his wife and as a sexual being, she had little time to ponder and to engage in a healing process after being raped. Kruse's love of Alice was expressive of both feeling and action, as we see in the letters. Alice's poetry, such as "The Gift," also proves informative: "I could give less, but all my life / Lies at your feet, to take or not. / I crave your clasp that shields from strife, / The Kiss you gave me, loving so. / I love your breath upon my hair, / Myself I love— you think me fair." Alice may well have agreed with Lorde, who stated in an interview, "My power as a person, as poet, comes from who I am. I am a particular person. The relationships I have had were particular relationships. They help give me my particular identity, which is the source of my energy. Not to deal with my life in my art is to cut out the front of my strength."[13]

As they sent expressions of love and intimacy across the miles, the two women also communicated the daily activities that consumed each of their lives, including Kruse's vast support of Alice's academic studies. A significant difference between this relationship and Alice's relationship with Dunbar, of course, is that he was not at all interested or supportive of her educational endeavors. Probably more than any concern he had with possible suitors, he did not want her to pursue her work or education. Kruse, by contrast, was very interested in Alice's studies and how she engaged with her instructors. Using a playful educator's tone, she wrote: "Be a good little girl, get your lessons and do not call your teachers ugly, they have brains and you can't expect them to have both brains and beauty."[14] Kruse found Alice's research on British romantic poets Samuel Coleridge and William Wordsworth quite impressive and appropriate for an English teacher at Howard. In 1909, she published her only known literary analysis article, "Wordsworth's Use of Milton's Description of Pandemonium," in *Modern Language Notes*.

Kruse was dedicated to Alice not only because of love but also because of respect for educational advancement. Supporting Alice's studies at Cornell meant that her chair of English could return to the little segregated school with an education that would bring them notoriety and respect. According to Alice's Cornell Student Handbook, presented by the Christian Associations of Cornell University, she was "welcomed . . . because more than any other institution whatsoever, it is the specific recognition of the spiritual vocation of the students." During the first term of her one-year stay, she took four English classes, two philosophy classes, and one history course. Later, during her second term, she enrolled in history, English, philosophy, and education.

Although she did not specify when she took it in her schedule, in her letters to Kruse, a German speaker, she noted that she also studied German. In fact, Kruse wrote little terms of endearment to Alice in German.

Studying at Cornell meant advancing the race, for both Alice and Kruse. But it was challenging. Alice had some experience in operating within racially and ethnically diverse educational institutions in the North, experiences she relished, as when she was able to teach at a school with a predominantly Jewish children population in New York. She had also studied at Columbia University. At Cornell, she faced challenges as a woman. Interestingly, although women were part of the student body, the focus of the Handbook is specifically on Cornell men. Under the greetings section, the following directive appears: "Every gentleman should be a student; every student should be a gentleman, as is the spirit that dominates life here. She, our Alma Mater, aims to send forth every year a class of broadminded, social, thoroughly trained gentlemen."[15] The first time the presence of female students is acknowledged appears on page 17, under "Rooms," in reference to housing space for women students. One has to wonder how a woman, a Black woman, with such strong feminist ideas and a decidedly independent spirit, could have endured being in such a male-centered, predominantly White institution—an institution that encouraged its students to "Get the advice of some College man, a Cornell man preferred, if you are in doubt about what to study."[16] Notably, this is very different from the catalog of Alice's alma mater, Straight University, which did acknowledge the presence of both men and women at the institution.

Regardless of the atmosphere for women, Alice networked as best she could among the small group of African American undergraduate students. According to Kruse's letters, Alice was doing much more than studying while at Cornell; she may have been looking for her next husband. Kruse's letters also reveal that Alice was involved with a White man, identified simply as Lanikins, an ill-advised move as far as Kruse was concerned. Alice must have written about this man consistently during October 1907, as Kruse made at least two references to him. On October 4, she noted, "Get all you can from Lanikins but don't get burnt yourself." With a tone that is more insistent and pointed than usual, she stated:

No matter how jealous I am you must tell me every little thing because you are mine; With me you have been comparatively happy with him—you would have after a while—hades—you thought you had it with Paul Laurence Dunbar—it would be worse with Lanikins. There could be, in this country, no happiness in a marriage between you and a white man—and there certainly could never be any relation except marriage—Take my advice.[17]

If she knew the details of Alice's family background, she did not say. Instead, she seemed intent on portraying Alice's love interest as worse than Dunbar.

Yet Kruse was motivated not only by her feelings for Alice but also by her own family background. Kruse had light skin, but her mixed ancestry forced restrictions upon her that might as well have marked her as Black in America. *This Lofty Oak* speaks of tensions between the German father and his Latin wife, which lead the daughter to feel estranged from him after they moved to the United States and her mother dies. In the novel, the father expects his daughter to follow his White German way of life and to deny a Latin identity. It is likely that Kruse did not trust White men. Nevertheless, without question, her motive was not simply to shield Alice from the prejudices associated with interracial coupling at this time but also to avoid losing Alice to another person, regardless of the person's gender and race:

> I love you Alice. I love you enough to die for you—if that meant life and happiness to you because of my love—I beg of you, don't play with edged tools. Both you and that man have "temperament," which as Miss Baldwin says—does make people do awful fool things sometimes—and you must keep your head, Alice.[18]

Is Alice pulling a card out of the same deck that her deceased husband played with when they were courting and later when they married? Extracting sentiments of jealousy through communications veiled as "honesty" seems to have happened quite frequently in Alice's relationships. Kruse pressed further:

> I wish I knew for sure that you are not happy without me and that you get worse—Then I would be happy—Alice—my arms are empty, my life is empty—I feel as if I cannot-cannot live the year out without you.[19]

These honest revelations appear almost always one-sided, with one lover expressing interest in the other and the committed lover responding with declarations of love and pleadings for attention. This particular letter is one of the most revealing about the intimate nature of their relationship, which clearly goes beyond friendship or sisterhood.

Alice's focus on Lanikins shifted by the spring. While it is not clear how long her relationship with this White man lasted, there are references in the letters to at least two other men. One is a man referred to as Jones, who was to escort her to an event; instead, she ended up being escorted by Henry Arthur Callis. Kruse expressed her support for Callis's presence: "I am glad it was Callis as that will shut up the mouths of the Negroes up there who say you were passing."[20] Callis was one of the few Black students and he was a leader among the Black male students. New York's legislature incorporated Cornell University in 1865 as a liberal institution "where any person can find instruction in any study."[21] Yet it had relatively few Black students in 1905. Alice had some problems connecting with the other African American students, who viewed her light skin color and perhaps the company she kept with Lanikins as signs that she was not interested in being part of the Black student community, a falsehood she addressed in her essay "Brass Ankles." Kruse's brief reference to Callis, who would later become a teacher at Howard High School and Alice's second husband, records that their relationship began before he came to Wilmington and became her coworker.

Callis, a founding member or "jewel" of the Alpha Phi Alpha fraternity, had entered Cornell as one of its fifteen Black students in 1905. Reared in Rochester, New York, a stop on the Underground Railroad, Callis's family had relationships with respected figures such as Frederick Douglass, who was a relative of his mother. Callis's father, an African Methodist Episcopal minister, had graduated from Hampton Institute in the class behind Booker T. Washington.[22] Armed with an interest in the advancement of African Americans, Callis entered Cornell with the goal of studying medicine. Alice and Callis had quite a bit in common: both were Christian, were descendants of enslaved people, were able to pursue higher education, and were committed to civic responsibility. Unfortunately, almost no information about their courtship exists in the archives.

Their commitment to education and the uplift of African Americans reunited the two in Wilmington. To save money for medical school and probably to be near Alice, Callis went to teach at Howard School and the two married on January 19, 1910. According to their marriage certificate, she was thirty-three and he was twenty-four years old. Actually, however, she was thirty-four years old. It was not uncommon for Alice to lie about her age on government documents. Nevertheless, scholars have surmised that they married quietly, so as not to violate the community's standards of respectability, including the school's rules against faculty members forming relationships and the fact that he was twelve years her junior. Still, there were few secrets among the Black elite of this era. Just as people knew that she had endured an abusive relationship with Dunbar, so they most certainly knew about her marriage to this younger man. Surely they lived together. (On the other hand, there was still apparently no gossip about the presence of Kruse, who was not only Alice's lover, before and perhaps after Callis's move to Wilmington, but also the couple's boss.) She had both met the expectations of respectability by marrying him and simultaneously defied them because she was older than her husband. It was a scandalous act.

Word spread to Fleetwood, and though he did not name his informant in his letter to Alice, it must have been a woman who knew of Alice's life in Delaware but maintained ties among the respectable Black circles of DC. Fleetwood responded to an inquiry from Alice with a ten-page handwritten letter on June 12, 1910. In reference to a letter he had received from a mutual female acquaintance, he stated that he was told, "'[O]ur dear friend is making a grave mistake, can't you go on and talk to her about it—and save her from herself."[23] To which, according to his letter, he advised the woman that it had been his experience that "the best way to further an affair of that kind was oppose it and secondly it was none of my business unless you asked advice."[24] Alice had apparently written to find out what he knew about her marriage to the "young man," as the older Fleetwood referred to him. Having earlier stated that he would not marry, he informed Alice now that his "first impulse" was "an expression of the hope that you would find in it something to repay you for the troubles of the past few years was true and beautiful."[25] Whatever he was feeling and trying to emote in this clumsily written sentence, he seemed to be taking a dignified stance and wanting to express his concern with her happiness first and foremost. For at least three pages of the letter, Fleetwood laid out the societal concern: it is not that she is married, it is that she is married to a younger man. Her choice placed her under a scrutiny that the younger man did not suffer, and her crossing of a respectable barrier certainly contributed to the demise of the marriage. Enjoying a romance, especially for Alice, meant that society's perception of her would always supersede her own desires.

In any case, the relationship may have been doomed from the start, considering that Callis's ultimate goal was to attend medical school and probably to have a family. His wife's own commitment to her family made it unlikely that she would abandon them and relocate. After leaving Wilmington at some unknown time, Callis went on to receive his medical degree from Rush Medical School and to remarry. When the two legally ended their marriage has not been determined, as no divorce documents appear in the public records.

Although reportedly few people knew about their marriage, Alice's choice of a significantly younger man shows her willingness to test the boundaries and expectations of respectability politics to pursue her individual desires. With no letters or diaries in which to refer for her insight into this relationship, the bold act can only serve as a clue that she had deep feelings for this man. Choosing Callis, despite the controversy of the age difference, allowed her an opportunity for public liberation following her abusive relationship with Dunbar. As a form of resistance to respectability, her marriage was an act of possessing the body, an act that empowered her physically and emotionally while she worked to advance the race through teaching.

Years later, Alice documented in her diary the unresolved feelings she harbored for the Callis years. In an entry on November 28, 1930, written during her marriage to her third husband, she remarked how good she had looked in preparation for the Bachelor-Benedict Ball, where she danced with Callis. "He has not forgotten," she observed. "Rather intense." She stated further, "[H]e was as eager and breathless about it as when he was a kid in Wilmington."[26] Avoiding any comment about how she felt about him, she focused instead on how she perceived his reaction to her. Stroking her own ego, she noted that he was married: "Promised him and Myra to dine with them Sunday."[27] Such descriptions of their interactions reveal how he made her the center of attention. Whatever the reason for their breakup, unlike the end of her first marriage, she and Callis remained amicable until her death, even socializing with one another's subsequent spouses.

After a visit to Washington, DC, she reflected on the demise of their romance in her diary when they met again in June 1931. She assumed ownership of the relationship ending. Writing in a way that only those closest to her might understand, she recorded a conversation that they had about their relationship on their way to retrieve Robert—curiously she called him by his first name rather than his pet name Bobo: "Arthur said—well, it was not much, the four years of our romance, the jewel around which his whole life was built—and a bit more." She replied that "[i]t was a beautiful thing that I hated to destroy." Either to him or to herself, she added, "Yet I knew that destroy it I must—to save him. Ruthless I was—but it was best for him."[28] She did not elaborate on why her behavior was "ruthless"—perhaps selfless, if we are to believe that her motives were for his good and not for her own.

Whatever she did, he appeared, at least in her eyes, forgiving and loving toward her. Although her dear Bobo was on this trip, she and Callis managed to spend a bit of time together alone, between sharing meals and his ferrying around both her and Nelson, who was financially bankrupt during this trip. The former Mrs. Callis emerged as happy and flirty in her thoughtful and girlish musings about the feelings she had for him. On June 5, she "walked[ed] slowly home through the beautiful streets thinking after all, love has been mine from many men, but the great passion of at least four or five whose love for me transcended that for other women—and what more can any woman want?"[29] Her contemplation of love gained and love lost was undoubtedly inspired by the fact that she was in the presence of her former husband and her current husband. She shared a moment of intimacy with Callis on June 6, 1931. Callis took her on a drive around the water in the morning before the arrival of his wife, Myra. "It was lovely, the water all ruffled up in whitecapped wavelets and we drove slowly and talked about the Brandywine [a Wilmington river] and held each other's hands and grew wistfully silent while I took off my hat and let the breeze blow my hair away."[30] At this point, she departed to visit the library. Both entries reflect that Callis *made her feel*. Notably, she used the words "beautiful" and "love" twice and characterized theirs as a romance. There is a feeling of freedom here: the nature's scenery provided the backdrop for the former lovers' feelings to resurface. At the age of fifty-six, twenty-one years after their brief marriage began, Alice felt that being in his presence returned her to youthful days. What we see here is the pursuit of love, the respect for the emotion, that she reserved a space for in her personal papers (i.e., her letters to Paul and her diary) and sometimes in her creative work (her poetry and fiction).

It may have been during that visit that she told him of a fellowship opportunity that recognized American citizens who addressed concerns of social welfare. She wrote to him on June 29 that she wanted him to use her name in applying for funding from the Carl Schurz Memorial Foundation and let them know his "contributions." Her goal was to work with the foundation in making it "bi-racial" by recommending a qualified "Negro." She ended the letter, "Love to Myra." Callis did not get the fellowship, much to her disappointment. As a doctor, Callis was sufficiently respectable and possessed other characteristics that made her willing to sponsor him for career advancement.

However, before they married and in the midst of the various love triangles among Kruse, Alice, and Cornell men, Kruse kept her vow to take care of Alice's family, who were very near the poverty line, according to Kruse. Her actions included giving Alice's mother a regular allowance of five dollars, which she assured Alice that she gave every payday, even if she had "forgotten to mention it."[31] She encouraged Alice not to discourage her mother and sister from taking in a boarder, a young man who took a space in the parlor. He was likely one of the teachers at Howard. By this time, it was certain that they had very little food to feed the family of two adults and four children, at least according to Kruse's observations. She also assumed the responsibility of trying to find summer employment as a "white" housekeeper for Leila, encouraging her to pass in order to ensure a good position. Although the Moore women were committed to making a living, no matter how hard they worked, in the absence of Leila's estranged husband, they never had enough to make the ends meet neatly. Their situation speaks to the struggles of Black women, regardless of educational background, who had fewer skilled job options and earned lower wages (then and now). In many ways, Kruse worked to move Black women beyond these restrictive boundaries.

Since theirs was not a public relationship, it is not clear how long Alice and Kruse maintained their intimacy. There was no need to continue to write to one another once Alice returned to Wilmington. But it seems clear that their relationship was minimized by the time of Kruse's death. In the first reference that Alice made to Kruse in her diary, she described a rift between Kruse and her mother. Following a newspaper article that told of Kruse having been placed in the position of helping her successor, Alice wavered between loyalty to her mother and sympathy for the one she loved. After a new principal was brought in to replace the aging Kruse, she wrote on August 27, 1921: "I can't gloat over her humiliation, as Mama does, remembering her sins against us." Despite whatever had occurred, she concluded, "I remember her good deeds and that I once loved her."[32] Yet later she took her with the children to a baseball game between the Black Sox and the Aberfoyles, noting, "It was like loading something into a truck to get her into the car. I sent Polly [Pauline] around with the invitation, hardly thinking she would accept, although she had asked me to take her some time."[33] Alice's frequent references to Kruse in her diary indicate that she remained fond of Kruse, visiting her often and giving her Christmas gifts, as the elderly woman aged and declined mentally.

Kruse, whose parents died when she was young, never married and seemed to have no relatives in the United States.

Without question, Alice greatly admired Kruse. Upon Kruse's forced retirement, in 1920 Alice dedicated an editorial to her as part of her "From a Woman's Point of View" series. The heartfelt acknowledgment of the venerable Edwina Kruse and her work as principal of Howard School, later Howard High, did not reveal Alice's own relationship with the woman. She wrote that Kruse developed a school that "gathered under its wings one of the finest little groups of intellectual men and women in the country—all due to the careful culling and pruning of the doughty principal."[34] She stated further:

> To have raised the intellectual standard of a community is no small task, but when you add to that, the enduring monument of a splendid school, and the education of thousands of boys and girls, you have an achievement well worthwhile, and a life that has been finely worth living.[35]

Alice, who by that time was a former educator of Howard, after having been unceremoniously dismissed from her post by the nameless "male principal [who] carries on the work which she set so firmly on her feet," used the power of her pen and the attention of her audience to illuminate the work of a woman and the work she did to "uplift" Black people. A seasoned writer, she implied that the "male principal" resided in the shadow of Miss Kruse, who had a national reputation that was celebrated by "educators who came from far and near, even though a blizzard was raging, to pay homage to the woman who set the intellectual pace for Wilmington."[36] Had it not been for the high standards of Kruse, Alice implied, "colored" children in Delaware would not have received a high-quality education that prepared them to pursue college degrees, advancing the educational level of Black people and possibly increasing their contributions to America.

There is no denying that Alice Dunbar contributed significantly to the growth and reputation of Howard. Her last name and publication record was often touted as a point of school pride and gave legitimacy to the school. Kruse's success as the longtime principal at Howard was partially due to her investment in Alice's professional development. Dedicated in 1869, Howard School, now known as Howard High School of Technology, meant a great deal to the segregated community, as it was the only high school that provided vocational education for Black people in the state of Delaware during segregation.[37] As chair of the English Department, Alice drew on her education at Straight, Columbia, and Cornell to build a curriculum that she hoped would prepare the students to pursue higher education. Although closely familiar with Black literary artists, her teaching journals reveal that she built an English curriculum focused on the European "classics." The Department of English's course of study was broken into six categories, including the classics, rhetoric, poetry to be memorized, themes, required reading, and current events. Each semester and year had different requirements, but an example of the first-term, first-year curriculum reads as follows. Under the category of the classics, she included the titles of Irving's *Sketch Book*, Lowell's *Vision of Sir Launfal*, Coleridge's *Ancient Mariner*, and Kingsley's *Old Testament Narratives*. Rhetoric lessons were drawn from Scott and Denney's *Elementary Composition*. Students were required to memorize Lincoln's Gettysburg Address, Wordsworth's "Sonnet on Milton," and works by Shakespeare. Themes encompassed a variety of areas, from selections from the Irving texts and narratives of the rhetoric section to themes based on stories of Samson and Ruth. Students were required to read *Pilgrim's Progress, Tom Brown's School Days, Up from Slavery, Treasure Island, Robinson Crusoe, Uncle Tom's Cabin*, and "others selected by the pupil." Here we see that she encouraged the students' own individual preferences and supplemented them with works on world travel, slavery, and self-dependency. Always a scholar of education, Alice challenged herself to become familiar with the works that were assigned to the students.

Alice saw this course of study as essential to intellectual growth. It also fit squarely with the Black club women's beliefs. As with their earlier mission, she continued to believe that Black students must possess the knowledge of their White peers in order to meet the standards set by them. In an essay titled "The Training of a Teacher of English," she argued that exposing a girl early to these works will prepare her for an occupation. She suggested a regimen of reading, studying, and memorization: begin with telling stories and nursery rhymes, then gradually move to Greek myths, poetry memorization, the retelling of stories, and fairy books. By the time she is nine, she should be familiar with the list of works above; in grammar school, pair these literary studies with history, geography, and sciences. Alice clearly desired well-rounded students and saw literary studies as the center of this achievement. Her ideal course of study would not be complete without "a year of travel or a year of study at foreign university."[38] Such ideas showed the importance of Howard to the Black Wilmington community, not only as a center of educational advancement but also as a cultural arts center. Alice proudly assumed the position of unofficial arts ambassador. In other words, she sought to use her skills to produce respectable Black women, which she defined as educated and knowledgeable. Anchored by her family and limited by financial resources, she hoped that her students would move beyond Wilmington.

A lover of the arts, especially all forms of performance, Alice often used her writing skills to entertain the community and to make a political statement or two. Wilmington was small, but the community had access to the arts. Alice's business travels and excursions would allow her time to see plays and hear live music when she traveled by train to New York, Philadelphia, and DC. Traveling shows starring Black actors often came through the city. She had much inspiration to join with her own imaginative writing and penchant for live performance. Having interviewed former teachers of Howard, including Pauline Young, George Chapell concludes, "Through the years the community came to Howard to enjoy the annual school play, to listen to the lecture series of prominent speakers, or watch the school's sports teams. One of the gathering points in the community, Howard High helped to keep Blacks together while facing the difficulties of racism and segregation."[39] In her position as the literary and drama specialist, as well as the chair of English, Alice organized many of the plays that the school hosted and continued to attend them after she was no longer employed by the institution.

In her archives is a copy of one such play about the colonization of Hawaii, which was performed at Howard in 1916. Since there is no title written on the actual script, scholars are at odds about the title of the musical. Whether it is *Hawaiian Idyll* or *Down Honolulu Way*,[40] it is a bit unusual, when compared to the recurring themes of her earlier work. This play focuses on native Hawaiians and their experiences with Christian colonization in the early nineteenth century. After entertaining a reverend, his wife, and their companion, a Queen sends her daughter to America to learn the ways of White men, while she remains home to learn their ways as well. What she learns are the ways of treachery and betrayal through being held captive in her palace by the Christian visitors as they beat and insult her people. Once her daughter learns what has occurred, from people who escape the island and find her at her host home in San Francisco, she returns and, with the aid of the prince who wants to marry her, frees her mother. Police from San Francisco arrive to arrest the Christians on charges of fraud. The Queen declares that Christianity is about love and not about the work of the people she has interacted with over the past year. Overall, the play offers a story in which attempts to oppress people are thwarted by the intelligence and courage of those people.

Hawaii had grown in popularity and interest, prompting Alice to write and produce what was more of a musical than a mere play for the Wilmington audience.[41] According to Lurana Donnels O'Malley, "The play was inspired by the real-life story of a Hawaiian princess. As niece to Queen Lili'uokalani, Ka 'iulani (1875–1899) was seen as a possible heir to the deposed monarch after the overthrow of the Hawaiian government in 1893."[42] Alice's documented interest in reading newspapers and literature would have exposed her to this history, though O'Malley makes clear that the play is influenced by the broad history of Hawaii and not by the actual events related to the royal family. Furthermore, a number of theater groups came through Wilmington between 1913 and 1916 and presented Hawaiian-influenced music and dance, elements of the musical that Alice wrote for her Howard audience. Her love of all forms of performance, dating back to her years in New Orleans, as well as her interest in international cultures and history, especially as they related to African American history, inspired her to write this fantastical play, replete with dancing, singing, music, conflict, and history.

Alice used the experience of the Hawaiians to revisit the history of African Americans. Typically, her fictional work does not focus on the colonization of Africa and the brutal treatment of people of African descent, even though her own mother was an enslaved woman prior to the birth of her two daughters. She used very direct language in this play, however, and one can only imagine what the audience may have thought. It is worth noting that she had been in her position at Howard for approximately eighteen years by this point, and the audience would have had a strong awareness of the world outside their own, considering the threats imposed by the First World War. It would not have been a stretch to consider the impact that racism had on people, in the name of Christianity, in various parts of the world. Alice had used fiction to critique Christian hypocrisy before, as in "Little Miss Sophie" and the 'Steenth Street stories. O'Malley concludes, "Although nothing in the play directly addresses an African American context, Alice implicitly asked her youth audience to connect the oppression of Hawaiians by paternalistic missionaries to the history of enslaved Africans in America."[43] Writing and producing the play must have been a highlight of her career as a reference to the play and its production appears in This Lofty Oak.

With Kruse's support, Alice was able to use her talents to provide Black students of the segregated school with the best education possible. Yet, as I will discuss, after Kruse's departure, Alice was eventually dismissed from her position at Howard. With Kruse, what is certain is that Alice enjoyed an erotic period as she developed under the guidance, comfort, and love of Edwina Kruse. In response to news of Kruse's death on Monday June 23, 1930, Alice lamented the loss of the woman she loved through acknowledged good and undisclosed bad times:

> Krusie died tonight at nine o'clock [of double pneumonia]. Poor deal old Ned-Odduwumuss. My mind goes back over the years from 1902 to 1909 [when D-N first came to Wilmington] when we were closer than sisters— till first Arthur [Callis], then Anna [Broadnax][44] broke up our Eden—and then to 1920 with our semi-friendship. Those first seven years! Well, she passed away. . . . When Baldy [Gertrude Baldwin, at Kruse's house][45] called over the phone . . .
>
> Krusie—her life spelled more romance than will ever be told. A friend she was—paradox of paradoxes—one of my worst enemies. Let her soul rest in peace. I loved her once. Twenty years ago, her death would have wrecked my life.[46]

Her dying wish to her niece was to have the novel, This Lofty Oak, published. In many ways, it stood as a love testament to the elder woman who allowed her the time, space, and means to escape from her needy family, pursue advanced study, and to meet the man who became her second husband, and, to further prepare for advancing Black children. After the physical, verbal, and mental abuse of Paul Laurence Dunbar, Alice must have been in need not only of refuge but also of healing. Kruse pointed her toward the bridge that led her to her time for transition. No longer the wife of Dunbar, as his widow she took the opportunity to begin living a life that would expand her boundaries. Yet she still felt bound by the expectations that were deeply rooted in her Victorian-inspired Southern upbringing. As she grew older, and as the country began to change in the early twentieth century, she would test the boundaries even more, embracing more fully the love she had for herself and for others.

IMAGE 1 *Alice Moore late 1800s*

IMAGE 2 *Alice Dunbar-Nelson, date unknown*

IMAGE 3 *Alice Dunbar, sometime between 1898 and 1902*

IMAGE 4 *Edwina Kruse, date unknown*

IMAGE 5 *Pauline Young, 1977*

7

Ms. Dunbar and Politics (of Love)

Beginning with her correspondence with Dunbar, Alice recorded her life by saving the letters, diaries, flyers, and newspaper clippings that gave insight into the triumphs and challenges of her public and private experiences. She consistently remained open and receptive to what the world around her had to offer, and she made her own efforts to contribute as best she could. Examining the chronicle of her life from her own personal perspective, we find a life—redefined. Alice's archives reveal several key points that defined the trajectory of her life: (1) middle-class African American women's resistance against racial and gender restrictions of the suffrage movement; (2) a woman's perspective of marriage as a partnership where gender roles are often blurred, especially when finances are precarious; (3) the struggles of African American political activists during the early twentieth century; and (4) the intimate relationships between African American women and men and African American women and women. What emerges in the dialogue between the diary, her columns, her essays, and her fiction is a critique of those patriarchal and white supremacist conventions that attempted to restrict Black women's progress, as well as Alice's resistance against these attempts as a political writer and activist during the early twentieth century. During this period of her life, more than any other, we see her navigate and even—redefine respectability—unapologetically.

After her marriage to Callis ended, Alice chose to marry another socially acceptable man, Robert "Bobo"[1] Nelson, a man two years her senior, on April 12, 1916. However, this man was not popular or a man of means. Remarkably, her former lover Kruse stood as her maid of honor. During their marriage (1916–35), she engaged in a period of recovery, where her coupling, as Ann duCille puts it, allowed her to return to her activist roots as she continued to explore new forms of writing. Nelson, like Alice, was interested in uplifting the race through publishing and politics. His social position as an average man prompts me to conclude that Alice must have had deep feelings for him and believed in his potential to be a good partner. The two worked together on *Master of Eloquence*, a collection of essays published in 1914, soon after they met and their relationship blossomed. Her diary illuminates her perspective on their relationship, including their fights and financial struggles, the loss of family members, travels for business and pleasure, their many career shifts, and her dalliances with another man and at least two women lovers. Together, the two worked to bring a voice and political empowerment to African Americans in the northeast. Alice's role as Nelson's wife was certainly complicated. He seemed not to have objected to her identity as the widow of Paul Laurence Dunbar, which, to some degree, allowed her to remain relevant in the literary world and to remain valuable on the speakers' circuit. As the widow of the celebrated poet, she often accepted invitations to read his poetry. On other occasions, she was billed as the wife of Paul Laurence Dunbar, and this identity served to draw attention to causes she supported, just as it also kept her visible and relevant. However, she did write of Nelson's occasional jealousy, his domestic expectations, and his inability to provide adequate financial support. For the most part, in this marriage, Alice was a partner. She fulfilled her desire as a woman to enjoy a relationship with a progressive man or a New Negro Man—one who did not attempt to limit her social activities based on societal gender expectations. What he suffered, so did she. They worked together, each with the respect of the other.

The University of Delaware houses a box of materials, including a "Women's suffrage scrapbook containing newspaper clippings, most of which relate to the women's suffrage campaign, primarily in Pennsylvania and the Mid-Atlantic region, in which Alice Dunbar-Nelson was active."[2] It is a carefully curated item that documents a period of her life when her freedom as a widowed woman gave her an opportunity to express her individual Black self in service to the race. Of the scrapbook, Ellen Gruber Garvey astutely observes, it "offers insights into the relationships between her speeches and the more general women's suffrage ideology of the period, and into her understandings of women's suffrage in the context of the needs of the black community."[3] As noted in Chapter 1, Alice had written an article in *The Women's Era* noting the influences that women had on their husbands' voting choices. Seemingly anticipating the debates that would rage well into the twentieth century, until the Nineteenth Amendment was ratified in 1920, Alice became actively involved with the movement to encourage Black women to seize their right to participate in electoral politics and Black men to support them. She also encouraged Black men, in particular, to support Black women by using their power to vote. The intersections between respectability and politics emerged as she used her identity as the wife of Paul Laurence Dunbar to advance women's political rights.

She entered a struggle that had begun shortly before her birth. Despite the promises of the Fifteenth Amendment, both Black men and women had been deprived of the right to vote. When the Reconstruction Act of 1867 was passed, requiring Confederate States to hold constitutional conventions, African American men, women, and children attended these conventions en masse. Their presence, especially those of the Black women, who outnumbered their male counterparts, showed that they were interested not only in exercising their right to vote but also in seizing political power. Several prominent issues emerged after ratification of the Fifteenth Amendment, which granted all men the right to vote. One question was: Should women vote, or should they stand in support of Black men, some of whom were able to vote (conditions in Southern states were always precarious) by right of the Fifteenth Amendment? Some women argued that women should stay home and leave the voting to men, while others went as far as taking up arms to protect their husbands and traveling long distances with their husbands and entire families on voting days. Elsa Barkley Brown observes, "African American women, unable to cast a separate vote, viewed African American men's vote as equally theirs."[4] Of course, this could be said only of the women who were married. In such a scenario, unmarried African American women, including widows, would have no man to influence or a vote to claim.

The second question was: Should the national movement support Black women, thereby jeopardizing the chances of all women? The influential National Women's Suffrage Association (NWSA), formed in 1890, was at the core of this debate. Leaders Susan B. Anthony and Elizabeth Cady advocated for "expediency," a strategy that "was to prove that the enfranchisement of White women would further, rather than impede, the power of a White ruling class that was fearful of Black and immigrant domination."[5] Threats to Black women gaining the right to vote were obvious at the 1894 convention, when the organization promoted literacy as a voting qualification. Black leaders, such as Francis Ellen Watkins Harper and Ida B. Wells-Barnett, spoke out against this and other tactics that represented class and racial preferences. Segregation in the group began to rise. Though Anthony and Wells-Barnett had a respectful relationship, Anthony would not support Wells-Barnett when Black women wanted to form a branch of the NWSA. Tensions rose further when, ignoring the challenges of Black Southern women and their efforts to gain the right to vote, the organization came out in support of states' rights in 1903. This tactic may have gained them support from Southern White men and women, but Black women were left to defend themselves, and that they did.

The year 1913 was a revolutionary year in the national women's suffrage movement, and Black women were active participants, literally refusing to sit on the sidelines. Wells-Barnett helped to organize the Alpha Club, the first Black women's suffrage club in Illinois. On March 3, 1913, the NWSA led a Women's March for Suffrage in DC, but Black women were told that they must walk behind the others, if they chose to participate.

Wells-Barnett, who had earnestly worked to earn a reputation for not cowering at prescribed boundaries, invited herself to walk with the Chicago representatives after the march began. Among the marchers were twenty-two young Black college women of the newly formed Delta Sigma Theta Sorority. Founded at Howard University on January 13, 1913, the sorority's purpose was to engage in political activities. Encouraged by Mary Church Terrell to participate in this particular event on a cool morning in March, the young women of the organization, with the support of Howard University, marched as they maneuvered past jeers and flying objects from onlookers. They also did this despite being told by the organizers to march in the back. Whether they complied or integrated themselves into the line with the other suffragists as did Ida B. Wells-Barnett is a matter of debate.

National coalitions included organized groups of women who were working state by state to change laws through rallies, marches, and meetings. Alice, who had been active with political organizations for years, increased her skills as speaker and organizer. In Wilmington, she formed political coalitions locally and further developed national networks. Starting in her own community, Alice joined with Emma Gibson Sykes,[6] Blanche Williams Stubbs, Mary J. Woodlen, Alice G. Baldwin, and other women to organize the Equal Suffrage Study Club on March 19, 1914.[7] With the exception of Woodlen, the women were teachers at Howard and would later become charter members of the Wilmington, NAACP chapter. Together they pooled their energy and ideas to form a coalition of organizations. They must have worked well together as they had also been involved with the Thomas Garret Settlement, a social service agency, that provided "a kindergarten, art and music classes, athletic activities, a health clinic, and meeting spaces."[8] Their first meeting occurred at the home of Sykes. Under the leadership of Alice as president, the women marched in a suffrage parade in Wilmington in May of that year.

In 1915, she became an organizer for the Middle Atlantic States in the women's suffrage campaign and joined the statewide women's campaign to have an amendment granting women the right to vote passed in Pennsylvania. Charged with lecturing throughout Pennsylvania, she mostly targeted African American audiences of both men and women, who also opened their doors to Whites. Her scrapbook[9] documents the many news articles that were written about her speeches to various church groups, club meetings, conferences, and festivals to persuade her audience of voters (men) and potential voters (women). She emphasized two main arguments, women's abilities to make sound decisions and the problem with Black men who assumed that voting women would neglect their families. If men worked with women to expand their rights, she argued, the race would be stronger and more capable of further advancement.

Newspaper articles printed about her speeches document her vocal attempts to challenge men's restrictions upon women. Yet she had to rely on a man's reputation to have access to this powerful group of voters. What is common among the articles is the emphasis on her identity as the wife of the poet Paul Laurence Dunbar. Dunbar had been dead for nine years by the time Alice became a suffrage leader and the articles were written. A woman who understood societal restrictions and comforts, Alice strategically kept his name and continued to accept invitations to read his work to audiences in various parts of the country, which allowed her to establish a reputation as a sought-after lecturer and to secure funds from these events. When she knocked on doors to speak to and about women and the right to vote, those doors were opened to a respected widow.

A couple of the newspaper articles strongly suggest that she created the story of an ideal marriage with Dunbar to market herself. Betty Hart articulates the problem with this: "It is ironic that a woman of such talent and energy should be remembered for what were probably the worst years of her life."[10] One article directly connected her marriage to Dunbar with her activism: "Since her husband's death in 1905[11] she has devoted herself to the uplift of the Negro race and her success has been noteworthy."[12] Mischaracterizing her as uninvolved in Black empowerment work before marrying Dunbar negated the career she had had as an activist involved with the "uplift of the Negro race" long before she met and married Dunbar. The article implies that Alice had no concerns and thoughts of her own before her marriage and, more strikingly, that she did not possess any interest in uplifting her race before their marriage. The writer ends by quoting Alice as directly crediting Dunbar with influencing her activist career: "She attributes her success to the encouragement and help she received from her husband." In fact, his letters show that he rarely encouraged her activist work but strongly supported her literary aspirations. Yet, as Ellen Gruber Garvey observes the article has the potential to garner men's support: "Inviting men to identify with Paul Laurence Dunbar's role not simply as a supporter of women's rights. . . . She offered him as a model for her male audience members to emulate."[13]

Another article even more clearly attributes Dunbar as the inspiration for her activism. According to the writer, Dorothy Deane, who was a member of the local suffrage group:

> Mrs. Dunbar said that Mr. Dunbar was an ardent suffragist long before she was. She said, that like many other women, she had always believed in suffrage, but she did not quite like the idea of going to the polls to register her ballot. One day while they were in Colorado, Mr. Dunbar drove her around to a voting place, so that she could see just how the women voted, and this of course converted her.[14]

The writer goes on to say that Mrs. Dunbar read a "suffrage story" or a poem written by Dunbar that "shows his sentiments." Whether or not this story about Colorado is true, it certainly served the purpose of endearing

Alice to her activist hosts, one of whom reportedly remarked that theirs was an "ideal marriage." She may have encouraged this thinking by informing the writer that the eight years of their marriage were "the happiest of her life." Such a fictitious comment places everything else that she alledgedly said to the reporter about her life with Dunbar into question. We may be reminded here of the stories she wrote during and about their marriage, which show the emotional turmoil between the two. Arguably, had it not been for her travels as a literary representative and posthumous agent of Dunbar, whose work she had always respected, his name would not have remained as valuable as it did on the literary market and lecture circuit. Still an unmarried widowed woman, she had more to lose by telling the truth about him than by taking liberties with his flawed character.

Her activist fervor was further minimized by the articles' attention to her physical appearance. In a statement that subjected her to scrutiny not related to her speech, the writer of the *Ledger* proclaimed, "[H]er exceptional beauty has proved irresistible to would-be opponents."[15] Another article described her as "[t]all and graceful, [with] a voice beautifully modulated and an easy flow of forceful logical arguments could not fail her arguments."[16] The *Williamsport Sun* described her as "a woman of unusual beauty."[17] Since her picture accompanied these articles, there was no need to add any descriptions of her physical appearance; the writers' choice to do so illustrates how women were undervalued for their intellect and political knowledge. In the cases where the descriptions were part of an announcement, they served the purpose of convincing audiences to attend. Such beauty would disarm her "opponents," as one journalist put it, and made her rather radical message more acceptable to men, who may have felt threatened by the idea of women voting. One has to wonder, if she had not been the wife of a known poet, regarded as a beautiful woman, or light enough to pass for White, would she have been invited to speak on behalf of important issues? On the other hand, the attention to her physical appearance was used to convince people of various ages and interests to attend the event, as evidenced by one article that announced her lecture and openly invited "White friends." Though identified as the wife of Paul Laurence Dunbar, it noted that "[s]he is herself an author," a "versatile person" with "literary talents" and a "marked ability as a lecturer and teacher." Lest her achievements dissuade anyone from attending, journalists described her as "youthful looking," "charming," and in possession of a "modulated voice," language used to entice people to come and "hear her."[18] All of these descriptions surely served the purpose of casting her as a nonthreatening, welcoming presence.

In some cases, such attention to mundane details overshadowed the purpose of her visits and her effectiveness. Vague details were given of her August visit to Pennsylvania, even though the anonymous writer informed the reader that the article was based on an interview with the speaker. The discussion of the actual speech is only two lines long. The first: "Pennsylvania should have been a pioneer woman suffrage state, and although the efforts of the suffrage workers to win the vote are commendable it is not to their credit that the tired and proved principal of equal franchise is still being debated at this late date." After commenting on her looks and listing her literary publications, the article includes a second reference to her work as a suffragist: "Concerning her plans for her suffrage work Mrs. Dunbar would say little, but states, through committees formed of negroes she hoped to get into closer touch with the negro masses than the white organizers had." What is lost in the "little" that she said? What was delivered in the speech? Attention was not given to answering these questions.

Other writers gave less attention to her social position and looks and more attention to the actual message. In an article on her speech to the Woman's Party of Darby, the writer described her "easy flow of forceful, logical arguments." By focusing on the major points of Alice's talk, the writer revealed her political platform and her method of appeal to the women's audience. According to the article, she emphasized how suffrage would help the race, how women could help their men, and how men would benefit from the increase of the voters. These were common statements made on the national level by suffragists. Working together as a community of Black men and women could unify rather than divide. Uninterested in minimizing or belittling women, her message remained similar to the message and work of the early Black club women who emphasized that the race could not advance without the work of Black women. She went on to appeal directly to the women by declaring that women's "ceaseless hard labor" had resulted in an increase of wealth and the growth of an educated class. In the same article where she is described as speaking of a happy marriage with Dunbar, the writer also described her as believing "in telling the truth," as she spoke to men about the "conditions" most in need of change. Her message to Black men was based on a historical perspective that she provided, which started with enslavement and progressed through freedom, educational advancements, men's right to vote, and the argument that freedom for women meant being self-sufficient. "The best way they can help themselves is to have the ballot," she reportedly said.[19] In these we see that she argued that the advancement of the race partially depended on the women's political power.

There were two specific arguments that she routinely addressed in her lectures. One was the absence of the woman in the home if she voted, to which Alice responded by discussing the historical absence of Black women in their homes—because so many went to work. She reminded the working-class men that they had no problem with their wives working to bring in an extra income. In a speech she delivered at the same rally as her old neighbor Mary Church Terrell, she informed the African American audience at the First Presbyterian Church that women voting would not affect the "home anymore than their church activities."[20] Alice was adamant that women had earned the right to vote, based on the contributions they were already making to their households and their communities.

Her sharpest argument was the wage-earning capacity of working women. To an African Methodist Episcopal audience, "she showed how the colored women represented equally with their men folks the earning capacity and impressed her hearers that had it not been for the women of the race adding their help to the men that the race would not have attained what it has in the way of achievement and moral achievement."[21] Again, she hoped to convince the men that supporting women's suffrage was a step toward unifying Black communities and families, as well as a move toward economic stability:

> We women, she said, want the ballot so as to join forces with you and gain for the race those rights we feel we are entitled to and which you know can only be gotten by standing by together as a solid mass. When the rights of the race are an issue the women will stand with the men on the matter and by doubling our vote we will then be able to show to the oppressor that we are a factor that should not be despised.[22]

Since her earlier days as a club woman in New Orleans, Alice had always focused on the treatment and status of women, and in particular Black women. Participation in the women's suffrage campaign was another way to advance Black women. One article captures the significance of her involvement in the state's campaign as one who "educated the women of her race to a fuller understanding of the merits of woman suffrage."[23] Her role, then, proved instructive to Black women as much as to men. No matter how much credit she assigned to her deceased husband for awakening her interest in voting, her deep involvement in the Pennsylvania movement was most certainly an extension of her interest in the advancement of women. She had always believed that the race could not advance if women were not recognized as full partners in the decision-making.

Her deployment of strategies that appealed to men did not stop with the idea of racial unity; she also appealed to Black men's sense of chivalry as a desirable and admirable trait in the early twentieth century. More specifically, she appealed to men's sense of chivalry to entice them to support Black women. Gaining equal suffrage was a test for Black men to show themselves as respectable. She stated, "[N]early every colored man who amounted to anything was in favor of giving the franchise to the women." And, to make sure they saw the symbolic importance of supporting women's right to vote, she told the men, "[I]f they are willing to deny the women of their race what white men were willing to give to theirs," then they "slap [their] women in the face" and "kick themselves" because a vote from women supported men's votes.[24] Interestingly, she used a metaphor that placed Black men as perpetuators of domestic violence. Her own experience would have told her that there was little sympathy for women in such relationships. But she asked the question: Do they see Black women as being as good as White women? Perhaps shaming them was the strategy needed to transform men's minds.

A second opposing argument that she addressed was a belief in women's lack of intelligence or ability to make informed decisions. Rather than try to disprove such beliefs, she shifted the critical gaze to the behavior of boys and men. Relying on her own experience as an educator, she informed the audience that girls stayed in school longer than boys, who tended to leave at the age of fourteen to work. She ended by addressing the selling of votes by Black men, an action that would not be taken by women; she proclaimed with a bit of humor: "[I]t would not be of any use to buy a woman's vote, for 'she never stays where she is put.'"[25] At this point, she took an authoritative tone as both an educator and a woman. Her address to the men was the result of the opposition she reportedly received from "colored men" as she traveled the circuit. This suggested yet another reason why she told the story of Dunbar being a supporter of equal suffrage: perhaps their poetic tragic hero could also be their political model.

Alice did not always limit her talks to equal suffrage, even if that was what the crowd expected. Her lifelong attention to the "advancement of the race" led her to speak on other matters as well. In Chester, Pennsylvania, she spoke briefly about suffrage and then in greater detail about the importance of and need for adequate housing. Reportedly, "The speaker denounced in emphatic terms the fact that colored families in many cities of this country were living in congested sections and that there was not ample room in their homes for the family."[26] Her extensive travels during this period may have prompted her to appeal to her hosts, the Bennet Colored Improvement Club, to act. Her long history with women's clubs and their work in assisting communities in need probably also inspired her to address such issues, which she did not seem to share with any of the churches she visited. Her collection of materials that document this segment of her activist life, complete with a carefully curated scrapbook that contains examples of her versatility as a speaker, shows a woman who was able to change her message and emphasize specific points according to the audience and the venue, while building on her keen observations and vast experience as a writer and activist.

As a result, Alice earned the reputation of being a respected and passionate suffrage speaker. Her presentations were often described as having received "an enthusiastic impetus," as "heart-to-heart talks" conveying a "plain truth" and bringing laughter from the audience.[27] While recording her appeal and the audience's reception, the news writers also recorded the breadth of her reach. She spoke to relatively large crowds of people. In Washington, Pennsylvania, for example, she "kept more than 400 persons interested for over an hour," evidence of "her power to captivate her hearers." The writer regarded her as "the best suffrage lecturer and one of the most charming speakers ever in Washington." The *Harrisburg Telegraph* begins its article: "Fully 1,000 persons heard Mrs. Paul Laurence Dunbar, widow of the famous negro poet deliver stirring lectures on suffrage."[28] Alice clearly enjoyed these engagements and the attention that she was given by the press—as evidenced by her assemblage of a scrapbook. In some ways she was living in Dunbar's shadow as the poet's widow, but for the first time she was also redefining herself as a political leader, lending her voice to a national history-changing political cause. As she did so, she and not Dunbar was lauded as the pride of the race. It was printed that "the race should be proud of Mrs. Dunbar; should be proud that one of its members has so thoroughly absorbed the details anent racial advancement, and can so conclusively and conscientiously present them to an audience."[29]

Some of her lectures occurred during the summer months, when she was not teaching at Howard, but she kept a steady schedule up to the date of the suffrage amendment vote. As she did so, she continued her appeal to men to vote for passage of the amendment. Papers in York County, Pennsylvania, where she was on the day of the women's suffrage vote, recorded her activities. She continued to address the points she had been making since June: women's place in the home and the impact of men selling their votes, while emphasizing that "intelligent" men were in support of women's suffrage. At this juncture, her addresses became more specific to Pennsylvania, as she tried to convince them that the high divorce rate in the state would decrease if women were able to vote, since such a right would make them happier. "The minimum of divorces in the West is undoubtedly due to the equality of sexes, she said."[30] On November 2, she remained in York County to make speeches and visit "all the polling places of the city to help boost for votes."[31] Unfortunately, the people of York failed to support Amendment One: 5,348 voted yes, while 12,090 voted no. According to one article, York was one of three counties expected to vote against the amendment. Most certainly she was in the area to try to change the inevitable. Although the amendment did not pass in 1915, the women's work served to educate people as the country moved closer to passage of the US Constitution's Nineteenth Amendment.

Despite this setback, Alice remained respected for her work as a suffrage activist and political organizer. She continued to make speeches as Black women continued to demand their right to expand their access to citizenship. "Distinguished Women to Meet in Baltimore" read the headline of a June 22, 1916, *New York Age* article that captured the work of the National Association of Colored Women's Clubs who met August 6–10 of that year to chart a path forward with "representatives from the various national race organization doe uplift." Under the leadership of Mrs. Margaret Washington, Alice Ruth Moore Dunbar-Nelson is listed among the "well-known women who are programmed to speak at the conference's" . . . : symposium on woman suffrage."[32] In 1919, she urged women to vote responsibly. In a speech, the *Cleveland Gazette* reported on July 7, 1919, that they should stay vigilant: "you should vote for me and not measures. . . . You should watch the sweet and oily politician, electing only the man who will remain sweet and oily after he wins."[33]

Her activism earned her an invitation to become an honorary member of Delta Sigma Theta Sorority. She had first been invited by the sorority to a tea on Howard University's campus in 1916 to speak about the importance of the vote for women. Surely the women's active interest in suffrage, the major issue of the day for Black women, and its make up of middle-class educated Black women, such as Mary Church Terrell, another honorary member, made the organization appealing to her. Alice's invitation to join the organization was inevitable. Her niece, Pauline Young, had been a charter member of the third chapter while at the University of Pennsylvania, also the location where Alice had done further postgraduate work. Once Alice became a member, she remained influentially active at the early stages of the organization's growth, writing the lyrics to the sorority's national song and often attending meetings and gatherings, as evidenced by the descriptions of meetings in her diary and the documents she left in her scrapbook. As a respected activist, her role in the sorority was to be a model respectable activist. On December 27, 1921, she wrote of one convention in Philadelphia, where Sadie T. M. Alexander, the sorority's national president, had asked her to speak on the history of Black women's activism, that her "voice was horrible, but [she] did [her] best. Made the same speech, practically, as in Montclair, on the development of the club idea among our women, and the big job of the young women of the sorority in inculcating race pride."[34] She correctly saw her position as a pioneer of the Black club women's movement as a precursor for the development of Black college sororities. A return to her beginnings remained purposeful for the new generation of Black women who had organized as college women.

The year 1915 was a busy year for the energetic activist. In addition to pushing for women's right to vote, nine years after the National Association for the Advancement of Colored People (NAACP) formed, she worked with community leaders, such as Edwina Kruse and Howard High School's graduate, attorney Louis Redding,[35] to charter a Wilmington chapter. As an organization that was founded to combat lynchings, Alice's interests and those of many Black folks aligned with the organization's anti-lynching campaign. According to the chapter's historical records, she formed a coalition of community members to protest a showing of Birth of a Nation by getting the City Council to "pass an ordinance banning moving pictures 'likely to stir up bad feelings between the races.'"[36] Adopted from a novel titled The Clansman, the film was cowritten, produced, and directed by D. W. Griffith to incite violence against Black men that was necessary to save White women, giving rise and purpose to the Ku Klux Klan. Through the NAACP she would work closely with luminaries, such as James Weldon Johnson, who became the national field secretary in 1916.

Leading the life of an activist had its risks. After nine days on the job, Ray Wooten, Howard's new principal, denied Alice's request to attend a social justice event on October 1, 1920. Being *the* Alice Dunbar-Nelson who had an established reputation as an activist, she went anyway, but when she returned to her classroom the following Monday, she found the lock had been changed. According to a newspaper article that was posted in several newspapers, the "widow of the late Paul Lawrence Dunbar, famous colored poet, was unceremoniously discharged from her position as teacher in the public schools of the city by the Democratic board for having attended the social justice pilgrimage to Marion, Ohio, October 1."[37] Implied here is that her removal was a political move by a rivalry party. It goes on: "Mrs. Nelson, who was among the colored delegation from the east that went to Harding's home, joining the thousands of other women assembled there for the purposes of social welfare," had been warned not to attend by Wooten. In fact, after the passage of the Nineteenth Amendment, the suffragists continued to agitate for women's rights and had gone there to meet with other women to hear the Republican senator and presidential candidate speak outside his home in Marion, Ohio. Wooten was not impressed and she would later see him as a man who was replacing women teachers with men.

He was, to be sure, in a position of power. She and Wooten gave the board their resignations on October 14; on October 15, the board decided to accept Alice's and to reinstate Wooten. In a letter to W. E. B. Du Bois, who knew Alice and had posted a "news item" about the firing in *The Crisis*, Wooten informed the venerable leader that she "was insubordinate to the extent that she absented herself from duties without an official permit of the Board . . . and against the expressed wishes of her principal." And, in response to not being allowed to teach until the matter had been "officially handled" she took him "to task in a most unprofessional manner in a local Negro weekly" and then refused to retract the statement when asked by the board. Without Kruse's protection, her eighteen-year career at Howard—a job she took immense pride in having— came to an abrupt end, and for the most part, with the exception of her brief stint at the Industrial School, this ended her career as an educator and her ability to earn a steady income. Consequently, the Moore-Nelson family suffered a loss of steady income. She would later encourage her husband to pursue the position of Recorder of Deeds in Delaware, but he did not earn the votes.

There were highs and lows, to be sure. In January 1921, the activist was one of two Black folks asked to serve on a committee charged to write Wilmington's new city charter. It was a prestigious appointment.[38] Despite all her work, by 1921 Alice felt hardly satisfied with the status of Black folks. She was not alone. Historian Rosalyn Terborg-Penn reports, "In spite of these efforts to implement their political rights, black women in the South were disenfranchised in less than a decade after the Nineteenth Amendment enfranchised them in 1920, and black women outside the South lost the political clout they had acquired."[39] While her diaries do not cover every year of her life, references in surviving diaries and other archival documents show that in 1921, Alice became chair of the publicity committee of the National League of Colored Republican Women and her active ties with the National Association of Colored Women were an attraction to the political parties that sought the women's vote and allegiances. But by the end of the year, she began to break with the party as she was no longer very active in this position or as an organizer for the Mid-Atlantic states. By 1921, she was no longer a participant with the State Committee. Lisa G. Materson sheds light on the inner workings of the political landscape: "Almost as soon as women acquired full voting rights, however, fracture lines appeared in the façade of solidarity that black Republican women tenuously maintained among themselves in presidential election."[40] Materson goes on to explain that the Republican's appeal to White Southerners meant that the Black members' efforts to have the federal anti-lynching bill legislation passed was ignored, despite Black women's commitment to supporting the Warren Harding-Calvin Coolidge ticket. Anti-lynching work had been a top priority for Black women, such as Ida B. Wells-Barnett, who had been leading since the late 1800s. Alice would respond by successfully working against the reelection of Delaware's Republican representative Caleb Layton.[41]

Showing her commitment to issues and not to political parties, she converted to the Democratic Party and served as "the director of Colored women at the Democratic Party headquarters in New York" where she had established ties within the Black middle class. Her position was to rally more Black women to leave the Republican Party and join the Democratic Party. Relying on her oratory abilities, she would make the case in "Why I Am a Democrat in 1924."[42] She began by getting straight to the point: "The hour has struck for all loyal colored women to come to the aid of the race by asserting political independence. The day of a new emancipation has dawned." By appealing to her peers, she hoped to use the history of slavery to inspire the women to see a conversion to the Democratic Party as an act of liberation. Hers was an emancipation proclamation for Black women.

As she had done during the suffrage movement, she told her audience— one that she knew well— why working with the Democratic Party was beneficial to advancing their position in the United States. The ballot would yield a series of rights as "American citizens," including "the right to live and work," "for her children to be educated and reap the fruits of education," and "[t]o live in sanitary surroundings."[43] She was appealing to them as mothers who could make a decision that would secure a better future for the race. In the past, the clubwomen had coalesced to advance the race as servants who would focus on the betterment of the uneducated class of Blacks. This time, she spoke directly to all Black women about what they could do to advance themselves, if only they would seize the power made possible by the Nineteenth Amendment. For Black women of the North, especially those who had come from the South, the possibility of change must have been appealing.

She then moved forward in telling them the problems with the party she had abandoned. It was, she would maintain, the party of old, the party of Lincoln, not the party of the twentieth century. The race had advanced long past slavery. She used Black men to illustrate this as she informed her audience that they had paid any debt owed the Republican Party through service to the country: "for centuries the Negro has been the mainstay of the greater portion of this nation" as shown through exploration, fighting in wars, and working in fields.[44] To leave doubt to her point she declared, "The Republican Party has disregarded this loyalty of the past fifty years."[45] Their disloyalty was shown by not honoring one request: "They only asked that the Dyer Anti-Lynching Bill be placed on the Statute Books of the nation. The Republican Party killed the Dyer Anti-Lynching Bill[46] after great beating of tom-toms."[47] In addition to betrayal, she also accused the party of fearing the Ku Klux Klan and keeping "out of Civil Service employment colored girls, merely because of their race."[48] Comparing the party to a man, she told her audience that the Republican Party is a "coward" and "No woman loves a coward."[49] In this, she would go on, the Republican Party was the slave. Why would the women, she implied, want to have any association with slavery?

Thirdly, she addressed the matter of "patronage." Charging it with years of disloyalty, she reminded the audience that the party could have placed Black men in positions of power: "why didn't the Republican Party when it came into power in 1921 begin to restore these office to its faithful and devoted and loyal followers?"[50] In other words, if loyalty has not been reciprocal for Black men who have had the right to vote, then what would Black women hope to receive from the party?

Lastly, she made the case for supporting 1924 Democratic presidential candidate John W. Davis by introducing him as a man from West Virginia who had Black friends. As a result he and his family had a "spirit of kindness and . . . strong sense of justice which knew and knows no color line."[51] Her point seemed to be to not only endear him to her audience as a man they could trust to represent them but also to humanize him as one they could accept as an advocate. She went on to tell her audience of times that he had spoken on their behalf, suggesting to her that he was not a coward. In one example, according to Alice, Davis, when he was solicitor general in 1914, had openly argued, "The protection of the Constitution was extended to an entire race—to all races—it is true—but it extended to the humblest member of that race."[52] She also presented evidence that he would use the law to condemn the Ku Klux Klan. During the New Negro Movement and at this point in her long activist career, Alice had moved past trying to make compromises with her White peers. Her stance placed her in opposition to Mary Church Terrell, who "tried to halt more defections . . . [by] pointedly sharing [ing] Davis' shameful record with African American women" and the party's record in "controlling the South."[53]

She spoke openly and honestly to make advances for the race and was willing to take criticism for her choices. Privately, however, her misfortunes of having lost her teaching job and the uncertainty of her financial stability led her to conclude that a "voodooist" had intervened in her life. The busy widow was not alone as she dealt with these challenges.

Her life partner, Robert John Nelson, had entered her busy life. Referred to as Bobo by his wife, he was born on May 20, 1886, in Reading, Pennsylvania. The youngest of eleven brothers and sisters, he was educated in public schools and crafted a career in publishing and in journalism. He married twice, first to Elizabeth Barber of Baltimore, who was the mother of his daughter, Elizabeth, and son, Robert Clarke. Although the son died in childhood, Elizabeth, though of poor health, lived much longer, under the primary care of her stepmother, Alice. Nelson was active in publishing and politics. From 1916 to 1920, he cofounded and edited the *Wilmington Advocate*, and from 1925 to 1930 he edited *The Washington Eagle* (DC). He was an active member of the NAACP and the United Negro Republican Association. He was also an African Methodist Episcopal church elder.

While the details of how they met and their courtship are sketchy, they had known each other for several years before their marriage in 1916. The two clearly were attracted to each other's love for racial uplift, as evidenced by their joint project, *Masterpieces of Negro Eloquence: The Best Speeches Delivered by the Negro from the Days of Slavery to the Present Time*, which Alice edited during Nelson's time as president of the Douglass Publishing Company, a small press based in Harrisburg, Pennsylvania. Released in 1914, the collection includes speeches from respected activists whom she had known and others whose work she simply included with the rest. Work on the project took place at least during the fall of 1913. It was not easy. She drew from her personal collections, made requests of friends such as Du Bois, and relied on information and requests she collected from revered Black collectors and scholars.

With the assistance of historian and collector Arthur Alfonso Schomburg, whose research and collection would evolve into the Schomburg Center for Black Culture of the New York Public Library System, she received access to books and manuscripts from his private collection that otherwise were not available. In October, she responded to Schomburg's inquiry about her health that she had been "rather upset" by being forced to stay in bed for two weeks in her residence at 918 French Street, a situation that "just about gotten [her] nerves on the raw edges." Being kept in bed meant that she had to allow a substitute to take her class, but to keep from "drooling in some insane asylum" she kept up her correspondence.[54] According to the editor, "The present volume does not aim to be a complete collection of *Negro Eloquence*; it does not even aim to present the best that the Negro has done on the platform, it merely aims to present to the public some few of the best speeches made within the past hundred years."[55] To draw the interest of potential contributors, she marketed the collection as being "the greatest speeches delivered by members of our race," with a dedication "To the boys and girls of the Negro Race, this book is dedicated, with the hope that it may help inspire them with a belief in their own possibilities."[56] Alice's coordination of this project reflects both her growing interest in African American letters and her love of politics, in its various forms. What she did not include may account for the almost apologetic tone of the preface, a tone that she takes with Schomburg: "I am so sorry to say that I am so ignorant as never to have heard of Rev. Pennington, but that is not strange; what I don't know about famous Negroes would fill the libraries of New York."[57] For the English teacher, her work became personally informative. She states later in the letter she wrote to him on September 23, 1913, "I am so glad you allow me to correspond with you; it is like a liberal education." By the time she wrote to him, she noted that there were "already 100,000 words in the hands of printers, and all that goes in now—my contract allows me 115,000—will be pure gold. If I come across pure gold that I must have, even if the limit has been exceeded, I am going to cut down in some of the lesser lights."[58] Of the references made in the letter, she did not include works by these "famous Negroes" such as Pennington, but she probably received help from Schomburg to include Henry Dumas.

Despite her attempts to collect the work of the best of the race, the collection has noticeable flaws. Alice's choices have been criticized by Gloria Akasha Hull and Manning Marable, two of the few scholars who have acknowledged this anthology. Although Alice included essays and speeches authored by Frances Ellen Watkins Harper, Josephine St. Pierre Ruffin, and Fanny Jackson Coppin, there is scant attention given to the multitude of issues facing women at this time, a remarkable omission for a woman who was dedicated to the advancement of Black women. Harper's "Address Delivered at the Centennial Anniversary of the Pennsylvania Society for Promoting the Abolition of Slavery" is the only one of the women's contributions that brings attention to Black women, but this is not a featured theme of the speech. After indicting Europeans and White Americans for their role in colonizing Africa, Harper looks forward to the promise of African American growth as she encourages the race to rely on themselves for uplift. Women's work is part of this uplift. She states, "Women, in your golden youth; mother, binding around your heart all the precious ties of life,—let no magnificence of culture, or amplitude of fortune, or refinement of sensibilities, repel you from helping the weaker and less favored."[59] Delivered in 1875, the speech conveyed a common theme that Harper often addressed in her work, that Black women had an important role in advancing the race, whether men acknowledged this or not.

A focus on addresses of the Reconstruction and post-Reconstruction Eras brought attention to the self-degradation of those Black leaders who seemed unsure about the status of the race and how to move forward. For example, Alexander Crummell's speech "The Black Woman of the South: Her Neglects and Her Needs" is the only one specifically about Black women. Presenting the address before the "'Freedman's Aid Society,' Methodist Episcopal Church, Ocean Grove, N. J., August 15th, 1883," he intended to provide an overview of slavery and how Black women had been mistreated, as well as the impact that mistreatment was having on the position of Black women at the time of his speech. Unfortunately, his indictment of slavery led him to conclude that the greatest sufferers, Black women, remained in a state of intellectual and moral degradation. He remarked, "She is still the crude, rude, ignorant mother." His speech resonated with Alice and the club women, who held such beliefs and hoped to help the "ignorant" Black mothers to advance themselves by providing proper training. But Alice's interest in this work suggests that even sixteen years after the turn of the century she was still preoccupied with the state of Black women, leading us to wonder if it was her lack of access to other, more recent pieces that led her to include these essays or if she honestly felt that Crummell's assertions were still prevalent. It may have been both.

Such concerns as those in Crummell's address were not unusual for the period in which they were expressed. In fact, he covered issues that led Alice to cofound the Phillis Wheatley Club of New Orleans. The concerns were common among the Black educated middle class of this era, who often focused both on how Black women were treated by Whites and on how they needed to meet a set of societal expectations. These expectations were largely imposed on Southern Black women, who were deemed as not having the culture that the women of the North, especially New England, had developed over a period long before Emancipation.

Fanny Jackson Coppin's "Plea for Industrial Opportunity" also engaged the theme of Blacks' lack of knowledge; she made her case for industrial education based on the idea that Black folks are incapable of doing much else: "We have our choice of the professions, it is true, but, as we have not been endowed with an overwhelming abundance of brains, it is not probable that we can contribute to the bar a great lawyer except once in a great while."[60] Coppin took a decidedly self-deprecating point of view. For an audience of 1914, a generation out of slavery, delving into educational opportunities and organizing political institutions—for example, the NAACP and the Universal Negro Improvement Association—the themes of Coppin's essays would not have resonated well with the progressive tone of the twentieth century. Indeed, Black America's middle class, especially those in the Northern cities, was trying to move forward, like Alice, and pursue education in a variety of professional areas.

Josephine Ruffin's "Open Letter to the Educational League of Georgia" implored Georgian White women to expand the interest they were showing in Black children by providing them with lessons in morals and good conduct. She stated:

What untold blessings might not the educated Christian women of the South prove to the Negro groping blindly in the darkness of the swamps and bogs of prejudice for a highway out of servitude, oppression, ignorance, and immorality! While lauding the white women for volunteering.[61]

She ended by saying to Southern White women that, if they need to seek counsel, the Black women of the North—notably not the Black women of the South—are available. Similar to Crummell, Ruffin looked at the Black Southerner of the Progressive Era through the eyes of Victorian values and her perspective as an educated New England woman. She did, however, place the blame of whatever she saw as lacking on Southern Black people among their former slave owners and charged them to take care of it themselves rather than to rely on good-natured Northerners.

Curiously, Alice's own contribution, though she was a champion for women's rights, included an address not about women but about the life of David Livingstone, a Scottish missionary who explored Africa. Relying heavily on her literary studies and training in European writers, the essay analyzes the contributions he made to the "Dark Continent," crediting his activities for helping to end the slave trade. For the most part, her intent here seems to have been to use his life to influence the "future generation," as she puts it in her preface and in the essay. She notes, "What has this modern romance in it for the man of to-day? An infinity of example, of hope, of the gleam to follow."[62] She portrays Livingstone as one who achieved greatness because he engaged in a "thorough preparation of work," operated on meager funds, labored earnestly, was patient, and so on. He also became one with the "savages," proving his ability to meet all challenges. While the future generation may have been impressed with Livingstone's drive, one would hope that they would not see Africa as the Dark Continent, home of savages. Hull regarded Alice's attitude toward Africa as another example of her use of irony. Yet, in this era, such thinking was common, and it is difficult to know if this woman, who like most Americans had little knowledge of Africa, used such language as "savages" as a form of irony or truth. It is worth noting that irony was a commonly used method of political critique that she used liberally in her op-ed pieces.

Her choice of essays may cause readers to wonder why she would silence the voice of Black Southern women who spoke widely and "eloquently" about what they knew best. If Alice's own work was not sufficient, surely the voices of Margaret Washington or Ida B. Wells-Barnett would have been acceptable to the readers. Had the tumultuous years in organizing Black women's clubs kept her from including them? Looking beyond the flaws of the collection, Manning Marable finds it a valuable contribution to African American letters:

Despite some important limitations and contradictions, *Masterpieces* is a remarkable resource for understanding the life of the mind of black America, and the power of its oral tradition. The Volume defines a set of critical issues that framed the context of the black experience in the 19th and early 20th centuries: slavery, emigration to Africa, abolitionism, the Civil War, Reconstruction, and Jim Crow segregation.[63]

Certainly, the collection provides an archive of Black intellectual thinking of the late nineteenth and early twentieth centuries as Black people struggled to define, identify, and navigate the changing American landscape and their place in it.

In addition, the collection stands as the first of many collaborations between the Nelsons—and may even represent the imperfections and prideful moments that mark the growth and development of this African American couple's atypical relationship in the early twentieth century. Alice's diaries document an ambitious couple and the challenges they endured in aiding one another to reach their own goals. We see this through Alice's point of view, which highlights her dedication to her husband, her spiritual aspirations, her love of family, and her commitment to advancing race relations and attaining women's rights. Such aspirations called for a relationship that could stand the strain of long and frequent travel, severe (almost overwhelming) financial burdens, and political tugs-of-war. Nelson was a favorable match for Alice. His own interest in politics and publishing allowed him to be supportive of her efforts. Remarkably, there is no evidence that he tried to hinder her ability to market herself as the widow of Paul Laurence Dunbar rather than as his wife. In fact, he strongly encouraged her to travel and to make political speeches, even feeling invested in her speeches. She recorded, "Bobo came in before I began to speak. I think I did myself proud, though Bobo was not pleased with my speech, as he thought I did not use enough of the campaign material which he had prepared in the various issues of the paper."[64] Nelson's response here reveals his attempt to be a participant in the message his wife shared with others. We also learn of her resistance, even if understated, of his attempts to alter her voice. Of him, Hull remarks, "Self-assured about his own worth and life, he never tried to hinder his prominent wife, although on occasion he could be jealous and domestically sexist."[65] For the era, Nelson was a progressive husband, shortly before his time. Curwood notes that "between 1920 and World War II" African Americans' view on marriage changed: "From a previous emphasis on respectability, African Americans developed a limited acceptance of sexuality separate from production and began to believe that respectable women might earn wages."[66] She goes on to say that "evolving gender roles" emerged by the Second World War. To be sure, the marriage of Bobo and Alice was exemplar of these characteristics. With him, she would tease out her identity as a respectable activist.

Nelson certainly benefitted from Alice's late husband's name as she was the benefactor of his estate and any profits related to the use of Dunbar's name. In 1920, Alice would undertake another edited collection, *The Dunbar Reader Speaker and Entertainer: Containing the Best Prose and*

Poetic Sections by and about the Negro Race, with Programs Arranged for Special Entertainment. Although the title says that the collection is exclusive to Black writers, she also included over twenty pieces by "members of the Caucasian Race."[67] Dedicated "to the children of the race which is herein celebrated, this book is dedicated, that they may read and learn about their own people" the book includes a collection of work divided in seven parts: juvenile, dialect (humorous), dialect (serious), dramatic, oratorical, commemorative, and programs. In the introduction, she cites the book's purpose is for the "development" of the minds of Black youth."[68] Her selections are to guide the youth in "self-reliance, noble striving, and ambition for high achievement."[69] This may read as an education philosophy that she followed in her lesson plans, modeled in her school plays, but that also emanated in how she depicts children in the *'Steenth Street* stories.

Her own contributions to the collection show her commitment to these virtues for respectable living. For example, in her poem "To the Negro Farmers of the United States" she pays homage to men's work as being a kind of "sweet service" anointed and blessed by God. Focusing on the "you" and "God," she lends her usual attention to nature to place the men in communion with God and Nature: "God washes clean the souls and hearts of you/ . . . Your glorious band, clean sprung from Nature's heart."[70] Their service is to meet the expectations of "the hope of hungry thousands, in whose breast/Dwells fear that you should fail."[71] As a result of their work, they shall receive a reward: "Tears, praise, love, joy, enwoven in a crest/ To crown you glorious, brave ones of the soil."[72] Alice's attention to these invisible people shows their importance in a society that often overlooked the importance of Black workers. Many of her youth in the era would likely find themselves in a similar situation, especially since working in fields was common among Black folks who lived in rural areas across the country. These men were models for the virtues she listed as admirable.

A second example is her speech about "The Boys of Howard." Here she addresses criticism of the Black male students: "the complaint has been made that the bond of your school does not measure up to the standards of the girls; that they are indifferent to the welfare of the institution which honors them by admitting them."[73] She goes on to say that they are loyal to the school and to the principal who was Edwina Kruse. Her purpose here seems to be to give voice to the boy's pride in their school and to void any criticism of them as lacking in devotion. What exactly prompted this short speech is unclear, but her sense that she must serve as a protective barrier to the boys and to soothe the obvious concerns of the principal (her mentor and former lover) are obvious. For Alice, advancing the race meant uplifting the potential of its youth. These two works also show a high level of respect for Black men and boys.

Her commitment to Black men was extended to her husband as well. If he was a supporter of hers, she depicted herself as a major supporter of his. She certainly hoped that the *Dunbar Reader* would help with their uncertain financial status. At times, as she expressed on August 15, 1921, she felt frustrated and proud of her attempts to help her husband to secure a position of standing: "I wish I could help him more than I do, yet I doubt if any man has a wife who helps him more. No flattery to myself either."[74] His bid to become Recorder of Deeds for Delaware, though never realized, was a major concern of hers, as evidenced in several diary entries. With the encouragement of friends, they strategized to garner the position for him when the state Senate refused to confirm another person. She did not reveal in the diary whether or not she shared her thoughts regarding the strategy of his male associates (it is very likely that she did), nor did she describe his strategy, but she certainly wrote of her opinions about their plans. A woman of action, she attempted to use her influence as a political activist by asking the chairman of the Delaware Republican State Committee to talk with Senator T. Coleman duPont about Nelson's candidacy, adding that if the party had a debt to pay for her service, it would be settled by confirming her husband for the position. When his name appeared as fourth on the candidacy list, she moved forward by writing a letter on his behalf, using League of Republican Women letterhead, and secretly borrowing twenty dollars from their neighbor to pay his train fare to Washington, giving him an opportunity to plead his cause in person.[75]

Not getting this position and his consistent lack of steady employment for much of their marriage put an enormous strain on their marriage. And she had more to deal with than securing a position for her husband; she was also caring for her mother who was in declining health. Alice paid for part-time help for her mother, which allowed her to work and organize and her sister to teach.

Despite the enormous level of stress she felt balancing her family life and finding ways to make ends meet, she kept up her activism. At times, remaining active meant that she could also receive a small stipend for speaking engagements and it also meant that she could leave her family and enjoy some time with other Black folks, especially her sisters in the State Federation of Colored Women's Clubs. There is a level of uncensored honesty in her diaries where she gave multifocal views that are not concerned with an audience. We may learn from her how some of the women got on her nerves, but she also delved into the contours of an event. Rather than stay solely focused on a person, she often connected to the beauty of a moment where she found peace and satisfaction. On June 30, 1921, she chronicled a drive with clubwomen, "through all this beautiful Jersey scenery to Montclair. It seems incredible—all this loveliness. My tired and tortured spirit is soothed by the coolness and green beauty of the hills and trees." She ended, "Violet and I rest in a big room with couch for V and bed for me . . . Slept. Ate. Went to movies." With these women, she found an escape from her home life. It is also through the writing of the diary and the engagement with these women who introduce her to Unity, a meditative spiritual practice, that she coped with her life's dire circumstances.[76]

In this marriage, for the first time in her pursuit of equality for herself and her race, Alice Ruth Moore found a relationship offering challenges she was willing to endure. Robert Nelson was far from an ideal hero, but then again, her lack of belief in the ideal masculine hero left her with no illusions. In Nelson, she found a social justice partner who worked with her to support a family and to build strong Black communities. With him, she could be the woman she aspired to be, a woman who could not only strive for social success but also feel love and supported in return.

8

New Negro Woman's
Love and Activism

Alice Dunbar-Nelson balanced her family life with her writing and activism. She led a life that entailed engaging in multiple major projects from one year to the next. During the New Negro Movement,[1] when Black arts and political resistance emerged, she situated herself in a variety of activities that involved both the arts and politics. In her movement from one project to the next and her membership in several organizations, it seems as though she was searching for something. Perhaps it was her way of finding and defining her Black self among the "mother race" in a way that would authenticate that self. Through active participation in organizations dedicated to protecting the rights of Black people, she could prove her allegiance. We also find that she did not choose to align herself with just any organization. Respected African Americans, such as W. E. B. Du Bois and Mary Church Terrell, were among the members of some of the organizations that she joined. Alice's last name of Dunbar had given her access, and she would continue to receive entry into certain spaces among elite Black people (even when she could hardly afford a train ticket) because of her affiliation as his widow and not for her amended last name Nelson. With them, she would address the assertion identified by Brooks-Higginbotham:

The politics of respectability, and this is the key thing about it, gives you a moral authority to say to the outside world, "I am worthy of respect. You don't respect me, but I'm worthy of respect. You don't treat me like an equal person, but I know that I am an equal person, and because I am an equal person, I'm going to fight for my rights. I'm going to demand equality. I'm not going to let you treat me like a second class citizen."[2]

Between 1918 and 1931, she would embrace her identity as a New Negro Woman or a respectable activist of the twentieth century.

As discussed in Chapter 2, Margaret Murray Washington had used the phrase "New Negro Women" to speak of Black women's mission to serve the uneducated class of Black people in their efforts to advance the race. Washington had probably taken the phrase from her husband, who in his essay "A New Negro for a New Century" had posited a similar perspective. Although the phrase had been used in the late nineteenth century by Booker T. Washington and his wife, among the twentieth-century generation of Black people, the term came to refer to their goal to "receive respect for their humanity, defend constitutional rights and privileges, and participate fully in U.S. society."[3] Erin Chapman notes that these activities "extended across class lines and permeated the modern art and performance of the New Negro Renaissance of the late 1910s through the 1930s."[4]

Harvard-educated Howard University professor Alain Locke captured the interests of New Negroes in several essays. In 1925, he articulated the meaning of the New Negro within the context of social change:

> Up to the present one may adequately describe the Negro's "inner objectives" as an attempt to repair a damaged group psychology and reshape a warped social perspective. Their realization has required a new mentality for the American Negro. And as it matures we begin to see its effects; at first, negative, iconoclastic, and then positive and constructive. In this new group psychology we note the lapse of sentimental appeal, then the development of a more positive self-respect and self-reliance; the repudiation of social dependence, and then the gradual recovery from hyper-sensitiveness and "touchy" nerves, the repudiation of the double standard of judgment with its special philanthropic allowances and then the sturdier desire for objective and scientific appraisal; and finally the rise from social disillusionment to race pride, from the sense of social debt to the responsibilities of social contribution, and off-setting the necessary working and commonsense acceptance of restricted conditions, the belief in ultimate esteem and recognition. Therefore, the Negro today wishes to be known for what he is, even in his faults and shortcomings, and scorns a craven and precarious survival at the price of seeming to be what he is not.[5]

Among the myriad of insights that may be gleaned from this passage, two are especially notable. One, Locke articulated the notion that the New Negro may be characterized by a stronger sense of self-respect, self-reliance, and race pride that had not been present in days past. While this is somewhat debatable, his emphasis on Black people's freedom to focus on themselves and one another speaks to a sense of progressive racial solidarity that was needed for survival. Two, he emphasized the importance of humanity as a concept, for only a human can desire to be "known for what he is, even in his faults and shortcomings." Although she was in her early forties at the dawn of this era, Alice's activities and interests reflected her commitment to Black people's right to full citizenship, as well as her interest in the changing representations of Black life in public performance.

In addition to her work as a voting rights activist, Alice became heavily involved with the efforts to support "colored troops" during the First World War, joining at least two of the Negro First World War support organizations. African American men had been strongly encouraged by Black leaders such as W. E. B. Du Bois to join the armed services and to prove that they too were patriotic Americans. Although women were not allowed to fight, they were able to support the troops through their involvement in various organizations.

At the age of forty-three, Alice sought multiple ways to support African American troops and to prove the commitment of African Americans to America. Her correspondence shows that she sought opportunities to volunteer in France. As she pursued a service position, she decided to establish a chapter of the Crispus Attucks Circle for War Relief, which named her the official representative of the state of Delaware. Its motto was a quote from Abraham Lincoln, "Let Us Keep Step to the Music of the Republic," and its purpose was to raise "$1,000,000 for war relief among Negroes." This was an ambitious goal for Alice, who was struggling with her own finances. Yet, despite her affiliation with this organization, she joined another, the Circle for Negro Relief, Inc. This organization boasted of more well-known people than the other; included on its General Committee were Governor Frank O. Lowden of Illinois and famed educator Mary MacLeod Bethune. W. E. B. Du Bois was a vice president and on the board of directors. Based in New York City, the organization had an advanced structure that allowed for the establishment of units of twenty-five members who would each pay a dollar for membership. They were encouraged to work on "special projects" designed to attract members. Units were charged to collect items that could be sent to the "colored men in the Western Camps." To raise money, in addition to the annual collection of a dollar per member, buttons were sold at five cents each and fundraisers were highly encouraged. Their mission was to cover the needs of Black men who served. The literature clearly stated, "Whatever the Red Cross shall do in its broad field for the general army and for the cause of humanity at large, this 'Circle for Negro War Relief' will do specifically for the colored people of the United States, as they may be affected by the world war."[6] They hoped to counter the segregation of the Red Cross with an equally supportive organization for Black soldiers. In her essay "Negro Women in War Work," she would give a nod to the organizations by describing their goals:

The Circle of the Negro War Relief and the Crispus Attucks Circle organized in Philadelphia in March, 1918, constituted the nearest approach to the Red Cross or other organization of this character through which the colored people cooperated during the war. The Crispus Attucks Circle did for Philadelphia what the Circle of Negro War Relief did for New York. . . . The one great project to which it directed all its energies was the attempted establishment in Philadelphia of a base hospital for Negro soldiers, in which Negro physicians and Negro nurses should care for their own.[7]

In this she made clear that she was not an advocate for integrated services and organizations as she argued, "They are needed in some places as schools, churches, and social organizations."[8]

Alice sought to do more, but in reply to her inquiry about volunteer opportunities, she was informed that, though the YMCA had cabled for six colored women to volunteer in France, the volunteers would have to pay 250 dollars for equipment. A month before, she had inquired with the YWCA about the possibility of volunteering in France but had learned that there had been "no call for colored workers as yet."[9] She was advised to volunteer with a hostess house in one of the American camps because "if she had knowledge of domestic science and had experience in the management of a cafeteria," she would qualify. Since there is no record of her applying for such a position, I imagine that she found cafeteria management incompatible with the skills she was hoping to offer.[10] Given the details of the letter informing her of the positions with the YWCA, it is more likely that there were no positions for colored women in France.

African Americans' interest in the war constituted a strategic attempt to further establish themselves as citizens by showing their willingness to overlook the horrors of the past through patriotic activities. As a member of the NAACP, Alice was involved with these efforts, using her time and talents to influence African Americans and to persuade White Americans of their loyalty. Caroline Stewart Bond, executive secretary of the Circle for the Negro War Relief, applauded her for a play written for an April 1918 issue of *The Crisis*, titled *Mine Eyes Have Seen the Glory*. At the time she wrote the play, she had developed a professional friendship with the revered intellectual, Dr. William E. B. Du Bois, who was editor of the organization's artistic journal. His archives show that she had been writing to him as early as 1917 about including excerpts of his work in *The Dunbar Speaker and Entertainer: Containing the Best Prose and Poetic*. She wrote to him: "You know I have always been in love with certain passages from the 'Souls of Black Folk' and 'The Quest of the Silver Fleece' and for some time have read them in public."[11] It is clear from his response that he knew her and trusted her to be responsible with the length of the excerpt she chose as he did not question her or give any specific restrictions.

A one-act play, *Mine Eyes* brings together the ethnic groups that had been isolated through prejudice and mistreatment in the United States, specifically African Americans, Jews, and Irish. The play focuses primarily on the African American characters, Dan, Chris, and Lucy, who are coping with their anger after the shooting death of their father, who lost his life while defending their home as it was burned down by racists. Lucy's foot was burned in the process, leaving her with a severe limp. Their mother died from "pneumonia and heartbreak." Dan was paralyzed from the waist down in a factory accident and sees his younger brother, Chris, the only one with the ability to support the family, as lazy. When Chris is drafted, his reaction is to seek a waiver based on his position as sole supporter of his family. He is finally dissuaded from his position.

Clearly written for an African American audience, the play's focus is on persuading them to look beyond the racial violence, such as lynchings and race riots, even if it resulted in the violent deaths of family members, and to serve their country. As a drama, it allowed other Black people to take part. Not long after it was published and circulated, Du Bois began to receive requests from readers to stage the play at their churches. Du Bois gave consent for three dollars and a requirement that they give "full credit" to *The Crisis*. One church, Pilgrim Church, corresponded directly with Alice by sending her their program. They printed a statement that expressed the reason for advocating that Black people support war efforts:

We of the colored race have no ordinary interest in the outcome. That which the German power represents today spells death to the aspirations of Negroes and all darker races for equality, freedom, and democracy. Let us, while this war lasts, forget our special grievances and close our ranks shoulder to shoulder with our own white fellow citizens and the allied nations that are fighting for democracy.[12]

When published, *Mine Eyes*, unlike the bulk of Alice's fictional work, blatantly targeted African Americans and celebrated race pride within an American wartime patriotic context. To persuade her audience, she referenced the history of African Americans who gave their lives for the cause of freedom, including Crispus Attucks and Civil War troops. She used minor characters, poor and themselves affected by the war, to boost the point that discrimination should not be a deterrent to serving one's country. Dan's expressed desire to rise from his wheelchair and fight is an inspiration to the younger brother, who can also hear the "Battle Hymn of the Republic" by the end of the play. The play was written to inspire individuals to contribute to the war effort and to show themselves as being American first and Black second. Dunbar High School in Washington, DC,[13] wrote asking her for permission to produce the play, demonstrating that even Black children were part of the race's patriotic movement.

As she became further involved with these activities, Alice adopted a Black soldier named Ernest Jones. In one of her letters she offered to send him books, which he stated he would be grateful to have. Jones's letters from his post in Fort Thomas, Kentucky, provide an informative and personal account of the conditions that Black soldiers endured, as they were crammed into a diverse community of Black soldiers from various parts of the country. They also give a perspective on serving within a segregated army while hoping to prove worthy of full citizenship rights. References in the letter to seeing a portrait of the "old alma mater" and to people named "Razzle" and "Stewart" suggest that this may have been one of Alice's former students from Howard High. But patriotism was not the focus of the letters. Jones told of his frustration with being quarantined, the result of a meningitis outbreak, an experience he felt was "worse than prison and for twenty-one days." The experience was made worse by their isolation from a city, leaving him without access to "moving pictures." All they did, he reported, was "drill, eat, and sleep." Jones's honest description of his miserable experiences proved the need for Black Americans to find ways to support Black troops. Jones's letters highlight a sense of universal humanity—what he suffered and hoped for lay in a longing for comfort and safety. Furthermore, for her part, we learn that Alice was not simply involved in activities that were public but worked to develop personal relationships with the troops she publicly spoke for.

Before her termination from Howard in 1920, her patriotic activities found her extremely busy, particularly in 1918 as she became actively involved with organizing a patriotic or Flag Day Parade that took place in Wilmington on June 14 to support the troops. Always interested in public pageantry to promote a cause, she felt that their patriotism needed a public platform as well. As a result, she formed an organization, of which she was president, and solicited donations to cover expenses. Their goal was to march in solidarity and to culminate the event with patriotic speeches. Aiming to give Black people an opportunity to show their commitment to the country, she sought and received advice from all over the country on how things should be done. J. Richard Browne wrote to recommend that she personally invite several prestigious individuals in the area.[14] An African American woman named Rosa wrote to her asking that she include a banner, saying, "'Loyal—in spite of injustice' or 'Loyalty rewarded by prescription'—I don't care what it says, just as long as it says it." Rosa's frustration in articulating a proper slogan in some ways represented the frustration that the conveners hoped to alleviate by organizing the event. Its purpose was to show that "every Negro is loyal to the U.S. [and] is more loyal than any other citizen." Members of the community saw this event as a proper way to be heard and seen. Six thousand Black people were reported as attending, earning it the distinction of being called "the greatest day in the history of Delaware."[15]

No matter how they presented themselves to the rest of America, they were always colored. Later in 1918, Alice was given a year leave of absence from Howard by Kruse to tour the South as a paid representative of the Women's

Committee of the Council of National Defense. Black newspapers across the country, including Chicago, Illinois, Savannah, Georgia, and Washington, DC, gave notice of her appointment. The *Broad Axe* of Chicago, Illinois, posted accolades to well-respected "coloreds" for their work. Alice's name is listed among the other Black leaders who supported efforts to get the support of "colored" citizens. The article goes on to introduce her as "Mrs. Alice Dunbar-Nelson, who has helped to mobilize the colored women of the country for war work under the auspices of the Women's Committee of National Defense."[16] In another article that was specifically about her appointment, it was made clear that she had leadership experience including serving as "head of the English department of the Howard High School" and is well known as a club woman, having served for several years as secretary of the National Federation of Colored Women's Clubs. Of course, her last name kept her in a place of prominence as "the widow of the late Paul Laurence Dunbar, the poet, whose productions are familiar to every household in the land." The writer returned to her work as an "author of note" and as a "newspaper and magazine writer of recognized ability and far-reaching influence."[17]

Her job was to focus on Black women of the "various State Divisions of the Woman's Committee to assist them in perfecting any organization they may have in hand."[18] A confirmation of her itinerary shows her scheduled to visit "Louisiana first, Mississippi next, and then Alabama." For this tour, she was given very strict guidelines as to what she could explain to "Colored Audiences and Committees" and what she must avoid. Her platform, for example, could include discussing the meaning of the war, with an emphasis on Blacks' hatred of Belgium because of their occupation of the Congo. A letter dated September 15, 1918, outlined the ten points she was to address: (1) the meaning of the war; (2) the meaning of the war to the Negro; (3) what Germany's victory will mean to the Negro; (4) what the Negro can do to help win the war; (5) women in the war; (6) the Council of National Defense; (7) the Women's Committee; (8) the wishes of the colored women under the Women's Committee; (9) hopes for reconstruction after the war; and (10) the need of combined forces of colored women to help make the country a loveable place for the race.

A woman who was well known for and proud of her oratory skills, Alice must have found a prescribed list of speaking points a great challenge to follow. This outline clearly was designed to manipulate African Americans' desire for acceptance in a country where Jim Crow was still integrated into the fabric of the South and racial prejudice was widely felt throughout the country. Yet Alice was to rally the spirit of Black women and to convince them that Germany was against "them." For example, Point 3 clearly defined the enemy, Germany, as being against "Africa: Morocco, etc.," and having an undesirable attitude toward "a. dark skinned faces; b. black soldiers; and c. subject peoples." Ultimately, if White America failed, then Black America would fail as well. The war's benefit for Black people could mean a change in social restrictions and increased economic access. Therefore, Alice was to emphasize that Germany was an enemy to the Negro by speaking about Germans' attitude toward dark-skinned people in America and Africa. Black citizens could help by volunteering to fight as they had in past wars, and women could volunteer with the Red Cross or by supporting the Women's Committee. The stated hope was that if Black folks worked to support the country, the country would be more accessible to them and their children after the war. In sum, Black people were promised an opportunity to have full citizenship. This must have caused a conflict with her as she would later address violence against Germans in her novel, *This Lofty Oak*. Alice had studied German, loved a woman of German ancestry, and wrote stories about German children.

Nevertheless, working as a war supporter gave Alice an opportunity to travel and to use her rhetorical skills. Although there is no record that she deviated from the script, her background suggests that she at least would have made the speech her own. For one thing, she was from the South and left it to enjoy freedom with as few restrictions as possible. She was also an intelligent woman with analytical skills and a strong sense of politics. Most importantly, she often tested boundaries by crossing borders.

Always interested in class and women's issues, she reported her interest in helping domestic women to organize a labor unit. In response, she received a reminder of her mission from the resident director: her goal must be to stay focused on supporting efforts to organize local and state units of the Women's Committee and not to sponsor any new organizations. She could speak in front of a labor unit if invited but could only speak on the points "confined to the war, to war work, and to the work which women have been asked to do and are doing through the Women's work." Given her independent nature, one can only imagine that Alice did not take kindly to these restrictions on how she could use her voice to help Black women. Notably, African American women and White women were being organized separately, casting an unspoken but obvious shadow over the promises that the National Council was asking Alice to make to Black Southerners. If she spoke and organized them in the same way as White-women-only committees had in states like Florida and Alabama, they would be more successful than the "joint organization." Overlooking the contradictions, however, she continued her work in earnest.

Despite efforts for integration among Black men who sought to earn respect through their service, racism would remain prevalent. As noted by Chapman, "African American men returned from the trenches of World War I determined to make democracy and black 'manhood' a reality in the United States."[19] They were not welcomed. James Weldon Johnson would label the summer of 1919, when race riots broke out in twenty-five cities across the nation, the "Red Summer."[20] Much of this violence targeted Black veterans. Claude McKay would pen what would become one of his most popular poems, "If We Must Die," in response to the racial violence. Tiring of violence and seeing little change, Alice and other Black leaders would turn away from supporting war in favor of peace work. The fight for racial equality continued.

Alice Dunbar-Nelson's activism would lead to her joining with other Black leaders to protest against the unlawful and discriminatory arrest of Black soldiers in Houston. Led by James Weldon Johnson, who was joined by other prominent Blacks, such as Mary Church Terrell and John Hope,[21] the delegation met in Washington, DC, to plan their presentation of a petition signed by over 50,000 Black citizens, which asked President Warren G. Harding to pardon the sixty-one soldiers who had been convicted for their participation in the Houston race riots that occurred in August 1917. Between 1917 and 1921, a series of riots had targeted Black First World War troops upon their return home, but none of the attackers were prosecuted. As a result, and later with the support of the NAACP, the Dyer Anti-Lynching Bill was introduced by Republican congressman Lonidas Dyer of Missouri in 1918, but it was never passed. In the midst of this violent and bloody turmoil, Alice joined with others to lend her voice to create a safer nation for Black Americans. More specifically, the contingent presented a petition signed by 50,000 people asking the president to "pardon 61 members of the 24th U.S. Infantry (colored) now serving longtime sentences in Leavenworth Prison, convicted of rioting in Houston, TX in August 1917."[22]

In her diary, she described how they met to strategize as they dealt with the pressure of serving the community in the public eye of the press. Johnson called them to meet a day before their scheduled meeting with the president for what Alice termed a "dress rehearsal." With the necessary detail of a skilled writer, "Friday also came a letter from James Weldon Johnson saying that the Committee to meet the President on the Brownsville case will have an audience on Wednesday, September 28, 1921 at 10:20. He wants all those who are going to be in Washington Tuesday night to meet him at the 'Y' Dress rehearsal, I suppose."[23] With money she reluctantly received from her husband (she "did not like to ask Bobbo for her railroad fare"), she went to DC, where the group discussed the pros and cons of touching on the issue of the Ku Klux Klan's involvement with the lynchings, as had been reported by the press.[24] She reasoned, "If we did, it might give the president a loophole to escape from the responsibility of the Houston affair."[25] What emerges here is the group's attention to planning and strategizing the best ways to address the murders of Black people. This is more than an elite gathering. Alice's involvement at this level of activism shows that she had established a national reputation among her peers as a respectable activist. Certainly, keeping her identity as Dunbar's widow helped, but her involvement with organizations dedicated to uplifting Black people further expanded her identity and gave her an opportunity to network among peers who lived in other parts of the east coast. To be sure, Dunbar's name may have gotten her attention, but it was her talent and hard work that her fellow activists admired.

They were certainly aware of the historical significance of the moment. Their meeting began with a photograph of the contingent, including an unnamed "weasel" whom Alice said she had never seen before, and then their entrance into the Oval Office. Using her writing skills, Alice set down a remarkable detailed description of President Harding, who greeted them with a "charmingly intimate manner," had a complexion that was "swarthily ruddy," and was a "big man" with a foot size that she found "astonishing." Johnson's reading of the group's statement showed his nervousness, though he had previously "had audience with President Wilson."[26] Noticing that his face was "cold and depressing," Alice was not impressed with President Harding's response. Using her journalistic style of writing, she gave a summary of his words while providing simultaneous parenthetical interpretations of their meaning. According to Alice, he was unsure that the "executive (delightful impersonality) had final word" and informed Johnson that he had heard a "great deal" about the incident when he was in the South "(southern viewpoint, of course)." He would look into it. To this she responded in her diary, "Bang! Went the door of hope."[27] Harding ended by refuting any claims that the KKK was targeting Black people.

Clearly, they sought a commitment from the president, especially since Johnson had outlined three grounds for their petition and ended by informing him, "The eyes of the colored people will be focused upon whatever action you may choose to take."[28] They left with his sympathy but with no promises of a pardon. Johnson's statement and his nervous demeanor remind us that these were ordinary men and women, artists and activists, who dared to use a measure of power—the influence they had garnered through their talent and hard work—to give voice to the violent mistreatment of Black people.

Alice's final thought was to provide an assessment of the office as "huge, gloomy."[29] Perhaps these words capture the mood as well and, in Alice's style of sarcasm, serve as a description of the president. A portrait of the event shows her standing among the men and not the women, thus drawing criticism from the women, whom she did not name but addresses in her diary. It is a fitting representation of how often she challenged gender boundaries and entered into political spaces intent on revising the narrative. Ultimately, she succeeded in recording a historic closed-door White House meeting and the attempt of Black activists and artists to effect change in a racially hostile and violent society.

Through her diary she provided documentation of a rare historical event, the occasion of Black activists meeting with a president in defense of Black veterans. They brought to the fore an issue of tense race relations of the early twentieth century, at a time when there was not only a war but also the emergence of Black arts giving voice to a new generation of Black Americans. Although it was not published until well after the New Negro Movement, Alice's diary provides a richer, fuller look at the issues that were of major concern not only to the artist-activists but also to segments of the community that did their share to change the landscape of America—in this case protect the Black troops of the First World War. She and the others understood that if the veterans were not recognized as worthy of respect, then no Black person was safe in America.

Her ongoing connection to Washington, DC, involved more than activism. Although she was married, she also had an intimate relationship with Emmet J. Scott, who was Booker T. Washington's chief aid and in 1917 became Special Advisor on Black Affairs to the Secretary of War under President Woodrow Wilson. Scott had been born in 1873 and married Eleanora J. Baker in 1897. To say the least, he was a well-known man among the Black elite. Alice made a brief but revealing reference to him in her diary that suggests the relationship was more than one mere occurrence. She noted that she had a "Dream Book," probably a scrapbook dedicated to their affair, and that her "Sonnet" commemorated the relationship. Published in *The Crisis* in August 1917, she uses references to nature to speak of love—"I had not thought of violets late"—and then goes on to compare her lover and mating to the spring flower, a "perfect loveliness that God has made." If Scott is the inspiration for the poem as she confessed, then he had stirred up a forgotten or neglected passion in her "Wild violets shy and heaven-mounting dreams./ And now unwittingly, you've made me dream/Of violets, and my soul's forgotten gleam."[30] Scott had published her essay "Negro Women in War Work" in his *Official History of the American Negro in the World War* (1919). He had also been present at Wilmington's Flag Day parade. Given her prominent work in representing Blacks' interest in the war and her frequent commutes to Washington, DC, from Wilmington, they probably met after she left Dunbar and during her strained marriage to Nelson. Their relationship most certainly overlapped with her relationship with Bobo whom she married in 1916. By 1921, however, it had ended as far as Alice was concerned. Whether he knew that is now a matter of conjecture:

> I was much amused . . . to see him slip the Army seal ring around his finger so that only a band showed—afraid doubtless that I had on the counterpart, and that it would be noticeable. When I saw him doing this surreptitiously, I made a point of showing both my hands . . . so that he could see that I no longer wear his ring.[31]

In fact, she may have pawned the ring to pay bills to keep the family afloat. Nevertheless, she basked in feeling that she still commanded his attention and in the tension of secrets they shared.

As with many of her collaborations, she was able to use the opportunity to give voice to the disenfranchised. "Negro Women in War Work" documents the contributions Black women made to supporting the war through their efforts to support Black troops. She begins by nodding to the "feeling of responsibility and seriousness of the women of the country" and then she moves forward by describing the efforts she characterizes as patriotic that were contributed by Black women through service as volunteers in the Red Cross where they donated "knitted garments, maintained restaurants, but were often denied canteen service"; registered to serve with the Nursing Division of the American Red Cross; opened and staffed Hostess Houses, "a place of refreshment for the women folks belonging to the soldiers"; were employed in war industries; and raised funds for loans and supplies. The essay not only documents their work as supporters of the troops but also illuminates areas where they tried to contribute but were denied because of their skin color.

Staying active with national affairs did not keep her from attending to the needs of women in her own community. When she moved to DC, she seemed not to have been as active a club woman during her time as Dunbar's wife, noting little in her letters to Dunbar other than scant references to meetings that she attended. However, by the early 1920s, her busy life included active participation with the Delaware branch of the State Federation of Colored Women's Clubs. Numerous programs show her giving greetings at state and national events on the chapter's behalf, though she was not the president. Serving the community in this capacity gave her and other women opportunities for empowerment.

A detailed diary entry of August 7, 1921, which is a record of events occurring on August 5, provides insight into her role as an executive board member when they convened their Sixth Annual Convention of the Delaware State Federation of Colored Women's Clubs. In conversation with the national president, Alice agreed that they should join the Northeastern Federation. She "became"—whether by majority vote or by some other form of action is not clear—the chair of the constitution and the resolution committees. Though twelve officers were elected without a hitch, there was clear tension between her and another woman whom she refers to as "Madam Lizzie." As is to be expected with Alice, there must have been some form of conflict or tension for the event to be worth recording. In this case, she applauded herself for being able to "look down upon [Madam Lizzie] from heights of indifference, thank God." When the event was over, she described her response to the women's departure in dramatic Alice style; she wrote of "putting old lady Hallie[32] on the moving train, pitching suitcase, umbrella, and bag after her. I took off my hat, fanned myself, and leaned breathlessly against the wall when the train had gone." Clearly, she saw herself as an integral part of the organization and enjoyed the hustle and bustle of life as an activist.

Their activities were not confined to organizing one-day conventions. An article titled "Clubwomen Plan to Block K.K.K" brought attention to the group, as it informed, "[M]embers of the Delaware State Federation of Colored Women's Clubs . . . held their sixth annual convention . . . yesterday."[33] The article placed the Black women in opposition with a nationally known terrorist organization. It states that National President

Hallie Q. Brown wrote to the mayor and governor regarding their concern that the "famous Ku-Klux-Klan is making clandestine attempts to obtain members and gain a foothold in the fair State of Delaware." The article goes on to cite a number of issues concerning the organization's attacks on human rights, including "being anti-Catholic and anti-Jewish, as well as anti-Negro," and its commitment to "defiance of the 15th amendment of the United States constitution." There is no counteraction noted here nor a plan to block the organization. Significantly, her archive does not show a response from the mayor or governor.

Although, as the article's title suggests, its main focus is on the KKK, it ends with more information related to the club meeting. After stating the names of the officers and the names of those who led songs, gave an address, and led the devotional service, it provides some brief information about the topics covered. As was normal for the club women, they spoke on "the guardianship of parents over children, intra-racial movement in this city, the necessity for industrial education for colored boys and suggested the need for a curfew law"—though who would be protected by this law and from whom was left unidentified. In sum, the state of Black families and education remained salient topics, as they had been in this work since the group's inception. What had changed was the interest in blatantly addressing racist organizations. This marks a significant shift; the women seemed to want to stay relevant as activists. Obviously, the post-reconstruction feeling of optimism among the first generation of educated Black people had waned and gone, as well as the hope that Black people would be accepted if they embraced the values of their middle-class White counterparts. But they were consistently concerned with the community, and their motto remained "Lifting as we Climb."

Another, more focused version of this article, titled "Mrs. Jackson Is Club Chief: Wilmington Honored with Presidency of State Colored Federation," identifies Alice Dunbar-Nelson as the chair of the executive committee. It focuses strictly on the results of the meeting and their gift of 21.85 dollars to J. Gregg, a professor from Tulsa, Oklahoma, who was requesting aid for those affected by the Tulsa riots.[34] Irene West, superintendent of the Colored Girl's Industrial School, in which Alice was involved, "asked for articles needed at the home" (details not given). Providing this small sum shows that the women continued the tradition of staying apprised of national events that had an impact on Black life. Surely their intent was to show solidarity with Black people who had lost lives, businesses, and perhaps hope.

The women did not just identify problems but also planned solutions, as seen when they opened the Industrial School for Colored Girls. Black girls who needed care and specialized education were sent to questionable facilities in other states, where "four or five deaths from tuberculosis" occurred, arousing "the colored women."[35] As a result, the women made plans at their 1919 convention to raise funds for a new school. The first donor was Mrs.

Bessie Bowser, who gave fifty cents at the convention. More fundraising resulted in the purchase of the "Grier farm on the Newport pike, eleven acres and a fourteen room house, with barns and outbuildings at a cost of $75,000," which needed remodeling.[36] Needless to say, the women proved to be successful in raising funds in support of their cause—a significant accomplishment, considering that they were not wealthy women. To place this in context, their own wages would have been the lowest in the country, when compared to men and Whites of similar educational backgrounds in the region. Yet they saw a need and sought to provide support for young Black girls. At the time of the school's founding, there was at least one other industrial school for girls in Delaware, but it did not admit African Americans. To ensure the sustainability of the facility, the women presented a bill to the state legislature that resulted in them transferring the facility and land to the state. As a state institution, the school established a diverse five-member board of trustees, appointed by the governor. Three were "colored," and two were White. Their perseverance paid off. The facility became a model for interracial relations among industrial schools for delinquent children in the state of Delaware. A remodeled room on the farm served as the school, beginning in 1922, the same year that the State's Board of Education began to oversee that aspect of the facility. Their presence meant that laws requiring school-age children to attend school had to be upheld and that they had to provide provisions for a teacher and books "but no other equipment, upkeep, or extra school supplies."[37]

Alice's involvement with the establishment of this school was similar to her involvement in co-founding a medical facility to make up for the New Orleans Charity Hospital's discrimination toward Black patients and to her involvement with the White Rose Mission that provided protection for Black girls not admitted to the other New York missions. Two years after her dismissal from Howard, her love of educating Black youth compelled her to work at the facility, although she received very little, if anything at all, for her work. As the head teacher in the public school department, she brought her skills as an English teacher and a lover of plays. In her three-act 1926 play commemorating Columbus Day,[38] she wrote parts for thirteen girls, which include Queen Isabella, King Ferdinand, and Native Americans with settings in Italy, the Port of Palos, and the Isle of San Salvador. In the first few lines, she used a dialogue between Columbus and his son to make a statement about withstanding criticism from peers: "I've had to fight so many boys at school, that I shall have to leave. They say you are crazy, and I know better" (Diego). As is expected, she presented the well-taught story of Columbus, who with sponsorship from Spain, proved that the world is not flat. She also included "friendly Indians" as welcoming to Columbus. Students might have learned not only the story well ingrained into American lore but may also learn the importance of standing up for what they believe, even in the face of criticism and public doubt. As a public speaker and activist, she must have seen these performances as ways to give her students a voice in a safe space.

The second annual commencement exercise program looks similar to those of Howard; the six graduates sang songs, including the Negro National Hymn "Lift Every Voice and Sing," participated in a play, and listened to an address. One difference here may have been that the young girls made presentations on social values, such as being ever dependable, earnest, loyal, and so on. Through oral presentations, performance, and memorization, she used drama to impart lessons that she hoped would provide the girls with tools to live successful lives.

She saw her work as necessary to combat a history of segregation and other forms of inequality in the state. In 1922, Alice would write about "Delaware's Inconsistencies" as a "state of anomalies, of political and social contradictions." She pointed to the state siding with the Union forces, but "rejecting the 13th, 14th, and 15th Constitutional amendments." She posited a number of contradictions in a myriad of spaces, including the University of Delaware, the local market, churches, movie theaters, and so on. By starting with the Civil War, she established that what continues in the state, including her city, is a historical legacy. By working with others in Wilmington and other parts of the nation, she tried to disrupt this legacy and to provide a new one.

Serving in her supervisory position at the Industrial School until she resigned to work with the American Interracial Peace Committee (AIPC) in 1928, Alice oversaw the courses taken by the girls, including, domestic art, domestic science, and laundry work, which gave them the skills to make their own clothes and linens, help on the farm, and can the produce. Ironically, if Alice herself had any experience making clothes and canning produce, she did not record it in her diaries. Not surprisingly, there was an expectation that the girls prepare themselves to become good wives. Theirs was a standard curriculum that would have been found in most schools for girls. Upholding traditional standards in education was a priority to Alice, who valued her career as an educator and had engaged in postgraduate studies. Industrial education produced respectable women, or at least women who had options. They could marry and/or pursue a college degree to prepare for a professional career. An article in *The Sunday Morning Star* celebrated the fact that there had been no runaway cases from the school since 1925 and that many had graduated from the eighth grade and gone on to other high schools and colleges, such as Tuskegee. In 1935, ironically the year of Alice's death, the state renamed the school Kruse School, in honor of Edwina Kruse. It was a fitting tribute to both women, who had worked together to advance Black youth.

As the country transformed and racial violence and injustice remained, Alice stayed busy. Notably, she relied on tools she had learned to use when a young woman—her organizing skills, group collaborations, and her speaker's voice. She and her fellow activists envisioned a better nation for themselves and the generations to come as they sought to assert the moral authority that Brooks-Higginbotham describes: "I am worthy of respect."[39]

9

For the Love of Family, Film, and the Paper

Between 1920 and 1927, Alice Dunbar-Nelson dealt with many misfortunes that caused her to reinvent herself as a woman and as an artist. Her favorite niece, Leila, known as Leila Jr., died after suffering from years of poor health, partially the result of having typhoid fever when a child. Leila Jr. was not the only one who suffered from chronic illness. Another niece, Ethel Corinne Young, worked about two years before her untimely death (1899–1930), and Alice's stepdaughter, Harriet Elizabeth Nelson (1903–24), also died from poor health. However, Alice's sister's only son (Laurence) and eldest daughter (Pauline) survived their mother and aunt. The young people's premature deaths speak of the hardships that the family dealt with for years—abandonment by fathers, first Alice's and Leila's, and then the abandonment by Leila's husband, as well as the struggle to earn a living that would provide for three women, four children, and later a husband and his sickly daughter in their home with their dog, Jack, at 1310 French Street. Yet all the children were able to get an education, even though not all of them lived long enough to enjoy a career. Such challenges caused Alice to work harder and to worry more. Her diary reveals bouts with depression, and she also recorded the ways in which she desperately tried to escape the pain of loss through a fascination with the film industry and by engaging in various forms of writing.

Taking care of her elderly mother and mourning the death of her favorite niece in addition to the family's constant financial troubles took a toll on her health. As she tried to find employment as a teacher in Washington, DC, she was unable to pass the required physical test. Her desperation and disappointment is obvious in her diary throughout the end of 1926 and early 1927. Dr. Murphy takes blood pressure. Varies from 162 to 178! Horrors! Examines heart. Irregular, but no valvular trouble. Insists upon a urinalysis, saying the one from the health department of Delaware not authentic. I leave sample. He tells me he will not pass me. Stumbling in tears, I flee back to [Bobo's] office. Things all black before me, so I run to Bobbo as a child to its mother.[1]

She is later told the specimen reveals low albumin. According to the doctor she probably had a kidney lesion. Feeling that her body had been violated, she stated in a February 3, 1927, entry that she "Never had my paddy-widdy so discussed before in my life, and by all kinds of gentlemen, from Senators and school superintendents."[2] Of course, for Alice, this would not just be a matter of medical tests, but the requirement of the tests allowed her an opportunity to think of the political implications of being examined physically because the laws mandated it. Indeed, her privacy had been violated. As a result, she would not be able to teach in Washington, DC, a job she desperately needed. Feeling powerless, she did what she usually did: escaped into the world of artistic performances: "Well, nothing to do but to eat, drop by to see Martha, go home, take a nap, and go out alone to the Dunbar School to see the 'Krigwa' players."[3,4] Perhaps, she could escape her own dismal circumstances and reimagine a better outcome if not for herself than another woman.

When she lived in New Orleans, she and her sister were involved with the arts. She became president of the Whittier Club that consisted of men and women while Leila served as the club's librarian. The two had roles in a two-act play, "Marriage is a Lottery," in 1893. As she matured, she continued her love of the performing arts Alice loved both film and theater, even though the "only legitimate theater . . . relegated them to the second balcony for shows." She may not have enjoyed dealing with the facilities, but she was especially fascinated by film, which was the best example of a changing world through the use of evolving technology. There too might she find a new self as a screen writer. Hull notes, "Being a movie addict who devoured all types of pictures, she attempted to market film scripts—scenarios and melodramas—to the Realart Pictures Corporation."[5] On November 29, she received a rejection letter for the submission of a screenplay based on her short story, "The Bayou St. John." In response she wrote on November 30, "I see now the kind of stuff the Reol people want and I realize that I can hardly hope to come up to their standard as long as I have the kind of thing in hand that I have. However I have sent them stuff an will await their verdict." Yet, her most ambitious attempt was working with an established filmmaker. Oscar Micheaux, the renowned African American filmmaker, was documented as coming to her Wilmington office[6] on several occasions, giving Alice the opportunity to pitch her work to him. In her diary, she gave an honest, uncensored critique of Micheaux's work:

The picture shown was a new one "Deceit," which was altogether too slow for comfort. I slept in spots. Poor action, bad English, and too many close-ups. Best thing was the acting of the child. Evelyn Preer is getting too fat, and so is Cleo Desmond. Colored actresses are not particular enough to details anyhow.[7]

She was not in the habit of sharing such criticism of Black art in her columns, but, as expected, her diary served as a confessional. Whatever annoyed her most about African Americans she wrote about in her diary. Hoping to improve the quality of the films, she "hinted to Micheaux that I'd like to collaborate with him, showed him 'The Goodness of St. Rocque.'"[8] Similar to her short stories, her screenplays and stage plays almost always focused on romances, which she felt were timeless enough for adaptation for the screen. On September 16, 1921, Alice noted plans for a collaboration:

We had a two-hour conference last night about movies. He has done some work in producing and distributing. Micheaux says his trouble is in distribution. White, a business partner, seems to have it down to a science. I went over the despised serial, "9—19—9" and we have decided to film it. But we shall have to wait until April. In the meanwhile, we will try out a five reeler. He showed me a bit of the new picture he is working on. His English is as execrable as Micheaux. But he can't be told, of course. I shall go to work on the picture.

Early-twentieth-century technology caught her attention as a method of bringing drama from the stage to the screen. In particular, *Nine-Nineteen-Nine: A Motion Picture Play in Eleven Episodes*[9] revisits her earlier concerns with women as vulnerable and reliant on men for protection. The film is typical of the love-story genre that she had explored in much of her work and that she hoped would appeal to White audiences, as it told a rags-to-riches story of the rich trying to exploit a poor young woman and her sister. Similar to her short story "The Decision," the screenplay follows a young woman, Hope Dudley, and her younger sister, Jeanette, who are left without provisions after the death of both their parents. As a result, Hope, whose age is not given, agrees to the terms of her compassionless uncle, who gives her the choice of marrying his unlikable, ambitious assistant and to remain married to him for nineteen months. If she is able to keep the marriage certificate away from him for that period she will inherit his fortune, but if Hollis, the assistant, is able to retrieve it from her, she must remain married to him and he will have control of the fortune. Hope eventually is able to triumph over Hollis with the help of a kind man, the story's hero, Robert Niels.[10]

When Hope agrees to the conditions, what exactly does she consent to? In essence, this story—with its rather weak storyline—acts as an allegory for female sexuality and erotic desire. Hope's name represents the longing and desire for stability that she is unable to acquire without a husband. Hollis's greed could be read as typically masculine. Men at the time had access to salaries, while women endured limits to their career choices and received unequal wages for their work. Hope is further exploited by her uncle, who makes her work for the money, forcing her to give herself—her body—to his assistant so that he can attain control. She is willing to consent to the terms of the will to secure not only her future but her sister's as well. Alice also noted that Hope did not want to hinder Hollis from receiving his portion too.

Nine-Nineteen-Nine is not nearly Alice's best work. The so-called screenplay is thirty-five typewritten pages and lacks dialogue as well as character development. It appears more as a brief, fast-paced description of a series of action scenes that reiterate the idea that Hope and her sister need help and that Niels is their hero and Hollis the villain. Moving from an unspecified big city, such as "Wilmington, DE, Baltimore, or Philadelphia" to New Orleans, from cities to rural and remote areas, where mayhem occurs under the cover of darkness, we are introduced to a number of stunts that include miraculous escapes from commandeered trains and fast-moving cars, people tied up in mansions, explosions of safes, and fights on scaffolding. Other than the proposed sexual exploitation of Hope that is reminiscent of works like "Little Miss Sophie," it is difficult to believe that Alice Dunbar-Nelson, women's activist, wrote this piece, but it is clear that she chose the damsel-in-distress story common for films in the early twentieth century—and, quite frankly, in contemporary times as well—knowing that an audience would not be interested in seeing a woman character who was not stereotypically vulnerable in the presence of a man. Only one that could survive the mayhem of her circumstances might find a place on screen.

Niels is educated and immediately falls in love with Hope. He willingly risks his life for her, after seeing her only twice and learning during their second meeting of her sad story. His interest in her, in effect, allows him to redeem and protect her virtue from corruption, to help her remain a respectable girl by societal standards. If Hollis is able to retrieve and keep the marriage certificate, he will also have access to his reluctant wife's body. Niels hides the certificate in a safe in his office or even on his own body, thereby placing himself in between Hollis's sinister plot to harm the innocent woman. If Hollis is able to get the certificate, as Hope has agreed, she will become his in fact. Although she seems unlikely to consent to having sex with him, in every scene he proves himself to be a man who would enjoy taking from her to meet his own desire, as evidenced by his constant threats to her and her sister's lives. Power is what he seeks and has been given permission to seek by his former employer, Hope's uncle, if only he can find the marriage certificate and keep it in his possession until the appointed deadline. Little is known about Hollis except that he latched on to the uncle, hoping that by doing the old man's bidding he would inherit his fortune. He uses the 100,000 dollars he was given by the uncle to hire people to help him secure the marriage certificate. What we might glean from this is that Hollis is interested not just in having a share of the money but in having the entire amount as well as everything else, including Hope and her sister, that is considered an asset of the estate.

Hope has willingly sold access to her body for the money that she can inherit from her uncle. Before she knew of her uncle's pending death, she earned a modest income from a new store clerk job. It is there that Niels first sees her and becomes interested. Rather than keep the position, she agrees to marry a man whose love for power will jeopardize both her life and the life of her younger sister. Several times he holds a gun on both her and Jeanette, and at one point he even threatens to harm Jeanette if she does not divulge the location of the certificate. Hope still refuses to give up the certificate or strike a deal with him. Of course, giving it to him will ensure that she has no negotiating power, but why she consents to this arrangement is unclear. Alice did not give an age for Hope, nor anything about her educational background or their financial circumstances, only saying that their family's finances were drained by medical bills accrued by the father's prolonged illness. Are they homeless? Starving?

Hope emerges as a symbol of the depraved and desperate who attempts to move beyond her meager circumstances to attain a certain status, no matter what. In other words, the screenplay is a story of desire for all involved and could be a criticism of the corruption associated with American greed. Infatuated with Hope, Niels is able to be an engineer by day and a hero by night. Hollis has the opportunity to ascend to a status revered by the American greed for power. Hope, a hyperfeminine character, is a means by which the two men are able to prove their masculine bravado. Their desire for what she possesses—her sexuality and virtue—motivates them and is at the heart of this screenplay. Ultimately, there is a tension between upholding respectability and disrupting it. Respectability wins when Hollis fails to take possession of the certificate by the deadline.

While *Nine-Nineteen-Nine* dealt with class and gender, she would also use the form to engage the issue of racial violence among the White middle class. A much more developed screenplay, at least in terms of direction, is "The American Crime,"[11] a script she sent to American Gallery Films in Hollywood at some unspecified time. It is about the lynching of a Black man named James Smith by or witnessed by twenty-three people. Written under the name of Alice Dunbar-Nelson, it was likely written in the early 1920s, around the same time that she was actively pursuing a deal with Micheaux and other film producers. Given its detail to direction of shots: "LONG SHOT straight on to CAMERA. Five cars on a dark road, racing along, headlights glaring," it was likely written after *Nine-Nineteen-Nine*, which does not give attention to detail as does this script.[12] Telling the story is a nameless narrator as Alice decided to silence the voice of the participants and survivors. This may have served as Alice's response to *Birth of a Nation*, a film that sought to justify lynching as a necessary form of saving White women from Black brutes and that she successfully fought to have banned from Wilmington theaters. Alice, however, had been doing anti-lynching work for years, including her position to push for an anti-lynching bill. Using film to bring attention to the work of activists in the area was a logical next step. Here she indicted the Americans who did not look like murderers: "They strike you as rather nice people."[13] As the audience looks at the screen, in-between the narrator's lines are visuals of "CLOSE SHOT (on screen) Negro comedian, showing the whites of his eyes in stereotyped fear. DISSOLVE TO CLOSE SHOT (on screen) leaning Chinese face, complete with mandarin's cap, thin mustache cap, thin mustachios, and 'sinister' lightening."[14] Her point here is literally to show how children, who symbolize "good people," are taught racial images that may lead to them becoming involved with a lynching, either as perpetuator or observer. "The child's growing up. He's learning the dirty words of America," states the narrator.[15] She would go on to include signs of hatred by the Ku Klux Klan and to intersperse more racist language targeting Jews and Mexicans and to show a neighborhood's push to keep out Black homebuyers. The screenplay ends with the narrator declaring, "YOU, THE DECENT PEOPLE—YOU MAKE THE AMERICAN CRIME POSSIBLE—DON'T BE A SUCKER!"[16] This work is a rare find in her body of work. It significantly differs from *Nine-Nineteen-Nine* as she confronts American racism and indicts not only known white supremacists but also "the nice folks" who engage in the everyday practice of racism in their neighborhoods. In some ways, she unveils the imperfections of White privilege and fears associated with it. What if the person has financial stability, what is the next threat?

Alice had more experience writing plays and she had some experience producing them, at least as school dramas. In sharp contrast to the screenplays, Alice's play *Gone White*[17] is more than a romance; it critiques public performance by teasing out the intersection between class and racial identity, leading to questions of morality. It focuses on the dilemma of Allan Cordell, a man who has an engineering degree but can't find a job because he presents himself as African American. Cordell loves Anna, a poor brown-skinned woman who is not light enough to pass for White as he eventually does. People in their small community predict that they will never marry because of his educational status and his skin color. For them, Anna is a burden who is preventing her lover from pursuing the lifestyle he could achieve, if only he takes the advice of his aunt, leaves their town, and passes for White. Anna, following the counsel of Allan's aunt, sends him away by telling him that she will marry John, an older, more established man who wants to support Anna, the grandmother, and the orphaned disabled relative whom she cares for. Allan leaves, marries his White employer's daughter, has three children, and passes into a successful life, which he tells Anna about twelve years later when they run across each other on a pier. By then, Anna has aged from the experience of losing her grandmother, her cousin, and a three-month-old baby, as well as from caring for her husband, who fell on bad physical and financial times after leaving the war. Allan proposes that they leave their lives behind and start a new life but changes his mind when he thinks of the costs. He proposes that Anna become his mistress, but she refuses him and returns to her husband, who learns, from Anna, that their status can be regained within five years' time. For Alice, it seems, all romances can be happy if money is recuperated at the end. Furthermore, upholding respectability is often rewarded.

Stories about passing were prevalent in film and in literature during this era. Micheaux tackled this issue in several of his films, including *The Symbol of the Unconquered* (1920). Rarely did Alice write about people consciously choosing to pass; when she did, the person who made the choice was a man. As in "Stones of the Village," in which the protagonist secures a law degree and ascends to the position of judge, in *Gone White* she allowed a male character to achieve status as an engineer. If these men claimed Black (the "mother race") as their racial group, the race would be proud to have them, but, in the case of Allan in particular, he is labeled a "Nigger" and a coward for abandoning his background. Unlike "Stones of the Village," in which the protagonist has lost his family and never had childhood friends, Allan has maintained his racial identity well into adulthood; consequently, he receives the wrath of the members of his community, who judge him harshly for the decision he makes to abandon them. Yet it appears that they expect him to make this decision when he stands in comparison to his brown-skinned fiancée. For them, the problem that he faces is his ability to make a living, for poverty will never suit an educated man who can pass for White. Observers may have compassion for Allan, whose heart is broken by the woman he loves and who announces valiantly that he would never leave her and pass for White to make a living. Whiteness changes Allan, as Anna learns when she returns to the pier and talks with him about his first proposition, that they leave their spouses and move to another country where he can make a living and they can love each other. Although Anna does not have any children, Allan is perfectly willing to leave his. He reasons that his wife will divorce him soon afterward and marry another. He does not show any concern for the impact that his sudden absence may have on his children. Passing requires a level of callous disregard for loved ones and of the passers' ethical and moral values. It is not until Anna talks with Allan the second time and realizes that he has changed his mind that she declares her unwillingness to accept his amended proposal to become his mistress. At that point, she sees him as having become tainted by his "Nordic" blood.

White is associated in this play with corruptness, especially given the history of White men and Black women as Alice knew it. Allan's racial identity as a White man gives him privilege and, in his estimation, cause to exploit Anna. Anna's dilemma and Allan's privilege are similar to the situation of Lillian

Hart in "In Our Neighborhood." In response to Lillian's father's death, Mrs. Hart expects her daughter to consent (as far as consent goes) to a relationship with an upper-class White man, a match that she initiated before his death. In the case of Gone White, however, Anna is older and sees her choices. She chooses to remain a respectable member of her Black community, which also shows her allegiance to the community. In both her fiction and her drama, Alice critiqued White privilege as a means to exploit Black vulnerability. In the twentieth century, Alice used Anna to subvert the idea of respectability as exclusively belonging to White women. If the standard for respectability was established by Whites, then Black women not only reached that standard but also, by their personal choices, could uncover the hypocrisy of sexual exploitation or the reality of not meeting respectability standards. Through the character of Anna, Blackness becomes pure and desirable.

What does money represent in these works? Why is it a symbol of happiness or a test of accomplishments? The answer may lie in what is given up to attain the money, wealth, and status. In Nine-Nineteen-Nine, Hope nearly loses her virtue and her sister nearly loses hers, just to win the game of keeping Hollis at bay. Hope wins the game with help, but if she had remained a store clerk she would have eventually married Niels, who fell in love with her upon seeing her the first time in the store. Playing and winning a man's game, however, puts her in possession of wealth and secures her and her sister's independence. Niels is a bonus. In Gone White, Anna marries a man who can give her financial stability, but her dedication to caring for those who need her most allows her to receive the news that they will move back into their comfortable lifestyle as a reward for her goodness. And this is common in Alice's works, where the attainment of wealth is a typical conclusion. Women in her time had to work extraordinarily hard to attain a fraction of what was given to men because of their gender status. As I have mentioned, money in her writing is a reward for respectable behavior. However, though money is a symbol of status, it is also a symbol of the inequality that existed in Alice's troubled America. Her own experience demonstrated this challenge: no matter how many degrees and certificates she earned, she was usually unable to pay her bills or to maintain the lifestyle of a middle-class woman without having to find ways to cover up the day-to-day struggle that she and her family endured after she courageously left her first husband.

If Alice could not gain notoriety from making films and publishing more of her fiction and poetry, she would find another way to contribute to the fledgling Harlem Renaissance and the evolving political environment. Women had earned the right to vote in 1920 and were moving into elected government positions, earning law and medical degrees, expanding their opportunities beyond nursing and teaching. Recognizing that the 1920s was a decade of change in America, Alice found a new love for the race and her place among Blacks. During this period, she enjoyed a successful run as a columnist in Black newspapers, writing about her reactions to issues that affected her as an African American woman. As Black writers and artists began to enjoy commercial success, marking the artistic era of the so-called Harlem Renaissance, Alice responded with imagination coupled with her witty, sarcastic narrative style.

During this decade, she embraced her love of writing by becoming heavily involved with the Black newspaper industry. Living a public life through her work as a journalist and activist caused her to engage with the politics of respectability even more. She could use her influence as a journalist to "advance African Americans as a group," by showing the African American middle class in the best light.[18] She made use of her own love of the arts to write about the emerging work being produced by Black writers and performers. At the same time, she became even more interested in the growing film industry and continued to write plays. Notably, as she redefined herself in her personal life, she remained steadfast that Black people should show themselves a respectable people; at times, how she defined respectability was inconsistent.

Alice's active involvement with politics complemented a shared interest in writing with her husband, whose own ambition fueled his attempt to establish a career as the publisher of the *Wilmington Advocate*, a weekly newspaper, with her full support. As she shared in his work, she felt the pressure of managing their household, including Nelson's daughter, who was chronically ill, and caring for her own aging mother. Their attempt at owning and operating the *Wilmington Advocate* led to two years of misery, which she recorded in her diary. But Alice was a talented woman who could always find a space for writing.

In 1920, Alice expressed her hope about her husband's pending deal to purchase a secondhand printing machine that would not only print their newspaper but could produce other printing jobs as well. It was a risky venture. Black newspapers had emerged during the antebellum years and grew significantly during the period after slavery, well into the twentieth century. Mainstream presses did not speak to the issues that were of great concern to Black readers, such as racial violence and Black business openings, nor did they take note of the accomplishments of African Americans. As early as 1690, Black people had begun to publish, but the more successful paper in the industry, *Freedom's Journal*, was started by free Blacks in New York in 1827. Published by John Russman and Samuel Cornish, the paper covered topics including "religion, science, politics, children, fashions, crime, U.S. and foreign news, speeches, and ship sailings."[19] It became the example that later Black newspapers would follow. Scholars estimate that thirty-six Black-owned and Black-operated newspapers had been established in six states and in one US territory by 1865. Louisiana had three, and all of those were located in Alice's hometown of New Orleans. These were the only known Black newspapers published in the South during this period.

During the Reconstruction and post-Reconstruction Era, well into the twentieth century, particularly the Harlem Renaissance, Black newspapers had to consider what they would publish to appease a new Black audience that was not enslaved. Some Black journalists, such as Ida B. Wells-Barnett, turned their attention to bolder issues, such as lynchings. As an investigative reporter, Wells-Barnett was under constant threat by racists and eventually left Memphis, Tennessee, to protect her life and to engage in forms of activism where the threat was less prominent. Overlapping this period was Black newspapers' shift to "yellow journalism." Shortly before the Nelsons ventured into this industry, it had been well established that Black publications, including newspapers and magazines, were influencing their target audience. J. Edgar Hoover made this obvious when he began to monitor their content. In particular, he noted interest in the editors of *The Messenger*, a Black radical newspaper and literary journal, and the NAACP's *Crisis*, which also featured news and literature; however, "An assistant attorney general explained to a South Carolina congressman in September 1919 that the Justice Department only went to court against publications" if it was sure to win. Hoover pushed to indict editors under peacetime sedition laws by linking Black people with communism.[20] Monitoring of Black presses persisted. Between 1919 and 1920, Congress introduced seventy peacetime sedition bills, but the presses' denouncement caused them to fail.[21] This did not save states from passing laws that limited what was printed.

History proved that there was much to consider for any Black person who entered this industry, including government disruptions, White backlash, and major financial challenges. Though she and Nelson wanted to give voice to Black Wilmington and to amplify her own voice, Alice learned that operating a newspaper entailed much more than writing. She wrote in her diary about the challenges of working with a man she referred to as "White," whom she initially hoped would help the paper achieve success but who, she later stated, did not have the credentials he'd claimed; therefore, she considered him incompetent. In fact, she grew to despise his presence. White seems to have been a partner in the printing venture and was to aid with bringing in orders that could produce additional revenue. Unfortunately, the printer often broke down. While she did not state how Nelson met White, we might assume that Nelson did not share his wife's assessment of the man and was unwilling to bid him farewell. His reluctance probably had to do with the fact that they had borrowed an undisclosed amount of money to purchase the machine, but the only way to pay back the loan was through profits from the printing. Though Alice was a prominent part of the paper, it is clear that she was not in control of its operation, leaving her to submit to the will of her husband.

Through her liberal engagement with her diaries, which at times served as a confessional and a testimony of her sincerest thoughts and feelings about the major events in her life, she shared details of the effort that she put into the business. Always ready for a new adventure, she dedicated her time and talents to making the paper and the printing business successful. Her entry of August 27, 1921, gives a detailed account of one of her workdays:

> I cannot get time to do anything but work on the paper. I took to-day off—I always take Saturdays off, and usually Fridays too, but today there was so much to do with room cleaning, and settling the elderberry wine and making jelly, and washing Duke [the dog] and two weeks ironing to do—that I was fagged out and very cross when I had finished. The new big work we have is sending out the extra thousand papers into Delaware County to take care of the judgeship contest there. Bobo landed that, and of course, all the labor falls on me. For two weeks now I have typed lists of names, cut them into strips, and pasted them on the ends of the papers, and attended to that end myself, which meant all day Friday gone. I shall see that some other way of attending to it is done next week. It's too wearing and too much of a waste of good time and energy.[22]

Though short, her description shows her frustration with fulfilling the traditional wife's role—ensuring the cleanliness and order of the home—while also working outside the home in support of her husband and his newest venture. Their financial condition would not allow them to hire domestic help, as she had when she was married to Paul Laurence Dunbar. No matter how tired she was, she expected of herself and was expected to find the "time and energy" to do it all.

Throughout September 1921, Alice quarreled with White over her car. They were in such poor financial shape that Alice eventually sold him her car—a vehicle she could not drive, let alone afford—with the expectation that he would take over the payments. Apparently she also expected that he would serve as the family's chauffeur when needed, as shown when she became infuriated by his refusal to take her family to the cemetery to place flowers on Leila Jr.'s grave. Not only would he not drive them when she asked for this ride and others, but he also reportedly was not in the habit of making payments. As tensions grew between them, working together became an insurmountable challenge.

How Nelson felt about their conflict was not recorded. Nelson was an ambitious man who strove for success; this was certainly one of the reasons Alice married him. Feeling that they could change their fortune by purchasing a printer, he moved forward. On October 20, 1921, she proudly stated that their partnership plans with White were official: "We are going to print our paper this week on our own press." In order to keep the paper operational, Nelson's wife worked with him to raise money by selling shares and ad space. As with any press, advertisements were sought to pay for the costs associated with printing and distributing the papers. "What small amount of advertising they did have consisted mainly of personal ads from middle class blacks playing up values espoused by newspapers, such as 'intelligence, sobriety, moderation, and industriousness,'" as well as those seeking work or promoting business skills.[23] Even the well-known abolitionist Frederick Douglass struggled to maintain the *North Star*, later renamed *Frederick Douglass's Paper*. (He reportedly invested more than 12,000 dollars of his money in the paper over eight years.) Alice's role in this area proved frustrating and embarrassing. She recorded a time when she "felt damn tired of running to the Republican party with my hat in my hand begging for a pittance that I don't know what to do."[24] Although it is impossible to know the impact of this reluctant partnership, accepting the loans certainly made them obligated to support the party's platform. At times, they had to borrow money from relatives and from banks. Their finances were so unstable that they regularly borrowed from one source to pay for a loan from another. It was not unusual for them to write checks to creditors knowing that there were insufficient funds in their account to cover the checks. Alice was never able to live off her writing. Publishing, especially for Black women, was difficult and required the support of a benefactor or a full-time job.

Lacking control of her life left Alice with a feeling of vulnerability and, in effect, stunted her ability to enjoy her life, as she sacrificed to support her husband's dream. As elated as she seemed about the new printer in the October 20 entry, she also expressed her shame and frustrations:

> Everyone seems anxious to see me have a job. Bowse[25] said to-day she heard I was to teach at Dover, and she was asked about it. Makes me sore. They think my husband can't support me; he can't as a matter of fact, but that's no one's business. Since my pay has been cut off, we are in straits most of the time, especially since every cent he can rake and scrape goes into business. But he will be able to some day, and handsomely too.[26]

Respectability politics dictated that she show herself perfectly poised in public; however, racial politics dictated the limits on her income. After her unexpected departure from Howard, the only school for African Americans in the area, teaching at one of the public schools for White children was not an option. During this period, their household income came from her speaking engagements and royalty checks from Dunbar's publisher, as well as Leila's and Pauline's teaching salaries. Alice maintained her reputation as a popular speaker in several circles, including both literary and political.

Suffice it to say, working together on the paper induced a great deal of stress and strain on the couple's marriage as they tried to stay afloat financially, run the paper, and remain active in other local activities. In her diary, Alice pointed to White's incompetence and financial challenges as reasons why the paper did not thrive. Her lack of reference to any employees other than her, her husband, White, and one other man indicates that they were woefully understaffed and in over their heads. In a fit of frustration, Alice expressed her concerns to her husband. Often prone to dramatic and rhetorical performances, she presented herself in her diary as a woman who was unafraid to speak her mind, even to her husband; he was also open about his frustrations at times. Her diary shows how their financial challenges had a severe impact on their life that left her depressed, ashamed, and physically ill. In a sad way, marriage may have taken a physical toll on her aging body, as she endured liver and kidney problems that probably stemmed from her early domestic abuse. It also reveals much about their marriage, the marriage of African American middle-class activists, and the ways in which she humbled herself as his wife. At one point, Alice spoke of her wish that she could find work to help her husband with the finances. In another passage, after she had failed to maintain her car payments on the car she later signed over to White, she shouted at her husband, "I am tired of being the man."[27]

An independent woman who never showed reluctance to work or a desire to rely on a man, Alice in this period of her life felt a challenge to her sense of self. If she could not earn her own wages, Nelson was expected to pick up the slack as her husband. His inability to do so challenged them both publicly and privately. Nelson and Alice had clear roles. He expected her to look clean and neat when he returned home in the evenings. She hoped that he would take some responsibility for ensuring their financial stability. Several references suggest that they maintained separate finances and that she was in charge of managing the household's budget. She prided herself on her ability to do so. On one occasion, she returned a watch to a jeweler. She wrote in her diary that the man complimented her by expressing his wish that his wife would manage money as she did. She also mentioned times when she lent Nelson money that she had earned from her lectures. It was important to her that she contribute, a far cry from the late-nineteenth-century days of women relying on their husbands to care for them, a system practiced in her first marriage. Yet Alice had always tried to define her role as wife, since that marriage. The Nelsons' definition of marriage seemed rooted in openness and not in how they filled the traditional roles of man and wife. Yet the tension of not meeting expectations tested their commitment to one another.

After losing her job at Howard, Alice hoped that running a successful newspaper would shame her enemies. Unfortunately, the paper closed after two years. Her diaries lapse, leaving scholars to wonder why they were unable to keep the door open longer. Hull surmises, "Because it was substantially financed by Republican Party interests, it was subject to the vagaries of partisan politics, as well as the negative effects of racism and powerlessness."[28] This may be another reason why she was no longer the state representative in 1921 and one of the reasons why she left the party and advocated for a Democratic Party presidential candidate in 1924. Of course, the lack of consistent funding and staffing problems also contributed to the paper's demise. Given her frustrations with the paper, Alice probably felt as though a heavy burden had been lifted.

What is known about their newspaper and its importance to the community Alice recorded in her diary for there are no copies in her archives or elsewhere. In her entry of December 10, 1921, she provided some detail of her contributions to the content and also remarked on the poor quality of the printed version. She noted, "Forgot to chronicle the labor problem." Given that there was a lack of journalists on staff, she probably wrote the local stories; national stories would have come from the Associated Negro Press. She went on to remark that the story idea had been prompted by an acquaintance who rushed into the office to tell of her brother's problem with finding a job, which lasted more than a week. Sympathizing with the woman and fellow community member, Alice asked, "What can one woman do when another comes to her with tears?" Moved by the lack of labor opportunities, she wrote to someone who was able to hire fifteen people. Such an entry reveals what would not have been printed: her office was more than just a place where papers were printed, and her presence in the community amounted to more than teaching, writing, and lecturing. Although she did not provide any information about the details of these editorials, she remarked that "Bobbo said the first one was a classy piece of writing."[29] She also commended herself for writing "two of the best editorials I ever wrote"—"We Need More Ghosts" and "The Advocate's Doll Baby." Here we see the part of Alice that remained consistent—the euphoric, erotic feeling associated with writing. Alice, with rare exception, had a deeply symbiotic relationship with writing. She had a strong sense of audience and experienced great satisfaction when she wrote something that pleased her readers.

10

The Respectable Activist's Love
for the Harlem Renaissance

In the 1400 block of North Claiborne in New Orleans a plaque was unveiled on November 4, 2018, to commemorate the existence of Straight University's last surviving building. One of its most famous alumni is acknowledged on the plaque: "An 1892 graduate of Straight became a poet, journalist, political activist, and preeminent figure of the Harlem Renaissance." Although her writing career began well before the Harlem Renaissance, she has now been associated as belonging exclusively to the era. In fact, her most successful work during this era was as a columnist. In this role, she was the eyes and ears of the cultural movement. Through her writing, she would mold a view of the era for readers and provide support for her fellow artists and amplify her activism.

Judging from a note that appends a loose scrapbook collection divided into three sections—social, political, and economic—Alice was clearly preparing for some sort of presentation.[1] Her notes reveal that she would compel the audience to think of how the terms "social" and "political" should be defined. Then she would probe questions under each heading to draw conclusions. Column one begins with the "Social" category, in which she posed a series of questions: "What is his status? Relations? Way he is regarded? By himself? By others?" Under the topic of "Political": "What is his status as a citizen in commonwealth of nation? Mass intelligence? Mass reaction to nation and state?" Under "Economic," she simply wrote "self-evident" and underlined it. A separate area provides more detail about what she considered pertinent for consideration under the category of social status: Art, Literature, Music, Dramatic, Athletics, Education, Race Relations. The second column shows questions for consideration as related to the first column: "What he has done. What others have done with him; his influence in these fields." She concludes: "I. On himself. II.

On the world at large." A note in the file, possibly left by her niece or some curious scholar, speculates that Alice may have been preparing notes for a lecture at the Industrial School for Colored Girls of Delaware, but this file of carefully chosen, meticulously organized articles, pasted on the back of the Industrial School's letterhead over a period of approximately one year (1933–4), also represents the main concerns of her life. In fact, her focus on the social, political, and economic contributions, accomplishments, setbacks, and contemporary status of the Negro identifies the themes she covered in her syndicated columns, written prior to the collection of these scrapbook documents.

Approximately four years after the *Wilmington Advocate* closed, Alice made use of her background in journalism when she wrote a series of syndicated op-ed pieces that were published in African American newspapers from around 1926 to 1929, under the titles, "From a Woman's Point of View," "Une Femme Dit," "As in a Looking Glass," and "So It Seems." She covered a variety of topics, usually two to four of them in one column, that targeted the interests of her Black audience, including racial violence and African American plays, films, and novel reviews. There was also coverage of women's equality and national politics. Often relying on a cynical and sarcastic tone to build to a resounding point, meant to straighten someone or something out, her opinion pieces closely resemble the bold Alice who emerged in her dairies. True to form, her editorials both record the state of Black America during the Harlem Renaissance and show her own transformation in her many and varying opinions about African American culture, which she drew largely from her perusal of numerous papers published throughout the country. When she wrote for *The Women's Era*, she had been a young woman residing in the deep South, and her opinions had most certainly been grounded in a lack of experience, a hint of naiveté; she had also had to meet the approval of activist Josephine St. Pierre Ruffin and those dignified women associated with the publication of the newspaper. These later columns, by contrast, were written in the voice of an older, more confident woman. Serving as a public intellectual gave Alice a sense of empowerment that was not often afforded to a woman in the mid-1920s. Although she continued to write fiction and publish poetry, her greatest contribution was through these op-ed pieces, which Black people of various backgrounds could access more often and more easily than they could her stories or poetry. Arguing for the importance of this genre of her work, Jaqueline Emery observes that "Dunbar-Nelson transformed the public space of the newspaper in order to cultivate politically engaged African American readers."[2] At the age of fifty-one, Alice, in her syndicated columns, conveyed her experiences as both a writer and an activist.

Using her platform as a journalist, Alice recorded the issues that she felt were of utmost importance to African Americans and spotlighted the burgeoning work of Black artists, emphasizing the importance of respectability. Her identity as a columnist differed significantly from the private writer of the diary, in which the focus is more often on herself and less on the community she served. Furthermore, the op-eds' emphasis on current political and/or social events meant they were short and to the point, giving them a broader appeal to a wide audience, unlike Alice's poetry and fiction, which described the lives of people the audience might not have known, such as those set in New Orleans or in an ethnic New York.

Alice's earliest editorials were written under the titles "From a Woman's Point of View" and "Un Femme Dit," published from January to September 1926. Jaqueline Emery also observes, "When Dunbar-Nelson 'From a Woman's Point of View' debuted in the 2 January 1926 issue of the *Courier*, it stood out for its miscellany of serious subject matter."[3] For the most part, she spoke about issues that related to African Americans, including their move, and possibly her own, toward a Black aesthetic and a criticism of racism. She also wrote of issues that pertained not to race but to women's political and social status in the years following the ratification of the Nineteenth Amendment. In sum, she documented the changing tide that Americans, regardless of race or region, had to respond to in one way or another. To be sure, she also recorded the responses.

Published in *The Pittsburg Courier*, one of the premier African American newspapers of her day, Alice's column ran until September 18, 1926. *The Pittsburg Courier*'s editor was an exemplar of the Black middle class, the same class that the paper targeted. Like many of his readers, Robert Vann had been born in the South—in his case, North Carolina—and moved to the North, where he earned a bachelor's and law degree from Western Pennsylvania University (now the University of Pennsylvania). Developing his interest as a journalist when he edited the university's paper, he later worked his way into the editorship of *The Courier*, challenging the popularity of *The Chicago Defender*. When Alice's column became a feature of the successful paper, she rivaled the success of George Schuyler, whose series of articles, titled "Aframerica Today," attracted much attention, thanks to his chronicles of a nine-month trip to towns, mostly Southern, that had over 5,000 African Americans. Vann eventually moved into "yellow journalism," or sensationalism, to increase his audience and secure a revenue. As a result, "[T]he sensationalism in the *Courier* increased throughout the 1920s, with frequently two or three large, sensationalistic front-page headlines on murder, crime, or interracial love, [and] its reputation still rose among whites."[4] Though she had entered a male-dominated profession, Alice found her place among the elite and commanded attention. Her presence showed how highly regarded she was as a columnist.

As a public persona and a voice of the Black community, Alice could exhibit in her columns a level of race pride that she had not expressed before. In her column of January 9, 1926, almost as a form of confession, she wrote that Blacks had "come a long way in appreciation of our own and the realization of our own possibilities."[5] "Our own" most certainly refers to the educated Black middle class, if not Alice herself, who often complained about people who wanted to hear her read Paul Laurence Dunbar's dialect poetry, work that she never accepted as his best expression of Black art. Yet she felt they had reached a point when "colored people" could no longer "feel self-conscious or humiliated when the old songs [are] sung."[6] Whereas earlier she had expressed shame of these Black expressions, she now acknowledged "sorrow songs" as "beautiful" and "authentic." Her embrace of Black expressions as artistic exemplifies a shift in educated Black middle-class perspectives as well as a renegotiation of respectability politics—in which self-expression no longer necessarily equated with lowliness of character.

She went on in this editorial to tell of a Black mother who proudly gave her little girl a "little brown doll." When the mother was insulted by another, who viewed the doll as ugly and expressed her own preference for a "Nordic doll," the mother stood her ground, even when the woman insulted the doll's hair, which was of a texture similar to that of the child holding the doll. The mother of the child with the brown doll responded, "It's not funny. And even if it is, its hair's heaps better'n yours!"[7] Although the race of the second mother with the preference for the "Nordic doll" is not given, the emphasis is on the Black mother's defense of brown skin and kinky hair (the exact nature of the texture is not specified). Alice's celebration of African features as beautiful reflects the Harlem Renaissance and the attention to art that depicted African Americans by such artists as Aaron Douglass. In the next section, she observed that the Negro had had an impact on Nordic dolls, which now had a "tinted complexion." "The Negro pigmentizes," she concluded, "all American life, literature, music, art, dancing, dolls, dress, oratory, law and love."[8] Significantly, much of her earlier work had focused on lighter-skinned women with straight hair or with ringlets that looked like her; by 1926, she had clearly been converted by the new perspective on and by Black people. This is one example of how she responded to new trends or movements, avoiding as best she could being left simply to observe quietly.

As a creative writer-activist, she fashioned herself as the journalistic voice of the New Negro social and political movement and the artistic Harlem Renaissance. In a later editorial of February 6, 1926, she gave her opinion on the purpose of Black literature: "Until the Negro realizes the sharp cleavage between the two [art and propaganda], his position in the world of art will be experimental."[9] Although she did not shy away from mothers purchasing little Black dolls for their children and schoolchildren singing sorrow songs in the company of White audiences, she remained steadfast in promoting the belief she shared with Paul Laurence Dunbar in her first letter to him, that race issues do not have a place as the subject of literature. In her columns, she wrote:

> The real novel about, by and for the Negro will be written only . . . when we learn to tell a story for the sake of the artistry and the sheer delight of a good tale, without an eye for the probable effect of the story on the consciousness of the white man.[10]

Yet she certainly wrote stories that tugged at the reader's consciousness, even if it was not always a racial consciousness. As I discussed in previous chapters, her short stories, such as "Little Miss Sophie," indict White men of the South and their exploitation of women of color. Her renditions of 'Steenth Street activities addressed those who neglected working-class children unless helping them would relieve their own need to feel guiltless. So her words here beg the question: When is propaganda for Black writers appropriate? Ironically, she may have been too harsh in her judgment, according to Richard Wright, who not long after, in his 1937 essay, accused Harlem Renaissance writers of catering to White audiences: "Generally speaking, Negro writing in the past has been confined to humble novels, poems, and plays, prim and decorous ambassadors who went a-begging to white America."[11]

Remaining consistent in her established reputation as an activist, Alice probed issues related to women's social and political status. She offered thoughts about the roles of women in "From a Woman's Point of View." Speaking as an older woman, she grew comfortable in her expressions, as seen when she included a section on younger women and their expectations of their husbands. Although this was only a brief observation, of about four sentences, it was a powerful, assertive statement on women's equality in marriage. Testing the meaning of respectability, she noted that in the past men had demanded to marry pure women, but now women were demanding the same of their husbands-to-be. One cannot help but revisit the courtship of Dunbar and how he exploited the social power structure through his manipulations of both her body and her emotions. Gaining the right to vote had most certainly given women cause to feel empowered, both at home and in society. Even if Alice was simply calling for women to make such demands of their male lovers, placing this issue in the minds of African American male and female readers would certainly influence their thinking.

Women's roles as community activists were often highlighted. Alice's personal life certainly influenced the topics she covered. A trained educator herself, she dedicated an editorial to the work of Edwina Kruse and other educators. One woman was Violet Johnson, who, like Alice, was a woman of the South by way of North Carolina who moved to the Northern city of Summit, New Jersey. According to the editorial, Johnson "transformed" Summit by giving a voice and presence to the town's "colored" people. Targeting the working class that had limited girls to "waiting" in hotels or catering to the wealthy, she opened a facility and provided recreational activities, as well as a home where girls could live and socialize. She also established a Baptist church, the community's first church. The result, according to Alice, was that the White citizens began to see their fellow Black neighbors differently and to show them more respect. Such thinking hearkens back to the concerns of the earliest days of the ideal New Negro, expressed by Margaret Murray Washington in her speech. Educators and activists like Johnson were prime examples of respectability that Alice presented to her readers as exemplary. She not only recorded the work of a small-town woman whom Americans might not have known otherwise, but she also underscored her hope that such activities would continue, that Black people would take charge of their own communities and rely on themselves to advance. This idea of self-reliance was prevalent among the Black club women, like Johnson, and in the perspective that they brought into the twentieth century.

One of the most pressing issues she consistently addressed in her activism, including her columns, was the problem of lynching and anti-Black violence as seen in her visit with James Weldon Johnson and the others to the White House in 1921. In 1923, she is known to have partnered with the Anti-Lynching Crusaders whose mission was "A million women united to suppress lynching." She served as the Delaware state representative. In response to Du Bois who wrote to her for a quote, probably for *The Crisis*, she opens the letter, "My dear Dr. DuBois," and provided, "Organize, organize, and again organize. Then vote for men, who are friends, of the race, irrespective of party or political superstition. And let the organization of our own race be so strong and compact that it will be felt as a force, wherever the Negro has the vote."[12] Lynching was a major concern of hers as it remained a major threat to Black men and, consequently, to the Black family. Her editorials would take on this issue for her Black readers. Lynchings always suggested that African Americans, particularly Black men, had acted inappropriately or had violated the unwritten rules of engagement with White women, compelling Alice and other Black journalists to provide a counter-narrative. Susan Jean concludes, "Lynchings rose across the South in the 1880s, peaked dramatically in the 1890s, and began to drop off slowly in the 1900s and 1910s and more rapidly in the 1920s."[13] Yet they still occurred.

Possibly delving into her interests in psychoanalysis, Alice offered a thought-provoking editorial in which she showed the intersection of race and gender by analyzing women of the Ku Klux Klan (KKK). She began by referencing Arthur Mann, former Kilgraph Secretary of New Haven, Connecticut, who characterized the KKK as "a national menace" in a letter sent to the press[14] on Tuesday January 5, 1926. She quickly dismissed this as a statement that revealed nothing new to "the general public" and went on to present a perspective that may have surprised her Black readers. While men "organize under the guise of patriotism and racial purity, overlooked, perhaps, has been what has motivated women to affiliate with the Klan." She wondered, "How they square themselves with their own conscience" in the face of "violence and mobocracy"? In order to provoke an answer, she considered a series of questions that showed empathy for these women. Were they born into a culture of violence and then convinced that violence was an appropriate way to live? Did they deliberately elect to become part of the culture of violence? Whatever the answer, "one cannot help but be sorry for them," for they have to "bear the burdens of their race and all the sorrows of womanhood."[15] This concluding sentence sounds more like Alice's sarcasm, as she was not in the habit of characterizing Whites as having "burdens," in her editorials. While she may have been empathetic in noting to her Black audience that the reasons were complex, she was not willing to absolve the women—individuals whom she had always maintained as being capable of intelligent thought—of their ability to know right from wrong.

Lynching remained a prevalent problem in the South well into the twentieth century, as evidenced by the attention Alice gave to racial violence in her editorials. On January 30, 1926, Alice informed her audience of the horrendous lynching of Nick Williams, which had occurred in Florida.[16] According to Jean:

Mobs in Florida claimed the lives of at least 303 victims between 1880 and 1951, placing Florida above such Border States as Kentucky and Virginia but below such Deep South states as Georgia and Mississippi in the number of lynchings. When Florida's lynching toll is measured against the size of its total black population, however, it ranks among the highest in the region.[17]

Another source notes that "rape or attempted rape was given as the reason for lynchings in 27.6 percent of the Florida cases between 1889 and 1918."[18] According to press reports, Williams was arrested for raping a seventy-seven-year-old White woman; while awaiting transport to the hospital so that the victim could verify his identification, a mob invaded the jail and pulled him outside for violent torture. Media reports that targeted White audiences received varying responses. Margaret Vandiver observes that, bending to pressures by the national media's coverage of Florida lynchings, the "*Ocala Evening Star* wrote brief straightforward accounts of events without justifications for the lynching and with only inflammatory language."[19] *The Evening Star* reported the affair in a similarly even-handed tone but finished the article by noting, "It is said that all indications and clues led to positive proof of this particular negro having committed the crime."[20]

However, Alice wrote a strikingly different report. According to her, the lynching occurred near a broadcast station, drawing "Northern visitors . . . out of their beds to see the horror" and hear the "yells and curses of the superior Nordics who need[ed] five hundred to kill one."[21] Continuing with her sarcastic tone, she labeled Williams a martyr for being the first to have been lynched by live broadcast, while his murderers upheld the purity of Nordic womanhood and the superiority of Nordic manliness. Although I find no other references to this event having been broadcast, this may be because the presses that covered the event were White Southern presses. Alice's coverage could constitute a historical record from a Northern African American point of view, with Southern influences. By questioning the reports of the White Southerners, she challenged the racist belief that Black men were lascivious by nature. Alice had been intolerant of violence and its intersection with race long before her abusive marriage to Dunbar. Indeed, she knew well, as the daughter of an African American woman and a mysterious father, the complicated history of interactions between Blacks and Whites in the South. Setting aside her own rape by a Black man, she knew of the exploitation of Black women by White men and the injustices that were likely to result. Notably, however, she removed rape from the argument and focused on the crime of racism. Laws did not favor or protect Black women from sexual violence, as far as Alice knew. A safer venture would be to use the cases of Black men to argue for the anti-lynching bill. Unfortunately, it was not passed.[22]

To address violent attacks on Black communities, Alice took interest in legislation that could deter such violence or at least hold violators responsible. As she wrote in her diary, her editorial of January 16, 1926 described opposition to the Dyer Bill, an anti-lynching bill that she publicly supported. Missouri Congressman Leonidas Dyer had first introduced the bill in 1918, but it failed to pass, even when it was reintroduced in 1922. As a primary goal of keeping her audience informed, Alice quoted her own statistics of lynching to her readers, "Three thousand, four hundred forty-five persons lynched in the United States; 2610 in the South. Of these 2400 admitted guilt."[23] Her purpose here was to dissect the meaning of each word and the corresponding statistics published by the Munro Work of the Negro Year Book and the National Association for the Advancement of Colored People (NAACP). Rarely did she use her pen to publicly speak out against fellow Black people, let alone the NAACP of which she was a member. Her concern was with what was lost in the dissemination of the numbers. She greatly respected Du Bois, who had also published her work in *The Crisis*. Yet she now risked backlash as she used her platform to inspire the Black organization and her readers to advocate for the bill based on her argument.

She began by pondering the meaning of guilt, then proceeding to question the semantics. In fact, she concluded that an admittance of guilt, in the Southern mind, is a confession that a rape has occurred. Similar to the earlier club woman Ida B. Wells-Barnett, Alice used her journalistic pen to interrogate the legitimacy of accusations of rape, when in fact "less than 2 percent" are guilty of rape. Arguing that the numbers did not reflect the punishments for "crimes of murder, arson, theft, and lesser misdemeanors," nor the number of women who were lynched, her goal was to ask the question: "How is one to get the idea over to the world that raping is not the chief cause for lynching?"[24] If African American men were accused of raping

White women and of being routinely punished for that crime, she argued, then there must be a good reason for the lynching. She went head-to-head with the NAACP, an organization started to combat lynchings, by calling for them to rethink their strategy and the impact that their publications of such crimes had on racial politics. Her evaluation highlighted the idea that African American men and women did not receive due process of law and that this could not be overlooked by focusing on the idea that all lynchings were the consequence of Black men raping White women. For some, this would be a justification to use the "rope and shot gun and torch" to protect innocent White women. If the case could be made that Black men being lynched was not the result of rape but a consequence of simply being Black in the South, then focusing on the crime of lynching would bring attention to that crime and, perhaps, shift the blame from the victim of the crime—Black men—to its perpetrators. In other words, community members lynching a person without a trial was the true crime that Alice, and others who agreed with her, hoped to address by pushing for the passing of the bill.

In order to preserve her identity and by extension her voice, "From a Woman's Point of View" changed on February 20, 1926, to "Une Femme Dit," translated as "One Woman Says" because "The title, 'A Woman's Point of View' got to be so popular that it cropped up in all sorts of places and the writer found herself reading articles that bore her title but not her imprint."[25] Seemingly frustrated with those who, in her estimation, appeared incapable of using an English thesaurus or dictionary that could enable them to construct their own title, she preferred to rely on French. Although she did not mention it, her attraction to the French language, which set her apart from the other women columnists, returned her to her place of birth, New Orleans, and the French-influenced culture that she had revered in her early fiction. French also gave her a sense of uniqueness that connected her to the growing population of Americans who had taken up residency in France. She compared the change to owning a hat that she preferred no one else to have. To avoid duplication, she would give the hat away if someone else bought a similar one. Like the hat, the choice of a French title for her column expressed a level of education, style, sophistication, and, of course, respectability that she wanted to be known for.

At times, she continued to address the controversial matter of sexual violation. When doing so, Alice used the word "rape," which marked another transformation, as she never used the word to describe what Dunbar did to her in 1897. In 1926, twenty-nine years later, she expressed an interesting perspective on the rape of Black women. After she posed the question "Will Uncle Sam Dishonor Our Women?" in reference to a marriage bill,[26] she concluded, "No one can dishonor a woman but herself . . . She may be insulted, defiled, even raped, but dishonor can not be put upon her, except in so far as she is a consenting party to the aforementioned proceedings."[27] This statement may, in fact, reveal how Alice dealt with her own rape by her fiancé:

she contended that a woman who had been raped was not consequently marked as defiled because of having power and control over who she was in all situations—if she consented to the rape (which was not possible), then she dishonored herself. Furthermore, if she thought of herself as dishonored, she dishonored herself. What Alice did not address here is the perception that people have of the woman who was violated. For her targeted Black audience, she became more specific about the history of racially motivated rape in the United States: "[H]as not Uncle Sam been a silent party to the rape of black women for over three hundred years. Think it over."[28] In other words, she asked, are Black women dishonored or dishonorable because of this history? Rejecting the notion that women, particularly Black women, did not have agency in their relations with men, Alice, in a brief statement of about ninety words, reimagined the sordid sexual history of the country and reclaimed respectability, just as she had in her personal life.

Rape, race, and women's rights, when they intersect, become political. This became obvious when Alice used her response to a marriage bill to make a statement about the historical rape of Black women, an obvious reference to the legalization of slavery and the lack of protection for enslaved women, as well as more recent cases of women who had been raped and received no legal recourse even when they sought it. She also made this connection two weeks later, in a March 13, 1926, editorial, when she stated, "Poor little Liberia has been raped on a rubber proposition, and for the first time in its history will have a white minister from this country."[29] Identifying the United States as the aggressor, she saw Liberia as a "dark nation" that had been violated. A nation of Black bodies, subject to exploitation similar to the reign of the "white fish—reptile, creature of prey, what not? Its simply white tentacles gripping, plunging, exploring, seizing, devouring all in its reach? Yes, sure it is white."[30] Although she had not traveled widely, she had clearly read widely; her work also reflects her exposure to African affairs through her political affiliations and Black activist connections, such as the club women, who always showed some attention to Africa. Her political writings engaged Schomburg, Du Bois, and other Black stalwarts she came to know when collecting for the *Masterpieces of Negro Eloquence*. It is not surprising, then, that those interests emerged in her column.

All issues could be made political to a woman who never seemed to tire of watching and analyzing national debates and the impact these had on local issues, women, and Black communities. Threats to Black people's constitutional rights were one of her concerns. In a March 26, 1926, response to a Missouri Supreme Court decision that the passage of the Fifteenth Amendment, granting African American men the right to vote, had had a negative impact on the country, she asked how African Americans should respond. After suggesting various activist approaches that involved writing—letters to White-owned papers, editorials for Black-owned papers, publishing statistics, letters to members of the Missouri

Supreme Court—she concluded that these tactics would be useful. On this rare occasion, she offered no argument that would affect direct change, as she had with the Dyer Anti-Lynching Bill,[31] though, in her subtle way, the suggestions she made were her way of at least offering a plan of action to her readers.

She moved on to the Nineteenth Amendment and, with a humorous tone, revisited the old arguments against granting women the right to vote. She reminded her audience that these arguments mostly targeted women who were wives and mothers:

> [W]omen would get up early in the morning, Monday morning, and vote steadily all day, Monday, Tuesday, Wednesday, Thursday, Friday, Saturday, and twice on Sunday. There would be no time for washing, ironing, cooking, scrubbing, sewing, baking, wiping the children's noses or getting them ready for Sunday school. Buttons would go unsewed and stockings undarned.[32]

Recalling her own tireless efforts to rally women and men around the suffrage movement six years before, she was able to wag her proverbial finger at those who attempted to hinder women from standing next to men at polling places. To some degree, this editorial acted as a moment of pause and as a celebratory reflection on the advancements that had occurred and her role in making them occur, even if there was much more work to be done.

Working with others to achieve their goals remained a primary interest for the editorial-activist. On at least two occasions, she discussed unity among Black people in political matters. Responding to a comment that African Americans disagree among themselves much more than do their White counterparts, she wondered if the speaker had not gone "temporarily insane." To this, she challenged the writer to think of Black people as a diverse global group of individuals, by querying the possibility that "twelve million people" identify as belonging to the same race, in the United States as well as those who live abroad—"Africa, Australia, Asia, South America, Central America, the East and West Indies and the islands of the sea. [Given] their diversities of language, tradition, religion, background, culture and what not," how could they agree on any one subject?[33] While she acknowledged the diaspora and the divisions of people of African descent, she dissected this diversity and advanced her belief that Black people have had a large impact on the world:

> Twelve million souls in whose veins, thanks to the white man, run the fires of Spain and Italy, the independence of England and Ireland, the cannies of the Scot, the slow poetry of the Scandinavian, the treachery of

the Greek, the methodolicality of the German, the passionate desire for self expression of the Russian and the Pole, some Mongolian here and there, some Malay, too, and the low cunning of the Balkans.[34]

In this statement, she acknowledged the African presence across the globe as well as the emergence of the African diaspora.

This rather long sentence placed Alice in conversation with the pan-African aspects of the period, led by Black intellectuals such as W. E. B. Du Bois and Marcus Garvey, who were engaging in conversations about African colonization and drawing political and cultural connections, but who had fundamental disagreements. Garvey, an immigrant from Jamaica's working class and leader of the Universal Negro Improvement Association, published *The Negro World* between 1918 and 1933; it boasted of circulation in Africa and the Caribbean. According to Jinx C. Broussard who recognizes the rare presence of Black female journalists, by 1924, a section written in French and a section addressing women's issues were added to the paper. Although Alice did not record the titles of the papers she read, it is possible that Garvey's paper, edited by his wife, Amy Garvey, was one of them. Furthermore, in 1919, Du Bois and other international Black activists and intellectuals convened the first Pan-African Congress in Paris.[35] Of course, Harlem was another center for these international conversations; not only did these individuals reside there during the heyday of their activist years, but New York, particularly Harlem and Brooklyn, attracted an increasing number of Black folks from parts of the South and the Caribbean. Alice spent a considerable amount of time in Harlem and DC as she records in her diaries. Du Bois and Garvey made it clear in their media outlets, *The Crisis* and *The Negro World*, respectively, that the two did not agree on how to advance the race, but Alice's point was that they did not have to, as long as some advancements were made.

This uncharacteristically long editorial, of several pages (in the Schomburg edition), had at least two purposes: one was to draw attention to the diversity of the Black world and the other was to answer more directly the question of African Americans' voting decisions and the idea that there should be agreement on only one Black candidate to represent the entire race in a political race. Alice rejected such suggestions as problematic, not because they might not empower African Americans but because the perspective came from a White person. Even White people were not known for their unity, she posited, giving the example of those who supported the KKK and those who did not. Defying depictions of Black people from White media perspectives was a primary concern for her as an editorial writer as it was when she wrote fiction. The irony is that the majority of her readers would have known that Blacks were diverse thinkers. However, she clearly felt that Black newspapers offered a safe space to critique narrow racialized opinions. She further rejected the idea that there was no unity among Black people on important issues:

> When it comes to the Dyer bill, for instance, or the Sweet case,[36] and similar segregation cases, or the question of Negro presidents for Negro colleges, or the appointment of worthy men to high office, if they are qualified, or Jim Crow schools in Northern cities—well, if anyone believes that "your people do not agree," let him read the files of the Negro newspapers of the last two years.[37]

In one statement, she dismissed the criticism and acknowledged the work of Black newspapers and journalists, who covered the social and political issues that affected the lives and decisions of their readers.

In a completely contradictory yet humorous opening statement on September 11, 1926, she remarked: "Politics in this column is taboo." Her reluctance, she clarified in the next statement, was that "Orders is orders, notwithstanding and contrariwise. I'm Organization enough to know orders and obey them."[38] Whether this was an imagined "order," or possibly one issued by a political party or even the publisher, as usual, Alice was aware of boundaries, but she persisted in her habit of ignoring them. However, this was a time in which she acknowledged that there are "orders" as she publicly navigated around them. She felt compelled to inform Blacks that they must "learn the white man's lesson—that race is bigger than imaginary lines of political demarcation."[39] While she had noted in an earlier editorial that Whites could not expect Blacks to agree on all political matters, she called for African Americans to put their own interests of racial uplift first and to ignore the "political self-interests" of "Caucasians."[40] Without going into specifics, she applauded herself for having followed orders, but in a sense she was putting the interests of the race first. She moved forward by comparing the African American relationship with political parties to feuding families. By using her columns to give voice to fears, experiences, and challenges of Black folks, she remained concerned with the importance of Black life in the state of Delaware and in the nation.

Apparently, Nelson tried to work with other Black publishers to keep the column in circulation. As editor of *The Washington Eagle*, he wrote to fellow publishers: "Mrs. Nelson is considered one of our most brilliant writers, and her column in the [*Pittsburg*] *Courier* attracted considerable attention and much favorable comment."[41] One response illuminated the competition she was facing: "I am carrying at least four distinct columns at the present time. I am hoping that the feature will have success and that in the not too distant future I will be able to use it." This was a typical response, as Nelson's checklist shows that twenty-seven letters were sent and the majority of the responses were no. Notably, the kind tone of E. Washington Rhodes, editor of *The Philadelphia Tribune*, showed the level of respect and camaraderie that existed among Black editors, if not for Alice herself.

Alice occupied multiple spaces at once. As a woman dedicated to uplifting the race by giving speeches and organizing with like-minded people, she imagined multiple ways to address issues of local and national concern. Writing was one of those ways. Speaking to a Black audience in print gave her opportunities to reach more people than she could have as a speaker, fiction writer, and poet, for it was much easier for her to publish a weekly column than it was to wait and hope for the acceptance of a poem or short story. In these columns, we also see both an old and a new Alice. While she remained committed to the ideal of respectability as a tenet of uplift, she also celebrated forms of Black artistic expression. This would become more obvious in her work focused on Black performance and art. To be sure, her journalistic work stood as a service to Black Americans of her day, as she gave voice and recognition to the Harlem Renaissance through her "looking glass."

It is not surprising that, as a patron of Black arts, she dedicated much of her writing during the era to critiquing Black art in its various forms. Moving past just changing the name of her nationally syndicated column, she relied on her own active interest in performance—films and dramas—and devoted a great deal of time to reviewing Black performance. Performance, as evidenced by the amount of time she gave to it in her columns, was central to the way in which she envisioned the evolution of Black arts and her role as one of its artists and ambassadors.

In the first editorial under the new name of "Une Femme Dit," she discussed *Lulu Belle*. Unlike her diary, in which she was more openly and honestly critical of Black actors, her column was decidedly more generous in praise than in criticism. Alice's work recorded the growing presence of Broadway plays that featured some aspect of Black life; it was a historical as well as a transitional time for Black performers. And of course, not all of these plays were written by African Americans. Notably, the decade opened with Eugene O'Neill's *The Emperor Jones*, which featured a lead Black character played by Charles Gilpin, an experienced African American actor.

Following the success of *Shuffle Along*, a controversial musical comedy about a theater featuring a mostly Black cast, came *Lulu Bell*, a play about a Black prostitute, played by Lenore Ulric, a White woman in blackface. But Alice did not join the critics who asked why the White writers chose to depict the worst aspect of Black life. Instead she asked, "And why should a white man do our propaganda for us?" She went on to compliment the play's scenery and backdrop and noted the similarity between Lulu Belle and Georges Bizet's *Carmen*: "[Edward Sheldon and Charles MacArthur] simply took the old story, popularized by Merimee, and set to music by Bizet, and not lately Russianized under the title of Carmencita and the Soldier."[42] Both Lulu Belle and Carmen were women who were seductive and unapologetic about their sexuality. Avoiding a racial propaganda critique, Alice applied a gendered and not a racialized lens to the character and the play, leading her to compare the storyline to Adam and Eve. She concluded, "Lulu Belle is Carmen, and Carmen is Lulu Belle, and both are ageless, eternal, universal. Of no race, no clime, no color, no condition."[43] Such beautiful "soulless" women can be found among people of all races, she concluded. Her perspective here marked a transformation: she, in effect, publicly granted a Black woman the right to be less than respectable if she chose, as a White woman or any woman of any race may choose. There is no overlooking the fact that the performer at the heart of this discussion was White. In Alice's earlier work, White characters or those who presented as White could be seen as metaphors for the ills of society, such as sexual exploitation. Performance, however, allowed for a celebration of sexual freedom that Black women, particularly middle-class Black women, really did not have in public spaces unless they were willing to deal with scrutiny. Lulu Bell and Carmen were not middle class but skilled workers. This distinction, in the era of the Harlem Renaissance where women, including Black women, were publicly and privately exploring their sexuality, inspired Alice to celebrate rather than denigrate these women, as members of society who were exercising sexual choices.

Such lines of inquiry would extend to her review of Black aesthetics of the period, as she reviewed the work of Harlem Renaissance artists. Along with these artists emerged a respected group of journalists and editors who engaged in the review of Black art and by extension dialogued with one another, either directly or indirectly. An example of dialogic engagement appears in Alice's April 17, 1926, editorial called "Negro on the stage or screen," when she responded to an article written by Lester A. Walton. Born in St. Louis in 1882, Walton served as a drama critic for *The New York Age*, coordinated a Black players company at the Lafayette Theater, and worked as a writer for *The New York World*.[44] He had been in this position for four years when Alice referenced him in one of her longest editorials. She used his words on the status of Black performers as a departure point: "The public no longer laughs at a Negro either on the stage or the screen carrying a chicken or watermelon, drinking gin, industriously wielding a razor or shooting craps."[45] Disagreeing with Walton, she concluded that his position in New York, which she labeled the North, had isolated him from the reality of African American theater; she suggested that he go to "any motion picture or vaudeville house elsewhere catering almost exclusively to a Negro patronage, and listen to the loud guffaws of joyous mirth when the minstrel type Negro appears."[46] Alice herself lived in Delaware and only commuted to New York for social engagements. But she maintained that representations like the ones Walton described filled the gaps and drew Black audiences who longed to see, and then support, any presentation of Blacks in film or on the stage. As with her rejection of her late husband's dialect poetry, she preferred that the public face of Black life and art reflect respectable standards of living—but for that to happen Black audiences would have to seek and demand such standards. To that end, she observed, "decent comedies are needed" to "delight the intelligentsia" and to "educate the submerged" Black audience.[47]

While she disagreed with Walton's assessment of the current state of Black performance, she admitted that representations of Blacks had gotten better over the "past quarter of a century."[48] Yet, focusing on some of the more "sophisticated productions," including *Shuffle Along* and *Chocolate Dandies* (1924), both Broadway productions, she argued that they lacked quality, including the props, backdrop, costumes, and intelligence. Observing further that the "female members of the cast always talk too fast, too shrill, too chattery," she was as harsh as she was in her diary.[49] Her preference was for a traditional "soft, beautiful voice" that she associated with the "melodious" voices of African Americans; instead, she concluded, the old stereotypes still prevailed. Alice was looking for the New Negro that Locke described. Though this was a transformative period, her clear preference for a level of sophistication that compared with what Micheaux produced—"I am reminded of Evelyn Preer's exquisite tones"[50]—as the standard for African American productions harkened back to the days when she worked to uplift African Americans by addressing what was embarrassing. She and Walton differed in defining the meaning of quality and how far was far enough when measuring the meaning of Black representations to African American and White audiences. Alice's engagement with a fellow reviewer elucidated the developing ideas that emerged among playwrights, actors, and cultural critics regarding the formation of Black theater during this era. Although, for the most part, Alice was not regarded as a dramatist (her audience may have known *Mine Eyes*), she situated herself within the center of the movement as an active observer of the arts and gave her voice to make the work of Black artists national rather than regional.

Moving beyond issues of quality, she also focused on storylines that included cheating, lying, and financial problems. Obsessions with money in African American theater prompted her to wonder if there was a psychological complex associated with money, especially given that so many Blacks lived in poverty. Notably, Alice herself was quite poor during this period and had written about these obsessions in her fiction and screenplays. She understood well African Americans' interest in money but dismissed it as fulfilling a psychological need to fill a paternal loss. And perhaps this explains her own literary attention to acquiring wealth or the lack thereof. She also knew well the impact that paternal loss could have on the standing of a family. Though living in dire need herself, she was by this point maintaining or publicly performing a middle-class social status through her writing and activist work. Nevertheless, what she seemed to question here was the idea of empowerment within the developing theater company.

Her conclusion was to compare Negro theater, which she felt was still at its beginning stage, to the Elizabethan theater of the 1500s. She argued that both the Elizabethans and 1920s Negro theater were "crude and coarse," but that the Elizabethans paid attention to the "refinements of their day and time." Of course there was no way for her to know what an actual Elizabethan performance would have looked like. But since she always indulged her love of the theater and film, at times scraping together her last pennies to see a show, she apparently wanted her money's worth and, to that end, expected her people to tap into their talents and make her proud by proving the advancement of the race.

She was much more impressed by African American writers than by Black theater. More so than in "From a Woman's Point of View," in "Une Femme Dit" she paid considerable attention to African American poets and their work. An experienced orator herself, she praised Langston Hughes on her editorial of June 5, 1926, for his ability to read his own poetry impressively, describing how he began to read by sounding boyish and then found his rhythm by chanting the verse and moving with the blues of the chant and swing. Hughes represented for Alice the tone of voice and performance that she saw as unique and beautiful among African Americans. She also praised Booker T. Washington and James Weldon Johnson, whom she knew, for their ability to deliver their arguments to an audience. Noting that they have "IT," she credited their oratorical success to their confidence as speakers.

Celebrated poet Countee Cullen, who was beloved by Du Bois, was featured in at least three of Alice's editorials that year. One recorded an incident that occurred in May of 1926, according to the poet himself and posted in various newspapers. Cullen had been invited to speak at the Emerson Hotel by the Baltimore City Club, but the members stood by quietly when he was asked by hotel officials to leave because of his color. Outraged, African American papers such as *The Afro-American* questioned the decency of Baltimore gentlemen: "Even if the hotel objected to a colored man speaking within its sacred walls, any host with a sense of common courtesy would have taken their guest to some congenial place." Fourteen days later, in conversation with others, Alice added a sarcastic tone to two short paragraphs in order to fuel the proverbial fire. She addressed the audience as if all of them knew what had occurred: "Now that the Emerson Hotel has insulted Countee Cullen," and ended the first sentence by warning the "unwise" not to demand that the "young poet at once take steps to break down discrimination."[51] Her method of addressing her audience presumed that there was a discussion she was entering and that she was only adding her voice to the community of voices, including those in her own social and political circles as well as those of the Black newspapers. Perhaps ignoring her own declarations that Black art should not reflect propaganda, which she often ignored, she encouraged Cullen[52] to write a poem about Baltimore "that may not be a saving sense of humor to transmute the black iron of insult into the white gold of poetry."[53] Alice's own work, I have noted, often "transmuted the black iron of insult" into her artistic expressions, even if she was too "respectable" to admit it. At these times, we see the ironies of respectability.

On July 24, 1926, she discussed a tribute to Cullen by a poet she simply referred to as Faun that had appeared in *The Chicago Daily Tribune* on July 6. Finding the accompanying poem racist, she dissected the poem and lambasted the poet. Clearly seeking to honor Cullen by stating that it mattered not that his skin was "dark / As the midnight jungle track," Faun appeared to emulate the language of Cullen himself in his reference to Africa in his signature poem, "Heritage."[54] Alice questioned the purpose of referencing his skin color, if the poet was really only concerned with Cullen's poetic abilities. "Those very first two lines," she observed, "reveal an ancient prejudice that trails slime over the intended tribute."[55] More verses paid tribute by referring to Cullen as having "a soul of a minstrel fair," a "blackamoor's frame," and of being a "scion of scorn and shame" as well as an "outcast," all of which he turned into "fame."[56] What motivated the poet's choice of words was not identified. In contrast to the idea that he was a gentleman, Alice concluded that the poet was a "Southern cracker," as there was no other reason why he would use such language to describe a respected man. She directly challenged him either to write about Southern chivalry or to forgo his Southern ancestry, which she associated with racism, and to "Come out in the open, and be a real critic, judging things as they are, and not as you would have them."[57] We see a different Alice here who, through sarcastic tones, did not concern herself with trying to make nice. Furthermore, she critiques respectability by ascribing it to Cullen—the subject of derision—in contrast to the poet. These were bold words for an African American woman to write about racism during this period, and they represented the strong and more assertive tones that appeared often in her columns.

By this time, Alice had become adept at interweaving issues related to race and art in her editorials. A third editorial on Cullen also included references to Hughes and Zora Neale Hurston, but as she had in the July 24 article, Alice was directly addressing someone she identified as racist. Responding to a *Chicago Evening Post* article that commented on an NAACP conference, in which the author reportedly concluded that the aforementioned artists had not made much of a contribution compared with "Nordic" people, Alice posted a poem titled "The Nordic Blues," which she said was written by an unnamed "Ambitious Youth" who was "too frightened, or too sensible to send it to a paper himself."[58] Since a copy of the poem is part of the Pauline Young papers at the Robert Woodruff library and her name appears at the bottom of the poem as the author, it is safe to assume that Alice wrote the poem, ensuring that it would be published, albeit anonymously. The poem is written from the point of view of a person claiming to want a "Nordic" identity and describing what enjoying life as a "Nordic" would mean. He "wants to have blue eyes, an 'dem straighten locks," "want to vote all day an' shoot all night," "want to burn niggers' houses ef dey move too high."

After each stanza is the line, "Got de Nordic Blues, dat's what I've got."[59] Her publication of this poem is yet another example in 1926 of Alice's direct and assertive critique of racism in America.

She dedicated most of her editorial career to "As in a Looking Glass," which she published between 1926 and 1930 for *The Washington Eagle*, edited by Nelson. In this column, she continued to cover many of the themes that she had before, including politics, women's issues, race relations, international issues in the African World, and Black performance and literature. The latter were at the top of her concerns as the Harlem Renaissance neared the end of the decade, and she promised to provide, as her readers had become accustomed to, a valuable perspective by interjecting her own ideology about Black performance.

On February 17, 1928, she published an extensive review of an untitled book edited by Alain Locke and Montgomery Gregory. The collection, *Plays of Negro Life: A Source-Book of Native American Drama*, was actually published in 1927, and the delay in the publishing of Alice's review suggests that books by Black authors were slowly circulated among the Black middle class, and even among the press. Ever dedicated to her public stance that there should be no resemblance of propaganda in the writings of Black artists, Alice provided a quotation from Locke to support her beliefs: "But it is not the primary function of drama to reform us."[60] She went on to state in her own words, "Now when the race as a whole gets that attitude of mind—that drama, poetry, fiction must not be blatant propaganda, but 'free' and 'subtle' in their preachments, we shall have advanced a far stage toward that pinnacle of artistry which is our present goal."[61] This statement came as close to a profession of her real attitude toward the relationship between Black art and propaganda as any she shared with her readers. Here she used the word "subtle" to describe the approach that Black writers should take in their "preachments," suggesting that she was not against the intersection of art and politics—or, more to the point, racial politics—but that these statements should not distract from the art itself. In the next section she listed the themes of the plays as lynchings, funerals, deaths, and rapes: "Plays that make your throat constrict with fear and pain, that leave your eyes hot with unshed tears, and your fists clinched with anger."[62] But their explication of "a phase of Negro life," she concluded, made them "worthwhile" reading.

One playwright, however, received harsh criticism from her. Frank Wilson, who published *Sugar Cane* in the volume as his play *Meek Mose* was running in New York, presented what she described as a "White folks nigger" in his work. Though his work was considered satire, she surmised that Wilson "believes in what his characters believe." The problem with this line of thinking, argued Alice, was that Wilson represented Blacks who saw something wrong when there was nothing wrong. In other words, they suffered from a case of paranoia brought on by their disbelief in racial harmony. She ended by asking Black Americans to be clear about their societal goals. Her approach here was an extension of her inconsistent philosophy regarding the purpose of Black literature. Should Black writers use it as a form of blatant propaganda or not? In this era, she had clearly come to accept that representing Black life in drama and fiction was acceptable, rather than representing racial inequality through racially obscure characters. During the Harlem Renaissance, the question was how to represent the problems of these Black characters in a way that would not result in repeating stereotypes. Though Alice may have shown moments of inconsistency about identity politics among African Americans, any suggestion that African Americans were incapable of complex thought, lacked unity, or were unproductive members of American society sparked vehement protests from her in all forms of her being. As was typical of members of the Black press, she identified the problems but rarely blamed fellow Black citizens as being part of the problem.

Casting a positive gaze on African American artists and activists was one of her goals. Unlike her previous columns, "As in a Looking Glass" provided many opportunities for its readers to learn of the events that occurred among the Black educated elite, of whom Alice was a proud member. Her September 21, 1928, entry recorded a celebration of Charles S. Johnson, the outgoing editor of the National Urban League's *Opportunity*. As an established writer, Alice had a developing relationship with Johnson and the journal. He had published her essay "Politics in Delaware" in 1924 and a May 7, 1926, entry documented that she had won honorable mention for her poem "April Is on the Way." She was present at the celebration of Johnson only because her niece, Young, who was a teacher at Howard, loaned her ten dollars to travel to the dinner. Alice moved from her assigned table to sit "near the speaker's table and close to Paul Green whose play 'In Abraham's Bosom' had just won the Pulitzer Prize." Through her own admission, Alice knew how to move around in elite literary circles, as documented in this particular column. She began her lengthy description of the "testimonial banquet" by filling the lines with nods to attendees such as Schomburg and James Hubert and noting that people came from New York, New England, Washington, DC, and other "sections" where the Black educated elite resided.

Her column, at times, clearly targeted the African American upper-middle-class society that she tried so desperately to remain a part of, despite her massive financial problems. In the next line of her description of Johnson's banquet, she stated, "The Café Boulevard, if you remember, is a picturesque place, admirably lending itself to such an occasion."[63] Her direct address referred to those of her readers who might have desired to sit at the table, meaning those who had managed to receive an invitation. Included in that list was a prominent minister, a professor from the University of Pennsylvania, and others in the writing profession. Given the affiliations of those individuals, it is likely that Alice had had some contact with these people prior to attending the event. Incidentally, she referred to her own presence there in the third person: "Alice Dunbar-Nelson voiced the gratitude of the teacher of English who saw her promising pupils given the chance to publish, otherwise denied them."[64] Relying on a lighter tone to contrast with some of her more pointed columns, this particular column served to celebrate the accomplishments of an African American man while demonstrating that he was not alone in his achievements. We are reminded that if the Black press had not had its own "society sections," these events never would have been broadcast as were those organized by affluent Whites.

Beyond these events, Alice showed growing interest in the experiences of people of African descent throughout the world. Black newspapers provided African Americans with opportunities to follow international affairs, encouraging them to spearhead efforts, as did club women and other Black civic organizations, to raise funds that could help their brethren. True to her lifelong interest in the treatment of Black girls in the United States, Alice brought attention to the case of a young Liberian girl she called Araminta, who had been relocated to America. According to an interview given to Alice, Araminta had been sold into slavery by her father for the price of twenty dollars and purchased by a missionary. The young girl was then adopted by a Black Baptist school, which paid for her board at the home of a Christian family as well as her expenses. Not only did Alice bring attention to the issue of selling girls in Liberia to settle debts, she also celebrated the work of African American organizations' intervention in these matters. Probably inspired by her knowledge of the exploitation of African American Southern girls, she ended with a touching and provocative statement from the girl, who was planning to return to her native home to work as an activist: "Lots of little girls are not so lucky."[65]

On March 15, 1929, Alice's love of both literature and international affairs emerged in her review of a serial work of fiction, "An African Savage's Own Story," authored by someone called Bata Kindai Ibn LoBagola, about a "Black Jew" who was kidnapped from West Africa and taken to Scotland. It is not clear if Alice ever learned that the work, reportedly an autobiography, was authored by a man born in Baltimore. Her interest may have been less in the authenticity of the text and more in the execution of the story. She avoided making a conclusion by describing it as "a serial which promises to be intensely interesting as it goes on."[66] Yet she was likely drawn to its story's premise—the intervention of Europeans in the life of an African. Although she often held African Americans' progress in various areas to European-centered standards, she drew the line at any form of nonconsensual intervention. Kidnapping would qualify. As she had with her play on the colonization of Hawaii, she made a statement here in support of work that critiqued the colonization and enslavement of Africans.

The treatment of people and their status as citizens remained at the forefront of both Alice's journalism and her activist work. As she had in her columns on Black arts and societal events, she used her public platform to continue to highlight the work of the National Federation of Colored

Women. In an attempt to bolster the power, size, and, by extension, influence of the group, she presented the idea that anyone with any worthwhile form of business to handle attended the National Federation of Colored Women's convention:

> Everyone who has a program to put over, an axe to grind, a bit of publicity to be gained, a resolution to be endorsed, advertising to put forth, a friend to meet, a date to make, someone to find, old acquaintances to seek, new contacts to be made, propaganda to spread, subscriptions to take to publications, articles for which to take orders.[67]

This may, in fact, be an example of propaganda, as she presented a clearly biased perspective on the federation's leadership: "The presiding of Mrs. Mary McLeod Bethune is a joy to behold. Absolutely fair and impartial, judicious, pleasant, cheerful, unruffled in the face of upheavals."[68] She continued by complimenting Bethune's ability to withstand the pressures and stresses of presiding over an organization's day-long business meetings. Bethune, who founded Bethune College (now Bethune-Cookman University), is presented as the perfect example of an educated Black lady, one that all middle-class women should strive to emulate if they hope to receive the respect of their peers. Alice also provided briefer profiles of other respectable ladies, such as Maggie Walker, who was a dominant figure "wherever she appears, and she appears everywhere, enthroned in her chair wielding her scepter of love."[69] A reference to "Sallie Stewart" in which Alice curiously neglected to refer to her by the title of Ms. or Mrs. leaves one to wonder if this was intentional. Nevertheless, she celebrated Stewart as the "unopposed candidate for the presidency for 1928-1930. You feel somehow in looking at her that the National Association of Colored Women will be in strong, firm hands, and that it will maintain its high standard of integrity and accomplishments."[70] She ended by giving some details of the decisions and progress made by the group as they moved forward.

At times, Alice would forgo her focus on African Americans' accomplishments and instead berate them for disregarding the laws of respectability. One incident is found in her October 19, 1928, column in which she described the behavior of the audience at the "first concert given by an artist of the race after a year's study abroad."[71] While the performance was taking place, the crowd—clearly made up predominantly of Blacks—continued to walk in and to make noise. Using humor to take the sting out of her whip, Alice stated, "Someone must have slain one of the ushers on the first floor for there was a cessation of bustle there."[72] This lack of respect for the performers led her to provide a list of observances about "the race" having to do with their lateness, their disregard for each other's feelings, and, lastly, their desire to be "seen and heard and not to see and hear." She concluded with a call for divine intervention granting the race "good manners, musical consideration, and the regard for the other fellow."[73] Although she relied on wit to criticize, her expectations were clear. Another column from December 28, 1928, described an incident or an urban fictional tale that featured a Black man who ate pig's feet on a streetcar. Once done, he discarded the bones on the floor. Alice's attention to the public behavior of Black people echoed an article written by Robert Abbott of *The Chicago Defender* ten years earlier, published in response to the influx of Black Southern immigrants. His column, "Things That Should be Considered," gave a list of rules related to public behavior, among them: "Don't use vile language, be drawn into street brawls, act discourteously in public, make yourself a public nuisance, etc."[74] Alice's firm entrenchment in establishing and maintaining middle-class values and behaviors never faltered. Throughout her life, she remained concerned with how Black people's lack of public decorum could impede the race's uplift and interest in Blacks living orderly lives.

Perhaps it was for that reason that celebrated artist Laura Wheeler Waring chose to make Alice the subject of one of her portraits in 1927. Wheeler had studied at Pennsylvania Academy of the Fine Arts in 1914 and later spent two years studying art in France. She taught at Cheney University and she had a platform for her art when she fulfilled W. E. B. Du Bois's requests to feature her art in *Brownies*, a journal for Black children. Of the painting, Professor J. Saunders Redding, graduate of Howard High, remarked,

> We shall see what the portrait painter sees in the character of his subject: we shall see, transferred by brush and paint to canvas not the beauty of the flesh alone, which anyone can see, but the beauty, which the artist discovers and which it is the artist's business to make others see. Failure to discover the essentialism element in the character of the subject means failure for the artist; and Mrs. Laura Wheeler Waring has not failed.[75]

The portrait now hangs in National Portrait Gallery in Washington, DC.

Alice was a woman who loved the art of writing and was respected by her peers because of it. After leaving New Orleans, she seemed always to have at least three writing projects on the table, in the form of journalistic pieces, plays, screenplays, short stories, and/or poems. Her artistic forms were fueled by her love for watching films, reading fiction, and attending plays. One of her real contributions to Black arts was her desire not only to be an active member of the early-twentieth-century Black arts movement as an observer and recorder but also to make her own contributions as a writer. Moving beyond the restrictions placed on Black women, including in the publishing industry, she was most successful in the male-dominated field of journalism. In this area, she literally used a woman's point of view to give voice to the concerns, triumphs, and struggles of the emerging African American middle class, and their respectable lives.

11

Love, Desire, and Writing

Writing, at times, was a labor of love for Alice Dunbar-Nelson. She continued to write fiction and poetry, but with rare exception she was only able to publish in Black-owned publications. This was especially true for her columns. After her column ended with *The Washington Eagle*, she began anew with "So It Seems,"[1] a column exclusively for *The Pittsburg Courier*. Her relationship with this paper proved useful in promoting her public image, as she received attention not only for this short-lived column but for more of the interesting moments of her public activist life—a life that would come to a rather abrupt end.

Part of the "Women's Activities" section of the paper, "So It Seems," featured a different photo each week of a more mature Alice, a light-skinned woman wearing wire-rimmed glasses, with her hair styled in a sophisticated bun. Accompanying the February 22, 1930, article, a prominent photo of her was located under the caption "Alice's Mirror," the implication being that she was sharing with her readers her reflections of the world. In this article, writing on her trip through the South, she paused to give a rather detailed review of Sarah Gertrude Millin's *An Artist in the Family*. The novel, written by a White South African, led Alice to comment on its "mostly white characters and the hero a typical wastrel with a supposed artistic temperament wrecking all with whom he comes in contact." She continued, "But Negro characters do figure in the book, and one, an American 'Negro' with the mistaken missionary idea, makes the climax of the book possible." This shift from focusing on the unfavorable to highlighting the favorable shows her ambivalence about this novel. On the one hand, she is miffed by the "Negro" character's attempt to reclaim an Africa that he "lost" hundreds of years ago; on the other hand, she berates Millin for the "unthinkable blasphemy of a black Christ on the Cross." Perhaps the real problem is that "Mrs. Millin has not read Countee Cullen's poem," a reference to Cullen's "The Black Christ." She concludes, "There is much food for thought in this book."

These columns do not appear to have been edited by *The Courier*. They were hastily written during Alice's travels, and at times the thoughts are incomplete. She moves on to a brief, two-paragraph statement about a North Carolina newspaper that did not capitalize the word "Negro" and tries to link the week's concern with this topic to her editorial of the week before. If readers wanted to know the significance of her concern here, they would need to have read the previous article. It may be that she was merely giving the audience insight into what she had observed and found interesting in these papers, such as the Greensboro, North Carolina, *Daily News*, and their representations of Black folks in the South.

In fact, she was wearing two hats—one as a columnist and the other as executive secretary of the American Interracial Peace Committee (AIPC), which had an office at 20 South 12th Street in Philadelphia. On June 1, 1928, she landed a job that gave her an opportunity for national travel and allowed her to receive a steady salary for engaging in "race" work. Rarely had race work or any form of activism provided a salary. Given the fact that her finances were precarious, leaving the family in worse shape than they had been in since she left the family to attend Cornell, having a steady income was extremely important. The aim of the organization was to "develop and enlist the active support of the Negroes of America in the cause of Peace," by building race relations.

A press release describes the kind of work Alice spearheaded as executive secretary. Much of her life in 1930 was consumed by saving a young man from death. When Theodore Russ, an African American man of twenty-two years, was arrested, tried, and convicted for "criminal assault" of a White woman, whom he had admittedly slightly cut in a brawl over the price of boot-legged liquor, the AIPC was asked to intervene. Attempting to have his sentence of hanging in the state of Delaware overturned, the organization rallied in collaboration with the Wilmington NAACP Chapter and Louis Redding, Alice's former student and the first Black lawyer in Delaware. Under Alice's leadership, they sent "letters, telegrams, appeals, petitions" to the governor that asked for a stay of execution "until further evidence could be found to prove the lad's innocence." Alice's skills as a writer and organizer were extremely useful in this position, but they were not enough. Unfortunately, according to Annette Woolard-Provine,[2] Redding, who was Russ's second lawyer, was unable to garner the support he needed to save his client's life. Russ was hanged twenty-five days later. As a competitive woman who took failures hard, Alice must have been quite disappointed by the loss of such a serious case.

Despite this failure, the organization was successful in other ways. Building on her love of the performing arts, Alice solicited the help of members of her network to organize a well-attended National Negro Music Festival in 1929 and 1930, which brought together notable Black musical performers from all over the country. She had asked her "dear Dr. Du Bois" to consent to adding his name to the organization's advisory board and invited him to attend the festival.

In their correspondence it is obvious that Alice knew she could rely on him for his support of her efforts. He paid for his three-dollar ticket for the May 25, 1929, event and was present, with guests, as she expected. In a letter to his wife, Nina Du Bois, dated May 20, 1929, he tells her that he expected to hear Florence Cole Talbert and Carl Diton, the Hampton chorus, and the Fisk, Howard, Lincoln quartets, and other people at a music festival.[3] For the 1930 festival, she would reach out to advisory board members to serve as patrons. Du Bois agreed that he "would be very glad" to serve in this capacity. Du Bois was a well-known man among his people, but his finances were immensely strained as he provided for his own expenses, those of a wife he did not live with regularly, and perhaps even his adult daughter. He lets his friend know his disappointment with her decision to assume that he wanted to pay for expensive seats. Of course, he bought multiple ones the year before and asked for prime seats. Assuming his needs the following year was an offense, however. There is no response in the record, but he wrote to her again on April 30, 1930, inquiring about an ad for the festival that he saw in *Opportunity*, a rival journal published by the National Urban League.[4] Du Bois wanted her to purchase an ad in *The Crisis* as well. Both journals had published her work. This letter shows that Alice always had to navigate Black communal terrains to maintain a balance as not to offend allies. Knowing this, she took him up on his "suggestion." As for his opinion of the quality of the affair, he shared on May 26, 1930, that he enjoyed the concert, especially the women and Fisk's choir, but that he did not like Howard University's choir. He advised that they should not be invited to return.[5] This is a rare time in the correspondence where he took a paternalistic stance and placed limits on her work. He and others may have enjoyed it, but it was not properly managed; consequently, that year the festival incurred debt. It would be the last year for the event.

Additionally, the organization engaged the youth by encouraging partners at schools to stage contests focused on reciting poetry with nationalistic themes. Winners received the Silver Medal for Youth Peace. Du Bois agreed to support her by serving as a judge for their high school essay contest in 1929 and 1930. Alice was good at using flattery to request what she knew was going to be a burden to the busy Du Bois. She wrote, "I know this is asking a great deal and I realize that you are very busy, but we feel that the young people who contest and who go to the trouble of writing the essays out to know that the very best possible minds are judging their work. Please do not say no."[6] His response to her inquiry tells of the respect he had for her and her work. Du Bois was most certainly fond of "My dear Mrs. Nelson" but that he saw the task of reading a large number of essays beyond the limits of his time. He presented a compromise, which she accepted, that involved sending him the best of the batch.[7]

Of greater interest to Alice was that working for the organization allowed her to indulge her desire to travel widely, to meet other social justice activists, and to build her reputation. Travel also gave her a welcomed distraction from her financial problems. Although she was not a wealthy woman, she often found ways to travel for her work. In addition to the event organizing, she set out on a tour of the South, including Maryland, Virginia, North Carolina, South Carolina, Florida, Georgia, Tennessee, Alabama, Mississippi, and Louisiana, where she visited many Black universities and colleges. By this point in her life, she only returned to the Deep South to represent the work she was doing for an organization. Ironically, her visit about nine years before was to support the First World War, as opposed to her current peace mission. She also listed California, Nebraska, and Iowa under the headline of "her southern trip."[8] Through the organization, she traveled across the country, giving speeches and working to form relationships with local chapters of allied groups that had similar missions. Her 1930 report of activities shows that she demonstrated great physical energy in "spreading the gospel of peace and interracial relationships."[9]

Alice's trip involved visits to thirty-seven schools, including six in New Orleans. She also reported visiting seven churches, twelve Young Women's Christian Associations, and twelve organizations and women's clubs. Based on the fact that she labeled three of the churches as White, the other organizations must have been largely comprised of Black members. Though Alice boasted of "reaching" 22,900 people on these visits, one has to wonder what the largely African American crowd that she faced took from her message of unity, especially if the point of the organization was to develop and expand relationships across racial boundaries. It is certain that their White counterparts of the late 1920s South were not widely receptive of any racial-solidarity messages. The onus of the unity, therefore, would have fallen on Black people. Notably, two of the churches labeled as "White" were not in the South but rather in Iowa and Hollywood.

Her column, "So It Seems," was a public outlet for Alice to share her observations about America. Traveling across the country by car and train provided her with an opportunity to expand her reputation as a "race woman," not only through her speeches but also through her column. In her reports, she gave descriptions of small towns and the activities taking place there that were relevant to her work. In Marion, North Carolina, a mountain town, she told her readers that the American Friends Service Committee "is doing relief work for the striking textile workers" by distributing clothing and food. In an effort to capture the scene, she described the "food shack" and "clothing shack" that she reached after being driven through "hills, ruts, rocks, and mudpuddles."[10] During her trip to South Carolina, she described the State College at Orangeburg (South Carolina State University) as a "big institution . . . housed in many modern buildings, doing some good work." She then described visiting a log cabin that had the "very latest things in kitchen equipment."[11] In observation of her trip to Tuskegee Institution, founded by Booker T. Washington, she shone a spotlight on the work of another "race woman" referred to only as "Mrs. Moton," who had "the true touchstone of greatness, genuineness, simplicity, modesty and that sweetness that some from living close to the heart of the world," as she continued the work of Alice's old friend from the Black women's club movement, Mrs. Booker T. Washington.[12] Alice's goal in these columns was to introduce her largely Black, northern, urban audience—many of whom had left the South and not returned—to the modern South and Black people's advancement, as evidenced by both their homes and their educational institutions.

Moving further South, she finally landed in New Orleans for a five-day trip. Her diary housed her private thoughts on this return. At the age of fifty-four, her trip back to New Orleans, where "it has been so lovely," gave her an opportunity to reminiscence about her past. A visit to her alma mater, Straight University, left her feeling that "the dream of [her] childhood had been realized." She felt "such a queer mix of emotions" at seeing "some of the same furniture here that was here then."[13] Indeed, she never would have revealed a lack of change to her *Courier* audience. Between her March 3 and 6, 1930, entries, she pondered her life in relation to the past: "Was I satisfied or disappointed?" She noted the changes as well through the marked change in a friend from second grade: "Think of seeing him after all these years! That stocky, grumpy, little second grader . . . who resisted my blandishments with all the strength of his seven-year old Creole body, now a stocky, grumpy, bald-headed pharmacist, still resisting my blandishments with all the strength of his 43 year old body!"[14] At Straight, she reported speaking to a crowd of "400" people, but despite her excitement at returning there, she would soon declare, "I know now where I shall want to spend the end of my life—here in California. The Spanish lure—the call of the blood. I have come home—home—home. My heart is singing, my pulses pounding, I am home. New Orleans did not feel this way, even though it be my birth place, But here—."[15]

From New Orleans, she began to head West, where she would have her most memorable moments of the trip, both public and private. She had an especially memorable time in Los Angeles. By this time, she had built a reputation for speaking on matters of race, and this was the first time she had had an opportunity to present her ideas and oratorical skills to a multiracial audience in the West. In anticipation of her visit, news releases began to inform potential audiences of her coming. On February 28, 1930, *The California Eagle* posted that the Los Angeles Civic League would be hosting "Alice Dunbar-Nelson, noted race woman, who will lecture at the Second Baptist Church on Tuesday night March 11th."

It was there that she took her first airplane ride. Hull finds that Alice's plane ride was the "most widely reported happening of her national trip."[16]

Her friends at *The Pittsburg Courier* published "Alice Takes to the Air" with an old picture of her. Alice was her own best publicist, as the article notes, "April 3—Word comes from Mrs. Alice Dunbar-Nelson, executive secretary of the American Inter-Racial Peace Committee . . ." According to the news release, likely written by Alice and sent days after the event, in order to avoid a twelve-to-fourteen-hour train ride from Los Angeles to San Francisco, she took a plane instead, where she was bid "bon voyage" by a "delegation of friends" at the Glendale Airport. The article concluded, "The flight was made on schedule time; and the San Franciscan engagement kept."[17] Alice had taken the plane "courtesy" of James McGregor, president of the Los Angeles Civic League, to speak at the University of Southern California's department of history, where she gave a talk and enjoyed a "spirited questioning on the part of the juniors and seniors who comprised the classes, the consideration of inter-racial relationships."[18]

Before leaving the city, she indulged her love of watching films. "My last day in Los Angeles (March 17, 1930) and a most eventful one . . . To the Paramount Lucky Studios. Saw a picture filmed. 'True to the Navy,' where Clara Bow is to be . . . Fascinating to see some of the sets I recognized."[19] *True to the Navy* was a romantic comedy released in 1930 about a counter-girl and her relationship with a sailor. The actress, Clara Bow, was popular during the silent film era and had appeared in over thirty films during the mid-twenties. She had, by this time, earned an Oscar nomination and was known for her sex appeal on screen. Having spent so much of her time and money watching and critiquing films over the last decade, Alice most certainly enjoyed this opportunity.

Newspapers made public what she shared with her audiences. In a rare printing of one of her speeches, on March 14, 1930, *The California Eagle* reported her thoughts on race and world peace:

> Here I am to talk to you tonight about "World Peace." Such a tremendous subject that most of us do not think of it at all, we just take it for granted. We have gotten into the habit of thinking that the subject of World Peace is for other people, that we have our own problems to solve, what have we to do with international affairs.

Rather than going into any specifics about the subject of world peace, she quickly shifted to the subject of race:

> I like to think of the Race in terms of the life of a man. The infant knows nothing more than its mother's breast, when it is warm and fed and comfortable. That is all, but as it grows older its horizon is extended a little bit but its prime concern is still food shelter and comfort; then it goes to school, its horizon is extended a little further, it is interested perhaps in its studies, some friends . . ., then a child grows and comes to

the adolescent period and it is interested in its friends, clubs . . . Then he comes to the man who goes to work and begins to make his contribution to society, is interested in civic affairs, interested in the community, his city; he votes for the president and congressmen. It is only when he realizes that he is a citizen of the world that this life of his is so bound up in all the rest of the lives of the world.

Her oratory technique was to humanize complex subjects chosen to appeal to her audience's sense of familiarity. In this case, she asked the audience to tap into their experience of maturing and use that experience as a metaphor for citizenship. Exercising citizenship, then, necessitates contributing to the good of all and becomes the responsibility of the individual for the good of the community and the world. Drawing from all that was important to her—racial equality, voting, politics—she made a speech that reflected the major concerns of her career.

Alice's introduction is a lead into a more specific statement she wanted to make about the problem with war. Relying on her experience as a teacher, she stated, "I have learned a lot from young people. . . . Young people ask questions and very intelligent questions and very important questions about World Peace and one thing that interests them is the absolute cause of war or just exactly what war is." She then went on to blame "old men." "Wars are made by old men, fought by young men and paid for by women and children." She concluded by making the case for peace as an "economic thing" and encouraged "we Negroes" to "begin at the bottom" by educating "the minds of the young people in fundamental principles of Christianity, educate them to go ahead with constructive building, putting away prejudice and hatred." Pointing to the youth as future leaders for the race, she pressed her audience to teach children that if they let go of hatred and prejudice, they would not become adults who were involved with wars. It is very likely that she presented the same ideas to segregated audiences in the South. According to the Black newspaper, *The California Eagle* (March 14, 1930), she was well received: "Mrs. Nelson has a pleasing personality and her lecture on World Peace and the Negro was easily a masterpiece in oratorical elegance and logic."[20]

As a representative of an organization dedicated to peace, Alice moved away from encouraging support of wars, instead discouraging Black people and others from participating in them, feeling that their purpose was to satisfy "economic greed," a perspective that echoed the concerns of Marxism, which had begun to influence African Americans and working-class communities of various races throughout the country.[21] Of course, Alice, who had spent most of her life in a state of financial instability, had always shown concern—through her writing and activism—for working-class communities.

Unable to sustain itself during the Depression, the peace organization ultimately folded. Alice admitted that by the time it had, she was ready to depart, since she no longer "believed" in the work of the AIPC.[22] Disagreements with members about the direction of the organization probably led her to make this decision. Nevertheless, her travels gave her an opportunity to build various kinds of relationships across boundaries.

One such boundary was her sexual attraction to women. Indeed, Mrs. Nelson loved women. The Harlem Renaissance era of the 1920s and early 1930s saw the emergence of sexually liberating blues music and was a time when Black people dared to test the boundaries of sexuality more publicly than ever before. Indulging their desires was risky as William Nelson finds that New York courts would punish people caught in same-sex liaisons: "Until the 1940s, judges routinely defended conventional Victorian morality for the twin purposes of preventing 'disorder and anarchy' and protecting 'our women and children.'"[23] Nevertheless, songs by blueswomen had moved well past the public boundaries of heterosexual respectability: "Went out last night with a crowd of my friends. They must have been women 'cause I don't like no men's."[24] Alice is also known to have visited A'Leila Walker's Dark Tower, a place located in Harlem, New York where legendary nighttime invitation-only parties were held and that was known to be a safe place for Black queer community members. In his study of sexuality during the Harlem Renaissance, Shane Vogel notes, "It is a mistake to think of a homosexual underworld, especially in the late nineteenth and early twentieth centuries, as segregated and isolated from an extensive heterosexual underworld."[25] Alice recorded her own sexual interests. On February 16, 1921, she wrote "You! Inez!" An unpublished poem of eight lines, it speaks of passion for Inez, who has "dusk eyes," a "flower soft," "red mouth," "curving arms." Alice's attention to sensual parts of Inez's body—her mouth and eyes—leads her to exclaim: "You! Stirring the depths of passionate desire!" This poem, unlike others that survived, speaks directly of sexual desire for a woman and was written, but not published, while she was married to her third husband. She *may have* also had an intimate relationship with Bessye Bearden, a journalist and activist who was the mother of the revered visual artist, Romare. She makes several references to them spending a great deal of time together during a visit to New York in an entry dated August 16, 1928. Bearden, who was married, was quite the socialite, making a good match with the socialite and middle-aged party girl. Both women, along with others, passed for White and saw a "most beautiful cabaret" she had "ever seen, and a gorgeous show" at the segregated Cotton Club. It "is pretty near day-break when we get home."[26] By February of the next year, she remarks that Bearden is "cool" to her and believed that "someone has told her something and she is breaking with me. Sorry I've lost both Geraldyn and her."[27] Whatever the nature of their relationship, it was one that she cherished and that brought her a great deal of pleasure.

Nevertheless, her love for Nelson did not deter her from exploring extramarital intimacies with women and other men. One such woman was Fay Jackson Robinson, whom Alice met while in Los Angeles while doing work for the AIPC—which perhaps explains why she developed such a fondness for the city. Perhaps Alice is the only one to document the fact that Jackson, a Los Angeles Civic League Executive Council member, was also associated with the AIPC in 1935. Recent scholarship on Jackson has focused on her undervalued career as a news correspondent, who spent time gathering news on domestic and international affairs. Born in 1902, Jackson had founded the first Black intellectual weekly newspaper by the time Alice met her. Certainly, their attraction was based on more than just their interest in world peace but extended to world affairs through the lens of journalism. After Alice's departure, Jackson became the political editor of *The California Eagle*, which carried stories of Alice's visit. Later Jackson became the first Black female correspondent for foreign affairs at the Associated Negro Press, in 1937.[28]

Writing on the Overland Limited train on her way back to the East, Alice revealed why Los Angeles was the place where she wanted to die. Perhaps too busy to record it earlier, she wrote of a night that she had spent with Jackson, who was also a married mother. Beginning March 17, 1930, she recalled that "marvelous Fay" stayed "all night" with her in a "little hotel." Two days later, she recorded, "Fay and I are awakened early . . . So we arose. And were soon dressed. NO water in our private bath." Leaving no doubt of the intimate nature of their relationship, she wrote, "All day I dream of the eight perfect days—of the romance, the beauty, the loveliness— and register anew a vow to return to California to end my days."[29] Her references here show that Jackson was as important to her as the beauty of California. At the time, she was clearly enamored with Jackson. Through their relationship, we learn of her personal perspective about marriage in a way we have not before. Recordings of this period of her life show how she tested the boundaries of respectability by enjoying romances with women while married.

As she wrote of Faye, she also wrote to her ex-husband Arthur Callis as she traveled back to the east coast. Remaining true to her nature of confident flirting, she wrote her disappointment in missing him while in Tuskegee where "[I] had washed my face and dolled up in my gladdest rags hoping I would meet you at the reception."[30] Writing to Callis as she basks in the romance of her days with Faye shows the tension between the simplicity of joy and the complexity of reality as she navigates private experience and public performance. Writing in its various forms betrays the convergence of identities that were the woman—Alice Ruth Dunbar-Nelson—who loved to love.

To be sure, her dalliances with Jackson during those eight days allowed her to have an erotic experience that also involved satisfaction derived from her writing and public speaking. Diary references to Jackson show Alice pining for the woman months after she returned to Wilmington. Upon her return, she wrote numerous diary entries that document her ongoing correspondence with the object of her California romance. As early as the return trip through Utah, she referred to a sonnet she had written to Jackson. Although she did not provide the entire poem, she shared a revealing line: "I had not thought to open that secret room."[31] Of this creative production, Audre Lorde writes, "For not only do we touch our most profoundly creative source, but we do that which is female and self-affirming in the face of a racist, patriarchal, and anti-erotic society."[32] Indeed, both married women were acting in defiance of patriarchy and anti-eroticism as well as the ideas of respectability; the only concern for society was their discretion. Yet, as scholar Matt Richardson notes, "Blacks who do not attempt to conform to dominant standards of heterosexuality . . . are clearly motivated against the basic conditions of . . . enslavement and colonization."[33] Those women would not forgo their pleasure in deference to the past. Indeed, Alice's time with Jackson gave her an escape from the strain of the financial problems plaguing her marriage and the problems of race that the activist women were trying to solve. Clinging to one another provided an opportunity for them to embrace comfort and security.

Alice's own diary, though treated on a conscious level as private, made public the intimate secret that the two women shared. Her diary has resonances of the "lesbian coming out story" as described by Monica B. Pearl: "The coming out story is a narrative of recognition and naming, a severing from an old identity and the community associated with it, and the adoption of a new identity and thus a reconnection with a new community."[34] Alice uses the diary to fully embrace her erotic attraction, the wholeness of who she was, with a sense of freedom documented in writing—freedom that defied the restrictions of respectability or at least redefined the meaning of respectability associated with proper middle-class living and the influences of a public expectation that restricted intimacy. Siobhan Somerville asserts, "Although individuals may desire to be 'in' or 'out' of the closet, one can never fully control the interpretation of one's status. One must therefore constantly renegotiate the boundary between 'in' and 'out' in a culture that simultaneously seeks out and erases lesbian and gay identity."[35] Alice and Jackson lived between the "in" and "out" of respectable boundaries. Any writing, from the diary to the poem, stood as a confession of the secret that they pretended to hold between the two of them alone. It is this "private" writing that betrayed Alice, or rather revealed a side of her that she revered as private, to her husband and to future readers.

Jackson was part of a romantic triangle that formed among her, Alice, and a woman named Helene. How the three women knew each other is not revealed in the surviving documents, but they most likely crossed paths on the social justice circuit and perhaps Black clubwomen circles. On March 29, 1930, Alice recorded her rage when she read a letter from Helene that contained a "mutilated scrap of a letter from Fay" to Helene. What it said exactly she did not share, but it was enough to reveal the affair to Alice's husband when he read it:

Bobbo got it, read it—he will read my things, diary and all—God, he pufformed. Called Helene and Fay horrible names. I don't know how I assumed an air of non-chalance and cool indifference—which threw him off. Inwardly I raged—at Fay's deceit, at Helene's asininity—hurting of me with Fay's letter, at Bobbo's meddlesomeness and coarseness.[36]

Alice's response showed her lack of interest in her betrayal of her marriage vows; instead she guarded her right to use her body as she pleased. In response to Nelson's confrontation, she gave a performance designed to distract him from this revelation.[37] Did she apologize or offer him an explanation? Opting to use her writing to focus on her reaction to his boundary crossing, she did not record his verbal response or hers, but the fact that he became aware of her sexual attraction to women, if he did not already know, leaves unanswered questions. Did they have an open marriage? Was he willing to overlook these infidelities because they were with women and not with men? Perhaps he was simply unable to confront the infidelities that occurred. In one entry dated Sunday, August 7, 1921, Alice wrote that, in opposition to the beliefs of Nelson, she told her stepdaughter that it was not a sin to wash clothes on Sunday. "Bob O would be horrified, for he is perfectly sure it is a sin to wash necessary clothes on Sunday but not a sin to type-write, write newspaper articles, go on excursions, cook huge dinners, commit adultery, or plan political coups which will result in another man's downfall."[38] Her diary offers examples of all these activities except, perhaps, adultery. Who was the adulterer in question?

Having come-out, in a sense, to her husband by leaving out a letter where he could find it, the affair persisted. Not able to resist the allure of this love triangle, Alice continued to record letters from Helene and her correspondence with Jackson. A day after Nelson read the letter, she wrote of rereading Dunbar's *Lyrics of Love and Sorrow* and her plan to copy some of the poems and send them to Jackson, "deceitful hussy."[39] Although Alice and Dunbar had never reconciled, her choice to use his poetry to honor the object of her affection reminds us that she always admired his poetic abilities and that, possibly, memories of their life together invoked both love and sorrow. Several days later, on April 2, she received a letter from Helene that included a "lock of her hair, scented." Alice wrote a dramatic response in her diary, saying that she had destroyed the letter and the lock, as it "seemed like a lock of her Medusa's hair. That curl actually seemed poisonously alive."[40] The next day she wired Helene not to send any more letters to the house; notably, she did not ask her not to send her any more letters at all. Her reasoning, she stated, was that she couldn't take any more chances that Nelson would read the letters. She went on, "Another outburst like that from him and I won't be responsible."[41] Again, she did not provide any details about his "outburst," but readers can only assume that she was referring to the reaction he had had to reading her letters a few days before.

Her writings consistently show her concern about his invasion of her privacy rather than concern about his feelings regarding the intimate relationship she was hoping to maintain with these women. Enjoying the exhilaration of erotic feelings and attention of these women was central to Alice. Furthermore, living through experiences separate from the burdens of financial stress and the needs of her family allowed her to find and claim something that was hers, so she embraced it unapologetically. This April 3, 1930, entry also included a sonnet that Hull believes is in reference to Jackson; given the number of sonnets that Alice wrote to Jackson over the next few weeks, this is probably one of them:

> You did not need to creep into my heart
> The way you did. You have smiled
> And knowing what you did, have kept apart
> From all my inner soul. But you beguiled
> Deliberately. Then flung my poor love by,
> A priceless orange now. Without a sigh
> Of pity at the wreck you made. Smashed
> The golden dream I'd reared. Then unabashed
> Impaled the episode upon a stupid epigram,
> Blowing my soul thro' smoke wreaths as you sneered a "Damn."

Her emotional expressions here are of a jilted lover. She wrote others but only provided single lines from them in her diary. On April 9, she received a letter and poem from Jackson about her and orchids.[42]

The relationship proved stressful. By April 15, Alice felt overwhelmed by the emotions that she felt as she read "wild letters" from Helene about the desire Helene felt for Jackson. As a result Alice "wanted to die. Cried myself to sleep."[43] Betty Hart's observation provides context for this moment: "man, simply indicate the restrictions that society placed upon the social freedom of women—specifically black women who were doubly oppressed by racial as well as social politics."[44] Her entries became more intensely emotional as she received letters and sent poems, though she did not provide details of what Helene wrote that made them "wild." Her preference was clearly for Jackson: "I'd welcome a daily letter from Fay." She did admit, "Helene loves me."[45] As all of this was going on, she continued to entertain her family, deal with her health issues, and continue her position with the American Interracial Peace Committee. She made no reference to sharing this relationship or her anguish with anyone outside of the three-woman circle. This part of her life was hers. She does not seem to have shared it with her sister and niece—her housemates whom she traveled with, partied with, and played cards with often. By June 17, she learned that Jackson had left her husband; she believed that both of them were after the same woman, "and John won."[46] Well into 1931, Alice continued to correspond with the two women. However, after she marked the year's anniversary of her trip to Los Angeles, she appears not to have seen Jackson again, and there are no more recordings of their correspondence.

As usual, travel as an activist supplied Alice with more opportunities to explore relationships. In the fall of 1931, Alice boarded a ship to Bermuda, where, according to Hull, Helene resided. Perhaps there, as in California with Fay, she cultivated "a longing for others who are like one, who understand."[47] Whether she went to be with Helene or not, Alice was met with much public fanfare. *The Recorder*,[48] a paper of Bermuda, recorded her visit as a distinguished guest and was careful to note that she was not simply the "relic of Paul Laurence Dunbar, America's foremost lyrical Negro"—as mentioned in an earlier article published on September 26, 1931, "Mrs. Dunbar-Nelson was herself distinguished in poetry and prose, was an international journalist, and was secretary of the Inter-racial Peace League of the United States, an organization that was doing immense good in fostering a better feeling between the races." Although she had published in a variety of genres since the death of Dunbar, as far as the public was concerned she was there to read his work, not hers, suggesting that she still lived in his shadow and was willing to if she could benefit from his legacy. To provide a more complete biography of her distinguished accomplishments, the article added knowledge to what they "did not know," which was that she had "been honored by the greatest purveyors of knowledge and general information—the British Encyclopedia."[49] While there, Alice presented one of her well-known and apparently still popular performances, known as "An evening with Paul Laurence Dunbar," which her Bermudian hosts billed as an elite affair followed by a social dance with music provided by an orchestra. In so doing, it showed yet another instance in which Alice, though struggling financially, seemed always able to move between class status because of her name and talent. In other words, she lived a life that valued masking.

Her intimate relationships with women reveal her unapologetic foray into her erotic desire, a willingness to embrace a self that shunned respectability. A year before this romantic triangle, in her diary entry of July 27, 1929, water becomes a metaphor for a sensual lover, a metaphor later confirmed in her description of a weekend resort trip she took with Nelson, family members, and friends to celebrate her fifty-fourth birthday. Water—how it made her feel both physically and emotionally—revealed sexually gratifying moments of the month she turned fifty-four years old. She declared:

> The water! Luxurious, voluptuous, lovely. Lapping, caressing, loving my bare body—when I get way out and slip my bathing suit down and no one can see me naked.[50]

> But the water! I came here for it. Weeks I dreamed of it. Here it is. No inconvenience too great for the love of it—even these hot days when it was calm as a mill pond and none too clean—I could wait. Lovely, luxurious, voluptuous water.[51]

Her ode to water—dreaming of it and declaring love for it—is instructive. But it is not just water, it is a body of water that appeals to her. Bodies of water inspired Alice to reveal a self that does not emerge elsewhere in the diary. In one entry, she wrote of a late-night swim in the lake with five of her female friends:

> Out not so far until up to our shoulders, the waves dashed over our heads. And we swam—matches of underwater swimming where the phosphorous made gleaming lights on the head—like miner's lamps. Swimming, swimming out to infinity—racing in under the pulsing water to the solitary light on shore.[52]

Apparently, there had been other times when the women swam together and "went swimming far out—we slipped off our bathing suits . . . let the water caress our naked forms."[53] She concluded, "The voluptuous caresses of my lover—the Chesapeake Bay—will soon be mine no more."[54] Notably, her husband at this time was on his way to the retreat. Although Hull sees that experience as an erotic moment between the women, I see it rather as an erotic moment with the water that is shared among women. It would seem that Alice's lover—the feelings that emerge from her contact with the water—helps to free the self that she often hid from others. To some degree, this may include her attraction to women, but it is also a love she had of herself, her nakedness, her aging body, by this point in her life.

Alice's diaries reveal that the Nelsons had a complicated relationship. It is no wonder why she continued to revisit marriage—more specifically the marriage that arguably brought her the most pain and disappointment: her marriage to Paul Laurence Dunbar. According to Hull, sometime between 1928 and 1931 Alice wrote "No Sacrifice," a short story featuring a relationship between Aline and Gerald, a writer, like Dunbar, who begins to correspond with Aline after he sees her picture in a journal that had published her work. The two eventually meet, become hastily engaged before Gerald sails to Europe for a lecture tour, and marry when he returns to the States. Almost immediately after they wed, Aline learns that her husband enjoys the company of a social crowd headed by a "tauntingly beautiful" socialite from Texas named Marie. At times Gerald leaves his wife at their home for long periods, while he has an ongoing affair with Marie. Feeling lonely and vulnerable, Aline starts a relationship with Owens, but upon her husband's return from Cuba, she finds him sick and near death. The doctor's prescription is to go into retreat at a ranch in Colorado, where the two begin to reconnect, until Owens and Marie intervene. Aline tires of Gerald's adulterous relationship, leaves, and finds employment and independence, but then she receives word that an uncle has left her a large fortune, as long as she does not give any of it to her husband for any reason. She gives up the fortune, however, to reunite with her husband, who is destitute and ill, a consequence of having been left by Marie for another man.

Similar to Alice's short story "The Decision" written shortly after she left Dunbar, "No Sacrifice" centers on whether or not Aline should give away the money (a symbol of her independence) that she has inherited to return to her estranged husband. The circumstances of the two stories are quite different, however. In "The Decision," Marion tells of physical and verbal abuse, emotional separation, and mental anguish. Furthermore, she expresses a lack of desire to trust or marry any man. She shows no pity for her estranged husband, only an obligation to share her fortune with him because he did provide financially for her while they were together.

Writing "No Sacrifice" during her marriage to her third husband, years after her separation from Dunbar, Alice was able to regard with hindsight her life with Dunbar and her multiple relationships with men and women. Presenting Aline as a woman who takes advantage of her choices was a way of empowering the character. Alice had reluctantly given up a teaching career to marry an abusive man; she would later rely on her teacher's training to sustain her family and marry twice more. Like Alice, Aline had a potential career before marriage; after her marriage fails, she uses her secretarial skills when needed to secure independence and financial security. She reconciles with her husband because she loves him, not for social prestige or other reasons, such as meeting respectability standards. Their reconciliation, then, is rooted in love and not public opinion.

The impact of Gerald's relationship with his lover changes Aline as much as her own relationship with Owens does. Yet her husband does not judge her for that relationship. Seeking and achieving wholeness, Aline must rely on her own skills, which gives her a sense of power and also a sense of peace through redemption. Ending the fictional Paul and Alice's relationship with reconciliation allowed Alice to write a harmonious ending to her relationship with Dunbar that she had never actually enjoyed. This ending signaled that she reached the point of forgiving him. Hull sees this story as a desperate attempt by Alice to write something she could sell for profit. While I do not disagree with her, "No Sacrifice" shows how marriage can change a woman—to free her from societal boundaries and allow her to explore new forms of expression.

In reality, questions about trust loomed between the Nelsons. At that time, her doubts about her husband's loyalty to their marriage appeared periodically, as in a December 5, 1921, diary entry: "He is awfully strong on that fourth commandment. I wonder if he has always been as strong on the seventh? I have noticed that the men who make the biggest fuss over a little pleasure on the Sabbath are the ones who enjoy the biggest Sunday dinners."[55] Perhaps it was these doubts that motivated her to have affairs with women and men. Christian beliefs were not a prominent factor in any decision that she made. Although she and Nelson had both been members of the church, she became disillusioned by active membership around the time when she wrote this entry:

> Many things will be forgiven in this world, but the circumstances destroyed my faith in Richard Trapnell, and turned me from the Episcopalian church will never be effaced from my mind. And the man who was responsible for that was a heavy weight to carry. . . . I was setting him up where no man had a place to be —in the place of God.

By this point, she had become more spiritual than religious and had taken to daily meditations with Unity and felt it to be a way to shield them from failures and misfortunes. In an undated letter to her husband about his unsuccessful bid to become a Recorder of Deeds, she outlined her efforts of support and then informed him: "God bless you dear Boy, and give you unfaltering courage. I am praying for you hard. And have all of Silent Unity's seventy members of the praying band, using their endeavors for you. I'm going to pray on Thompson and Ball. Your own adoring hopeful wife."

Despite Alice's doubts about Nelson's fidelity and her own relationships with women, the Nelsons shared their own sexual intimacies. Two years before meeting Fay Jackson, on the eve of 1928, Alice wrote, "My new mattress finally came. Bobbo and I will christen it together tonight."[56] Intimate flirtations came in the form of "playing poker in bed" as she gladly writes on October 23, 1927.[57] Thirty years after being raped by her first husband, Alice learned to embrace with a lighthearted and playful tone her relationship with her third husband and to form occasional intimacies with other women and men as well. In an undated draft of a poem titled "To My Husband," she shows her admiration for her husband as "Brave and strong and manly and true" and as one whom "I give myself complete and whole." Given the style of script she uses that was more consistent with the later years of her life, this poem may have been written with Nelson in mind.

Despite her complicated personal life and busy travel schedule, she stayed active as long as she was secretary with the AIPC after her return. In correspondence with Du Bois, she continued to rely on him and he obliged. In a letter inviting him to give a speech, "History in Colored Schools" at a teacher's conference she was organizing for October 4, 1930, she lightheartedly told him: "being the only speaker at the night session. That means that the other folks will talk all day long and you will listen to them. Then at night you can get back at them."[58] They would continue to correspond about the conference and the details, including who might be invited to attend.

In one of their last letters about the AIPC, she told him that "our good friends, the Quakers are unable to carry us longer and the Negro does not seem too excited enough about peace to pay for it." With no employment prospects, she goes on, "So I shall join the vast army of the unemployed after December. Have you a job for me in your office? I'm seriously looking for work, and must find it."[59] Given the precarious state of the economy in 1930 and the challenges of running *The Crisis*, Du Bois was unable to offer her employment. After her job with AIPC ended, regardless of where she traveled and with whom she had a relationship, there was no escaping her poor health. Nelson occupied various low-paying and uncertain positions after the close of *The Advocate* in 1922. He worked as the executive director for the Elks from 1929 to 1932, and he was also managing editor of *The Washington Eagle* from 1926 to 1933. He had an office in Washington, DC, which forced them to commute to one another while he boarded with family friends. At times this proved difficult for his wife, who felt the stress of the family's precarious finances. Her mother turned eighty in 1930 and required care that Alice paid for. On February 28, 1930, she shared her frustrations with Nelson during one of his weekend visits to home: "At last I got a chance to tell him of my desperate state. Debts. No money. Bottom dropped out of my job [a reference to troubles with the AIPC]. Confusion. Bafflement. Embarrassment. . . . He was very-quiet."[60] Nelson's response was to raise Alice's hopes by telling her of another business venture that he was pursuing. It was yet another dream deferred.

On Friday, November 6, 1931, she wrote, "Mama died at 9:40 or 9:39-1/2 at home." She described the event in brief statements: "At nine I went again. The breathing growing shallow. Called Leila. She sat by the bed. I put away cards and table. Went back and stood. At 9:39, Bobo's footsteps on the steps. His key in the door. A long last sigh from Mama. The end of Patricia Moore."[61] At the approximate age of eighty-one, Patricia Wright Moore passed. Alice had lived with her mother most of her life, and the loss must have been devastating, but she remained largely silent on how she felt about her mother's death. In the archives is a short biography, perhaps an obituary, that is a bit of creative writing for a twentieth-century audience:

> Patricia Moore was born in Opelousas, Louisiana, January 1, 1850. She was the daughter of Joseph and Mary Wright. Early in life she removed to New Orleans where she was married to Joseph Moore. Here she was confirmed in the Episcopalian church. Mrs. Moore moved to Wilmington about thirty years ago. While she was not a member of any church in Wilmington yet she was a frequent worshiper at Zion and Shiloh Baptist churches. Mrs. Moore was ill for more than a year and was confined to her bed for a year. She is survived by her two daughters, Mrs. M. Leila Young and Mrs. Alice Dunbar-Nelson; one grand-daughter Miss Pauline A. Young; a grandson, Laurence T. Young, a great-grand-son Laurence T. Young, Jr. of Chicago.[62]

Among other curiosities, absent from this biography is the fact that Patricia was born into slavery and the whereabouts of Joseph Moore. Both the politics of silence and respectability followed Patricia Moore to her death.

Their lives may have paused, but the stress remained. Despite the death of her mother, the Nelsons continued their political pursuits. Days after Moore's passing, Alice documented Nelson taking his frustrations out on her when a news writer leaked a false story that he had been appointed as the state athletic commissioner. "Bobo calls me everything but a child of God . . . says I'm a quitter, yellow, and what not." She excused his behavior as "peevish."[63] Several days later she received an invitation from President Herbert Hoover to attend a conference on home building and home ownership. When she found a way to attend (details not provided), he was "definitely grouchy."[64] She prided herself on being "tough" when it came to enduring his frustrations and on being able to maneuver around their financial shortcomings. Indeed, after surviving Dunbar, she may very well have seen his behavior as "peevish," but the fact that she recorded it implies that she was still emotionally moved by his words and activities.

Striking a balance between her role at home and her public activities was not always easy. One of her early entries reveals her regret at not being able to contribute financially as well as his desire to see her fill the traditional role of a wife who cooks and cleans. She wrote, "He said today he likes me at the office—evenings when he's there alone, but not in the daytime. Likes to run in the house and find me here."[65] After working all day at the music festival, she returned home with Nelson, who asked about dinner:

> Nearly cracked when I got home a wreck, and Bobbo asked me if there was anything to eat in the ice-box. It was too cruel. But when I got off my shoes, into nightie and bathrobe, and went down into the kitchen to eat the sandwiches he had cooked (fried egg) and a high ball, did not feel so near to tears. I might have bawled him out a plenty. And so, to bed.[66]

This episode, if accurately recalled, does not show that her husband was asking her to prepare a meal—but rather if one was readily available. The end result was his act of preparing food for the two of them, suggesting that, at least on that occasion, he did not expect her to assume a traditional role as cook in their home. There are other times that she described a meal he prepared for them. The incident begs the question: Was it he or she who expected her to cook after a long day in the activist field? In other words, to what extent was she able to let go of her feminist perspective in the home?

Regardless of what was going on at home, the pair was relentless and Alice's work stood out as her own and not as Nelson's wife. As shown by her former Howard student J. Saunders Redding who remembered her dedication and beauty in his memoir, the elder brother of Louis Redding and renowned professor recalled a 1931 speech she gave on the Scottsboro boys case, a case that involved the arrest of nine Black boys in Scottsboro who had been accused of raping two White girls.

I remember the almost weekly meetings. Especially do I remember one at which Alice Dunbar-Nelson spoke. The widow of Paul Dunbar, a Negro poet nationally famous at the turn of the century, Mrs. Nelson had been one of my teachers in high school and family friend. She was beautiful—tall, with ivory skin and a head of glinting red-gold hair—and she was also of great and irresistible charm. One thought of her as being saturated in a serene culture, even in divinity. I doubt that she had ever been much concerned with the common run of Negroes, and that night as she spoke to a large audience of all classes of a united people, she was like a goddess come to earth—but a goddess. In the end, with tears glistening in her eyes, she stretched her gloved hands and cried, "Thank God for the Scottsboro case! It has brought us together."[67]

Saunders complemented perspectives of Alice as a passionate orator. What is documented here is that as long as the specter of lynchings in any form (mob violence or state executions) was present she would continue to resist false accusations launched against Black men that would, if the public did not seize opportunities to speak against them, result in their deaths. In this case, nine poor young Black boys in Alabama had been accused of raping two poor White girls in 1931. Organizations such as the American Communist Party, the NAACP, and the Black press with the support of outraged Black people across the country eventually joined efforts to have the boys exonerated. Their success in this regard varied and carried on well into the late twentieth century.

Passion as described by her former student shows the effects of empathy. Caring for the self was necessary to carry the stress of being an activist. Despite her personal harrowing failures and disappointments and the pressures associated with her activist career, she sought means to escape the sadness. One such way was through her daily engagement with Unity, a spiritual practice that she had become involved with. She would go to a center for "noon meditation." In her archives, there are workbooks from Unity that show guided exercises designed to bring forth positive thinking and planning. Another way she tried to maintain a sense of peace in her life was to spend time in nature. During a trip, she wrote that she "had a lovely time exploring today—a rabbit in the sunken garden, squirrels in the big grove, thrush . . . —a lovely time alone."[68]

Being a respectable activist required giving much of the self to others, but she would learn to carve out space and time for herself. As we see through the life of Alice Dunbar-Nelson, activism's relationship to respectability did not leave much room for balance. But, as she got older and her body tired from the constant demands of lifting as they climbed and paying her bills, she had to find ways of escaping and tapping into the center of who she was. Her quest to embrace the fullness of herself was a lifetime journey.

12

'til Death Does the
Respectable Activist Part

After years of financial instability, the Nelsons moved to Philadelphia when Republican governor Gifford Pinchot named Nelson to the State Athletic Commission of Pennsylvania and as boxing commissioner in 1932. At some point, she had rejoined the Republican Party, which apparently paid them for the choice. Nelson had been lobbying for a position for some time, and his efforts had proved frustrating and disappointing, according to his wife, who almost seemed to foreshadow her own death: "Not having heard from Bobbo was naturally anxious to know . . . what luck he had . . . If Bobbo does not get something from Pinchot in the nature of a good position, it will kill him. He'll die of a broken heart, and the doctors will diagnose it as pneumonia or heart disease."[1] In her own humorous way, Alice wanted their work in politics to bring them both good fortune. When Nelson's job offer did come, it was the result of recognition for his work (and hers) and a noteworthy accomplishment that received recognition in *Opportunity*. He reportedly received a salary of $5,000/year (an equivalent of approximately $89,200 in 2021) with the post. References in other documents record that they were also given housing and a chauffeured car. Alice was now, for the first time in her adult life, on a stable financial footing that also matched her social circle. This was also the first time in her adult life that she could rely on a man. Hull notes, "Dunbar-Nelson had her own fancy personalized stationary and her own comfortable, well-appointed home" in Philadelphia.[2] There she could entertain the elite of the race, including her longtime friend Arthur Schomburg.

Nelson's position finally brought them the interest of the Black press as subjects and not as publisher or writers. On March 22, 1934, *The Pittsburg Courier* published the headline "Mrs. Alice Dunbar Nelson Injured." No longer identified as the widow of Paul Laurence Dunbar, Alice was

"Mrs. Alice Dunbar Nelson, wife of Robert J. Nelson, boxing commissioner of the State of Pennsylvania." The article goes on to note that she was in a car accident but that neither she nor her chauffeur was hurt. This slight reference to the chauffeur in the last sentence suggests the purpose of the eight-line article—to thrill its Black audience with the "near-death" experiences of a well-known, respected member of their community. Despite it being the era of the depression, these two had finally found financial stability for the first time in their marriage.

No matter where she lived, Alice would use her voice in politics. The Nelson's move to Philadelphia, a city where they spent a great deal of time prior to the appointment, found them keeping up their political engagement. Alice continued to give talks on politics, remain active with Delta Sigma Theta Sorority—writing the sorority's national hymn a few months before her death—and accept invitations to commemorate Paul Laurence Dunbar. In a "meeting held October 18, 1934 at South Philadelphia State Head Quarters Republican Party," she spoke against the New Deal and urged the audience to support the Republican candidate for governor. This was one in series of speeches. She received a letter from the incoming Republican committee chairman R. W. Thorne for speaking to the colored voters at Williamsport. Her interest this time was deeply personal as a letter written by Nelson confirms. If, George Howard Earle III, the Democratic gubernatorial candidate, won, he would lose his position as "the only colored man in the world who is a State Athletic Commissioner."[3] Earle was sworn in on January 15. Nelson held his commissioner's post until 1935, shortly before Alice's death.

Alice must have known that she was gravely ill. She was being cared for by Leila who had retired from Howard in 1931 and moved to Philadelphia to be with her sister. Leila wrote often to Young about her younger sister's condition. On July 26, 1935, she expressed her concern and hope for her younger sister's health.

> She had a light lunch at six o'clock. Last night before retiring she had a big plate of ice cream. Virginia [her doctor] says not to be alarmed because she is sure Aunt Alice will come out all right, of course, it will take time.
>
> I have been uneasy because her nightmares have been terrible. Virginia wants her to be quiet and remain upstairs. The breathing is better too, it has been distressing. So once more, I am hopeful.[4]

Alice, on the other hand, was not so hopeful. About a month later, she wrote details to Young about the location of documents and Young was entrusted with handling her business affairs, including corresponding with friends and colleagues about her aunt's health. Among these instructions was how to handle publication of *This Lofty Oak*, the novel she finished in the last days of her life, showing how important it was that the story of Kruse and the history of Howard be known.

Young was dedicated to her aunt as a second mother. Taking her cue from the women she knew and respected in Wilmington, Young herself was a respected and active member of her community. She must have been in contact with Du Bois during one of his visits to Wilmington. In a lighthearted letter to his friend, Alice, he jokingly spoke to her about what he had heard of her condition and concluded that she was an "interesting invalid" who was trying to gain the sympathy of her peers. Clearly, he was quite familiar with the family of women. He referred to her "lazy niece" and to notify her sister to properly brown the biscuits, adding, "I came near saying burned, but don't tell her."[5] This is a rare writing tone he took with Alice, showing his veiled concern for the state of her health. His friend passed about nine months later.

Bobo did his part to care for his wife. Alice wrote in an undated card to Young, "Robert roasted leg of lamb and making apple sauce." Alice and Bobo appeared to meet the standards of respectability through a marriage that cherished discretion. Despite the nontraditional nature of their union, they remained husband and wife until her death. If love is patient, these two loved each other well.

Friends, according to one notice in *The Washington Tribune* about her death on September 18, 1935, would blame her "prolific energies in the recent election campaign" for aggravating her chronic heart condition, possibly exacerbated by her smoking habit. In fact, she would die on that date at the age of sixty from pneumonia, which affected her heart. On page 10 of the September 28, 1935, edition of *The Pittsburg Courier*, the headline speaks of another way that her life, through her death, would interest those who knew her: "Alice Dunbar Nelson's Death Shocks Nation: Heart Attack Proves Fatal to Noted Figure in Women's And World Affairs—Career Brilliant and Useful." With the exception of the inaccurate age, the lead accurately summarizes the major points of her career: "Mrs. Alice Dunbar-Nelson, 63 years old, of this city, former teacher in the Howard High School, Wilmington, Del., and author and lecturer, dies in the University of Pennsylvania Hospital Wednesday night." In the five paragraphs that follow, the article gives a summary of her career as a teacher, journalist, editor, and political activist. The article emphasizes that she led a well-rounded, full, model life, not only by participating in service organizations such as the "National Federation of Women's Clubs, League of Independent Political Action, the NAACP, the IBPOEW (Improved Benevolent and Protective Order Elks of the World, Inc), and Delta Sigma Theta Sorority" but also by enjoying a social life as an "active member of the West Philadelphia Charity Bridge Club, Mercy Hospital Service Club, Pierian Book Club Sorority; Sophisticates of Douglass Hospital, Episcopalian." According to the article, "She had been in the hospital for a week suffering from a heart condition."

After years of health problems, her body finally gave out. She was survived by her husband, who by this time had also survived his own children, and her sister and lifelong friend, Leila. Two of Leila's surviving children, Pauline and Laurence, are mentioned in the article.

She would be remembered by others as well, including Julia Bumry Jones, who knew Alice and noted in her column "Talk O Town . . . Breezy Comment on Current Happenings," "She could deliver the most brilliant speeches . . . new, vitalizing talks that made you think[.] Political, social, civic phases of community life received her attention . . . she was marvelously versatile and oh, so charming." Surely Alice would have been pleased by her peer's assessment of her skills. Another editorial would have been just as pleasing, for it spoke to the public persona that she had strived to present to society. Under the title "A Gracious Lady Passes Away," an editorial writer in the October 5, 1935, *Pittsburg Courier* wrote, "She was the finest type of intelligent, cultured Negro womanhood and through her many contacts, personal and literary. She wielded a great cultural influence in colored American society. In addition, she performed a major service in improving interracial relations through her numerous contacts with white Americans." The writer adds, "She possessed charm and wit . . . a cosmopolitan mind, fine literary gifts, executive ability and lack of provincialism all too rare among our people at the time when she first came into prominence." She had been among the "Aframerican women" who had moved toward the "goal of culture" in the "past 30-odd years." Finally, the writer repeated what was commonly stated at the dawn of the New Negro Movement: "A group can rise no higher and improve no faster than its women. Mrs. Nelson helped our women aspire to higher and nobler things." J. Saunders Redding would concur: "She was the first lady in the affairs of her people."[6] Alice Ruth Moore Dunbar-Nelson had achieved the ultimate praise from her peers: she was in their eyes a respectable activist.

But she had defined the meaning of respectable in ways they had not known. There, within the narrow margins of respectability, Mrs. Dunbar-Nelson enjoyed moments of eroticism—some long and some short—as she matured and evolved through her love of herself, her family, her race, her community, her husbands, and her female lovers. In her diary, Alice expressed her desire "to float on and on and on into sweet oblivion."[7] After a funeral that occurred at her home in Pennsylvania at noon on September 23, 1935, her wish was granted when her ashes were scattered upon the Delaware River on September 24, 1935.[8]

NOTES

Introduction

1 Hull, "Brass Ankles Speaks," *Volume 2*, 311.

2 Hull, *Volume 3*, xxxiv.

3 I use Black and African American interchangeably. At times, African American is used for emphasis and specificity. Both are in reference to people of African descent.

4 Alice Moore changes her name at least two more times; therefore, I will refer to her as Alice throughout for consistency.

5 Hull, "Brass Ankles Speaks," *Volume II*, 318.

6 Wall, *Women of the Harlem Renaissance*, 88.

7 Hull, *Volume II*, 25

8 Ibid.

9 Ibid.

10 Ibid.

11 Richardson, *The Queer Limit of Black Memory*, 4.

12 Mitchell, "Silences Broken, Silences Kept," 436.

13 Brooks-Higginbotham, "The Black Church," 199.

14 Carlson, "Black Ideals of Womanhood in the Late Victorian Era," 61–2.

15 Ibid.

16 Spillers, "Mama's Baby, Papa's Maybe," 76.

17 Hammonds, "Black (W)holes and the Geometry of Black Female Sexuality," 306.

18 See works by Brittney Cooper, Patricia Hill Collins, and Vivian May. May argues that Black feminism is historical: "Maria Stewart's speeches of the 1830s can be considered the beginning of a written African American feminist discourse, or even the eighteenth-century poetry of Phyllis Wheatley . . ." These scholars have established that Black feminist activism and philosophies predate the women of Alice Dunbar-Nelson's era.

19 Brooks-Higginbotham, "Wresting with Respectability," ForHarriet, parag 3.

20 Hull, "Researching Alice Dunbar-Nelson," 315.

21 Cooper, *Beyond Respectability*, 9.

22 Lorde, "The Uses of the Erotic," 59.

23 Drury, "Love Ambition," 71.

24 Davidson, "Marginal Spaces, Marginal Texts," 51.

25 There are many different articles and biographical sketches written about Alice Dunbar-Nelson's work and life. Articles usually are limited to analysis of her New Orleans fiction.

Chapter 1

1 Blassingame, *Black New Orleans*, 1.

2 Ibid.

3 References to letters (ADN is Alice Dunbar-Nelson and PLD is Paul Laurence Dunbar) are taken from Eugene Metcalf's transcription of the letters, which I have compared to the originals found in Box 1 of the MSS 0113, Alice Dunbar-Nelson papers, Special Collections, University of Delaware Library, Newark, Delaware. I cite the dates to help with establishing a timeline.

4 Ibid., ADN to PD, March 7, 1899.

5 Alexander, *Lyrics of Sunshine*, 53.

6 Blassingame, *Black New Orleans*, xvi.

7 See "Alice Dunbar-Nelson" (1875–1935) by Pauline Young. Atlanta University Center, Robert W. Woodruff Library Archives Research Center, 2019. There are errors in this document or rather silences. One example is the omission of Henry Callis as Alice's second husband. Young lists Nelson as her aunt's second husband.

8 Ibid., 91.

9 Ibid., 86.

10 Stouck, "Identities in Crisis," 275.

11 Martin, "Placage and the Louisiana Gens," 57.

12 See Kenneth Aslakson, "The 'Quadroon-Plaçage' Myth." *Journal of Social History* 45 (3): 709.

13 "Fisk School," *Weekly Pelican*, 2.

14 Ibid., March 12, 1887.

15 Hull, *Volume* 3, 312.

16 Straight University merged with New Orleans University to form Dillard University in 1935.

17 Straight College Prospectus, 7. Straight College Collection, Will W. Alexander Library, Dillard University.

18 Prospectus 8, ibid.

19 Straight College Prospectus 7, ibid.

20 Perkins, "The Impact of 'The Cult of True Womanhood,'" 187.

21 Blassingame, *Black New Orleans*, 112.

22 Ibid., 118.

23 Giddings, *When and Where*, 108.

24 Brooks-Higginbotham, "Wresting with Respectability," parag 3.

25 Ibid., 49.

26 Cash, *African American Women*, 34

27 *The Women's Era* will be referred to as *TWE*.

28 *TWE*, Vol 1., No. 8, 1894. Library of Congress, Manuscript Division, Mary Church Terrell Papers.

29 Ibid.

30 Ibid.

31 Ibid.

32 To recognize Williams's career in education, there is a New Orleans College Prep school named in her honor. See https://nolacollegeprep.org/sylvanie-williams-college-prep.

33 "Fisk School," *Weekly Pelican*, March 12, 1887, 2.

34 Records for the schools during this period are unavailable.

35 Dunbar-Nelson, *TWE* VII No 7.

36 Ibid.

37 She married a prominent man who was the first Black man to graduate from Harvard's Law School and later became Boston's first African American municipal judge.

38 Ibid., 9.

39 Brooks-Higginbotham, "The Black Church," 188.

40 After Dunbar, both of her husbands were significantly light. She makes a reference in one of her diary entries of her niece Pauline spending time with a man she refers to as "ink spot" and "inky." Further, she engaged in preferences at Howard School. See *Integrating Delaware: The Reddings of Wilmington*. Newark: University of Delaware Press, 59.

41 Cash, *African American Women*, 38.

42 Giddings, *When and Where*, 93.

43 Feimster, *Southern Horrors*, 103.

44 Ibid., 102.

45 White, *Too Heavy a Load*, 24.

46 Ibid., 25.

47 Manuscript of speech, 1. See Box27, F459. Alice Dunbar-Nelson papers, Special Collections, University of Delaware Library, Newark, Delaware.

48 Ibid., 2.

49 Ibid.

50 Ibid., 3.

51 Ibid., 7.

52 *TWE* June 1895. Emory University's Women Writer's Project (online).

53 NACW 1896 minutes, 46.

54 Ibid., 52.

55 See *Unceasing Militant* for a detailed overview of the challenges Terrell faced in becoming the organization's leader.

56 At their 1896 meeting and under the leadership of Washington, they voted on the name of the organization, the officers, and on their articles of agreement.

57 *Southwestern Christian Advocate,* 4.

58 *TWE*, May 1895 Vol II No. 2.

59 A local newspaper reported that the Club received $95.00 for a group of young male entertainers who hosted a fundraiser.

60 According to the Dillard University website, in 1889, New Orleans University opened a medical department, including a school of pharmacy and a school of nursing. The medical department was named Flint Medical College and the affiliated facility was named the Sarah Goodridge Hospital and Nurse Training School. The medical college was discontinued in 1911, but the hospital, including the nursing school, was continued under the name Flint-Goodridge Hospital. (dillard.edu)Mrs. Caroline Mudge of Boston, Massachusetts, donated money to purchase a site for the hospital, which was renamed Sarah Goodridge Hospital in honor of her mother. After merging with Flint Medical College, the hospital was renamed Flint-Goodridge Hospital in 1915. In 1935, when Dillard University was formed, donations made to the university allowed for the purchase of the university's current site on Gentilly Boulevard in New Orleans and a new, separate site for Flint-Goodridge Hospital, which had been purchased by the university as part of the merger campaign. It opened on February 1, 1932, but closed in 1983.

61 *TWE*, Volume 2, I, 1.

Chapter 2

1 Davidson, "Marginal Spaces," 3.

2 Ibid., 54.

3 Curwood, *Stormy Weather*, 16.

4 Bell, *From a Girl's Point of View*, 211.

5 Ibid.

6 Ibid.

7 Ibid., 212.

8 Ibid., 217–18.

9 Ibid., 221.

10 Curwood, *Stormy Weather*, 16.

11 *Southwestern Christian Advocate*, 3.

12 Curwood, *Stormy Weather*, 18.

13 Ibid.

14 Ibid., 255.

15 Williams, "Report to the President," 6.

16 Dunbar-Nelson, "Violets and Other Tales," 12–13.

17 Ibid., 13.

18 Ibid.

19 Ibid.

20 Giddings, *In Search of Sisterhood*, 109.

21 Lorde, "Uses of the Erotic," 55.

22 Hull, *Color, Sex & Poetry*, 40.

23 Ibid., 41.

24 Ibid., 42.

25 Ibid.

26 Ibid., 12.

27 Washington, *The New Negro Woman*, 56.

28 Bell, *From a Girl's Point of View*, 221.

29 Gebhard, "Masculinity, Criminality, and Race," 344.

30 Hull, *Volume 1*, 137.

31 Ibid., 124.

32 Ibid., 125.

33 Dunbar-Nelson may be nodding to the idea of placage, popular among a practice that involved mothers of quadroons and other Creoles of color presented their daughters "to wealthy European men for the purpose of finding them a life partner." See Chapter One for more on this. Martin, "Placage and the Louisiana Gens," 65.

34 Ibid., 66.

35 *Southwestern Christian Advocate*, 8.

36 Ibid.

37 Brooks, "Alice Dunbar-Nelson's Local Colors," 12.

38 White, *Dark Continent of Our Bodies*, 37.

39 Hull, *Volume I*, 58.

40 Ibid., 149.

41 Brooks, "Alice Dunbar-Nelson's Local Colors," 12.

42   Stouck, "Identities in Crisis," 275.

43   West, "Religion, Race, and Gender," 18.

44   ADN to PLD, April 17, 1895.

45   Ibid.

46   Eleanor Alexander calls Alice Dunbar-Nelson racist (61–6). I address this claim further in Chapter 4.

47   Other well-known Louisiana writers, such as George Washington Cable, Grace King, and Kate Chopin, presented Creole communities to pose questions about racial identity, religious and social practices, and/or gender equality.

48   PLD to ADN, Feb. 16, 1896.

49   duCille, *The Coupling Convention*, 31.

50   Davis, *Southscapes*, 227.

Chapter 3

1   Tanritanir and Boynukara, "Letter Writing as Voice of Women," 2.

2   Hull, *Volume I*, 7.

3   A binary reading is possible, depending on the reader. Two of my students who identify as queer have argued that this poem may also be seen as a woman who is expressing desire for another woman. In effect, they see the use of Paul as masking this desire. I am thankful to them for offering an alternative reading that is quite plausible.

4   Hull, *Volume I*, 83.

5   Queer students have shared with me a queer analysis of this poem as being a desire of one woman for another.

6   Probably a reference to P. B. S. Pinchback, who also attended Straight.

7   Hull, *Give Us Each Day*, 268

8   PLD to ADN, July 9, 1895.

9   Ibid., June 4, 1896.

10   Alice Dunbar-Nelson to Arturo Schomburg. January 22, 1934. Schomburg Collection. Schomburg Center for Research in Black Culture, Manuscripts, Archives, and Rare Books Division.

11   Wiggins, *The Life and Works*, 67.

12   PLD to ADN, March 7, 1897.

13   ADN to PLD, October 6, 1897.

14   Curwood, *Stormy Weather*, 16.

15   Ibid.

16   According to Kevin K. Gaines in *Uplifting the Race: Black Leadership, Politics, and Culture in the Twentieth Century* (Chapel Hill: University of NC P, 1996),

the mission was "a settlement house for young black girls founded by Victoria Earle Matthews with the assistance of Booker T. Washington."

17 ADN to PLD, October 10, 1897.

18 Dunbar had a close friend named Sally, who referred to him as a brother.

19 PLD to ADN, November 19, 1897.

20 Metcalf, *Letters of Paul and Alice*, 243.

21 PLD to ADN, November 19, 1897.

22 Ibid., April 11, 1898.

23 Ibid., December 14, 1897.

24 Ibid., November 22, 1897.

25 Ibid., 13.

26 Sielke, *Reading Rape*, 19.

27 PLD to ADN, November 22, 1897.

28 Ibid., December 1, 1897.

29 Ibid.

30 Ibid., December 2, 1897.

31 Ibid., December 7, 1897.

32 Sielke, *Reading Rape*, 19.

33 Ibid.,16.

34 PLD to ADN, January 3, 1898.

35 Ibid.

36 Curwood, *Stormy Weather*, 13.

37 ADN to PLD, January 15, 1898.

38 Ibid.

39 Weir-Soley, *Eroticism*, 22.

40 Ibid., 22–3.

41 *New York Times*, March 19, 1905.

42 Kramer, "Uplifting Our 'Downtrodden Sisterhood,'" 246.

43 Ibid., 246–7.

44 Hartman, *Wayward Lives*, 28.

45 Ibid.

46 Ibid., 221.

47 Ibid.

48 Kramer, "Uplifting Our 'Downtrodden Sisterhood,'" 247.

49 Ibid., 248.

50 ADN to PLD, January 11, 1898.

51 Ibid., January 12, 1898.

52 Ibid., January 23, 1898.

53 Ibid., January 12, 1898.

54 Maritcha Lyons (1848–1929) was from a prominent African American family in New York. Lyons was a respected teacher and administrator in New York public schools and a clubwoman. She, along with Victoria Matthews, worked together in an anti-lynching campaign. More information about her is located in the Harry Williamson papers at the Schomburg Research Center.

55 Ibid., 256.

56 ADN to PLD, December 18, 1897.

57 PLD to AND, February 8, 1898.

58 Ibid., December 7, 1897.

59 Lorde, "Uses of the Erotic," 290.

60 PLD to ADN, March 8, 1898.

61 ADN to PLD, March 22, 1898.

62 PLD to ADN, September 19, 1895.

63 Ibid., March 21, 1898.

64 ADN to PLD, March 26, 1898.

Chapter 4

1 Gentry, *Paul Lawrence Dunbar*, 39.

2 ADN to PLD, August 12, 1898.

3 Ibid., August 31, 1898.

4 Ibid., September 13, 1898.

5 Ibid.

6 Ibid., September 20, 1898.

7 Alexander, *Lyrics of Sunshine*, 165.

8 Patricia Moore to ADN September 2, 1898.

9 If Alice kept a diary during this period, it is not in the archives. It is possible that she feared that her husband would read it.

10 Ibid., 166.

11 Hull, *Volume 2*, 75.

12 Ibid.

13 ADN to PLD, August 30, 1898.

14 Ibid., August 31, 1898.

15 Ibid., March 18, 1901.

16 Ibid., March 23, 1901.

17 This manuscript was not published. References are to the manuscript that is housed at the University of Delaware.

18 ADN to PLD, March 23, 1901.

19 Ibid., March 24, 1901.

20 Ibid., March 30, 1901.

21 Ibid., April, 1901.

22 See Paul Reynolds to ADN, July 27, 1900.

23 Pauline Young Papers. Atlanta University Center. Robert W. Woodruff Library Archives Research Center.

24 Manuscript p. 2. *Confessions of a Lazy Woman* manuscript. Box 14, F242. Alice Dunbar-Nelson papers, Special Collections, University of Delaware Library, Newark, Delaware.

25 *Confessions*, 1.

26 Ibid., 106.

27 Hull, *Volume 1*, 2.

28 Brooks, "Alice Dunbar," 10.

29 Hull, *Volume 1*, 12.

30 Ibid.

31 Brooks, "Alice Dunbar," 10.

32 Hull, *Volume I*, 5.

33 Ibid., xlv.

34 Weir-Soley, *Eroticism*, 2.

35 Ibid.

36 Hull, *Volume 1*, 75.

37 Ibid., 28.

38 West, "Religion, Race, and Gender," 13.

39 Brooks, "Alice Dunbar," 17.

40 Hull, *Volume I*, 6.

41 Alice Dunbar-Nelson wrote a series of essays for the *Journal of Negro History* that had been founded by her friend, Carter G. Woodson.

42 Ibid., 364.

43 Stouck, "Identities in Crisis," 286.

44 Hull, *Volume I*, 10.

45 ADN to PLD, March 25, 1901.

46 Hull, Volume I, 19.

47 Hull, *Volume 2*, 321.

48 West, "Religion, Race, and Gender," 24.

49 Hull, *Volume 2*, xxxviii.

50 Gebhard, "Masculinity, Criminality, and Race," 348. I agree with Gebhard, who argues against scholars, such as Akasha Hull, who believe the stories are exclusively about Irish youth:

Despite some critics' claims that the 'Steenth Street boys are Irish ghetto youth, only one of them bears a recognizably Irish surname. Her recurring characters—

Abe Powers, James Brown, Gus Schwartz, and Lesie Channing—have a more ambiguous racial and ethnic status, although they are most definitely not middle-class WASPS. Some of them might be black or mixed-race or even poor whites, and some might be children of Italian or German or Irish immigrants; in other words, they embody the population in the poorest New York neighborhoods.

When Alice lived in New York, she reported to Paul that she helped children of an African American and German mother, she taught Jewish children, and she taught African American boys and girls at the Mission and in the school system.

51 Hull, *Volume 2*, 137.

52 Ibid.

53 Ibid., 138.

54 Ibid., 141.

55 Ibid.

56 Ibid., 103.

57 Ibid.

58 Ibid.

59 Ibid.

60 Ibid.

61 Ibid.

62 Ibid., 105.

63 "A Celebrated Case," 14.

64 Metcalf, *Letters of Paul and Alice*, 12.

65 Brooks-Higgobatham, For Harriet parag 8.

66 Victoria Matthews to ADN, page 2. See Box 5 F126. Alice Dunbar-Nelson papers, Special Collections, University of Delaware Library, Newark, Delaware.

67 Ibid., 3.

68 Alice did not provide details, but James Young, Leila's husband of about five years, abandoned his wife and four children "because of personal, familial, and financial difficulties" (Hull, *Diary*, 214). As a result, Leila, the children, and Patsy Moore moved to live with the Dunbars in Washington, DC.

69 PLD to ADN, May 7, 1903.

Chapter 5

1 Eckman and Alsberg, *Delaware*, 67.

2 Marks, *A History of African American of Delaware and Maryland's Eastern Shore*.

3 Holland, *The Erotic Life*, 46.

4 For more information about the Fleetwoods, see "The Comprehensive Guide to Victoria and George Cross," HYPERLINK "http://www.victoriacrossonline

.co.uk/christian-a-fleetwood/4592071056" http://www.victoriacrossonline.co
.uk/christian-a-fleetwood/4592071056; and *Whispers of Cruel Wrongs: The
Correspondence of Louisa Jacobs and Her Circle of Friends*, edited by Mary
Mallard. Their papers are housed at the Library of Congress.

5 Hull, *Color, Sex & Poetry*, 65.

6 Ibid.

7 Christian Fleetwood to ADN, February 14, 1906, 1.

8 Ibid., 5.

9 Ibid., 1909, 1.

10 Ibid.

11 Ibid.

12 Ibid.

13 Ibid.

14 Ibid., 4.

15 Ibid., 5.

16 Ibid., July 13, 1911, 1.

17 Ibid., 3.

18 Somerville, *Queering the Color Line*, 6.

19 As far as I can tell, "Natalie" was not published during her lifetime.

20 Carbado, McBride, Weise, and White, *Black Like Us*, 3.

21 The narrator refers to him as Howard, and Marion calls him George. I will use
Howard in my analysis.

22 Bloomberg, *Tracing Arachne's Web*, 71.

23 Dubar-Nelson, *A Modern Undine*, 3.

24 Ibid., 5.

25 Ibid.

26 Ibid., 6.

27 Ibid., 13.

28 Ibid., 10.

29 Ibid., 67.

30 Ibid., 21.

31 Ibid., 36.

32 Richardson, *The Queer Limit*, 13.

33 Ibid., 10.

34 Ibid.

35 duCille, *The Coupling Convention*, 87.

36 Ibid.

37 Hull, *Volume 3*, 198.

38 Ibid.

39 Ibid.

40 Ibid., 200.

Chapter 6

1 Richardson, *The Queer Limit*, 6.

2 Shepard, "The Other's Other," 41.

3 Hull, *Give Us Each Day*, 25.

4 Hull, "Researching Alice," 316.

5 Edwina B. Kruse to ADN, October 22, 1907. See Box 8 F190. Alice Dunbar-Nelson papers, Special Collections, University of Delaware Library, Newark, Delaware.

6 Ibid.

7 Ibid., October 4, 1907.

8 Ibid., October 5, 1907.

9 Ibid., October 23, 1907.

10 Ibid, October 26, 1907.

11 Ibid.

12 Lorde, "Uses of the Erotic," 49.

13 Tate, *Domestic Allegories*, 109.

14 Kruse to ADN, October 12, 1907.

15 Cornell Handbook, 14. Alice Dunbar-Nelson papers, Special Collections, University of Delaware Library, Newark, Delaware.

16 Ibid., 15.

17 Kruse to ADN, October 19, 1907.

18 Ibid.

19 Ibid.

20 Kruse to ADN, May 25, 1908.

21 Cornell Handbook, 18.

22 Bradley, "Progenitors of Progress," 70.

23 Fleetwood to ADN, June 12, 1910, 3.

24 Ibid.

25 Ibid.

26 Hull, *Give Us Each Day*, 397.

27 Ibid.

28 Ibid., 432.

29 Ibid.

30 Ibid., 433.

31 Kruse to ADN, May 18, 1908.

32 Hull, *Give Us Each Day*, 67.

33 Ibid.

34 Hull, *Volume 2*, 110.

35 Ibid.

36 Ibid., 109.

37 Howard High School was part of the landmark 1954 *Brown vs. Topeka Board of Education* case, known for its desegregation of public schools. It was originally filed as *Gebhart vs. Belton*, when African American Delaware complainants filed for access to segregated Claymont High School.

38 Dunbar-Nelson, "The Training of a Teacher of English," 7. See Box 22, F13. Alice Dunbar-Nelson papers, Special Collections, University of Delaware Library, Newark, Delaware.

39 Chapell, 3. Unpublished essay, *The Delaware Historical Society TypeScript Files.*

40 This play has not been published.

41 O'Malley, "Staging the Color Line," 2.

42 Ibid., 3.

43 Ibid., 1.

44 Anna Broadnax was one of several teachers at Howard who lived with Kruse for years. She inherited the house upon Kruse's death.

45 Gertrude Baldwin also lived in the Kruse house.

46 Hull, *Color, Sex & Poetry*, 374–5.

Chapter 7

1 She spells his name as "Bobo" and "Bobbo" in her diary.

2 Taken from the Finding Aid of the Alice Dunbar-Nelson paper at the University of Delaware.

3 Garvey, "Alice Moore Dunbar-Nelson's Suffrage Work," 310.

4 Brown, "To Catch the Vision of Freedom," 82.

5 Giddings, *In Search of Sisterhood*, 124.

6 Sykes taught at Howard. She also marched in the 1920 national women's suffrage parade, was a charter member of the Wilmington NAACP chapter, and a board member of the Kruse School. *News Journal (Wilmington, DE)* (January 2, 1971, Page 29).

7 Boylan, *Biography of Mary J. Johnson Woodlen*, 1.

8 Ibid., 1.

9 News articles referenced in this section are located in the scrapbook.

10 Hart, "A Cry in the Wilderness," 74.

11 Paul Laurence Dunbar died in 1906, not in 1905.

12 Articles cited in this section, *Williamsport Sun* and the *Ledger* are found in her scrapbook in the UD archives. Given how they are cut, some citation information is no longer visible. *Ledger*, August 7, 1915. Probably the *Public Ledger*.

13 Garvey, "Alice Moore Dunbar-Nelson's Suffrage Work," 321.

14 Deane, *Williamsport Sun*, August 12, 1915.

15 *Ledger*, August 7, 1915.

16 *Swarthmore News*, July 30, 1915.

17 Deane, *Williamsport Sun*, August 12, 1915.

18 *Swarthmore News*, July 30, 1915.

19 *Williamsport Sun*, August 14, 1915.

20 Deane, *Newark Evening News*, October 9, 1915.

21 *The Advocate-Verdict*, October 30, 1915.

22 Ibid.

23 Deane, *Williamsport Sun*, August 12, 1915.

24 *The Advocate-Verdict*, October 30, 1915.

25 *Williamsport Sun*, August 14, 1915.

26 *Chester Times*, July 14, 1915.

27 *Williamsport Sun*, August 4, 1915

28 *The Harrisburg Telegraph*, October 27, 1915.

29 *The Pittsburg Courier*, October 26, 1915.

30 *The York Daily*, November 2, 1915.

31 Ibid.

32 "Distinguished Women to Meet in Baltimore," 2.

33 Ibid.

34 Hull, *Diary*, 134.

35 Louis Redding (1901–8) was a graduate of Howard during Kruse's years as principal. As a civil rights attorney, he successfully fought to desegregate the University of Delaware and was the lead attorney in Delaware's suit to desegregate schools, which was part of the landmark Brown v. Board 1954 decision.

36 Marks, Part 1, 13.

37 "Wilmington, Del.-Oct. 8," 1.

38 "Race Represented on Charter Committee," 3.

39 Terborg-Penn, *African American Women*, 19.

40 Materson, *For the Freedom of Her Race*, 109.

41 Ibid., 129.

42 References made to the copy of the speech located in the archives at the University of Delaware.

43 Dunbar-Nelson, "Why I Am," 2.

44 Ibid.

45 Ibid.

46 As of June 30, 2021, after nearly 200 proposed anti-lynching bills have failed, including the Dyer bill, lynching has yet to be outlawed. The last attempt stalled in the Senate.

47 Ibid., 3.

48 Ibid., 4.

49 Ibid.

50 Ibid., 7.

51 Ibid., 11.

52 Ibid., 19.

53 Parker, *Unceasing Militant*, 3401.

54 Alice Dunbar to Arthur Schomburg on October 19, 1913. Schomburg Center for Research in Black Culture, Manuscripts, Archives, and Rare Books Division.

55 Manning, "Preface," *Negro Eloquence*, vi.

56 Ibid.

57 Letter written by Alice Moore Dunbar to Arthur Schomburg on September 23, 1913. Schomburg Center for Research in Black Culture, Manuscripts, Archives, and Rare Books Division.

58 Dunbar-Nelson to Arthur Schomburg, September 23, 1913.

59 Dunbar-Nelson, *Negro Eloquence*, 67.

60 Ibid.

61 Ibid., 118.

62 Ibid., 427.

63 Ibid., v.

64 Hull, *Diary*, 75.

65 Hull, *Color*, 94.

66 Curwood, *Stormy Weather*, 14.

67 Dunbar-Nelson, *Dunbar Reader*, Table of Contents.

68 Ibid., Preface.

69 Ibid.

70 Ibid., 240.

71 Ibid.

72 Ibid.

73 Ibid., 226.

74 Hull, *Diary*, 58.

75 Ibid., 124–5.

76 Ibid., 51.

Chapter 8

1 I make a distinction between the Harlem Renaissance as the cultural expression movement among Black artists, writers, and performers and the New Negro Movement, which encompasses not only the cultural movement but also political and social reform.

2 Interview with Evelyn Brooks-Higginbotham, *For Harriet*, paragraph 8.

3 Chapman, *Prove It On Me*, 7.

4 Ibid.

5 Locke, *The New Negro*, 447.

6 "Necessity for Negro Relief" is a document located in the Alice Dunbar-Nelson papers at the University of Delaware.

7 Ibid.

8 Ibid.

9 Letter from Ruth Gregling to Alice Dunbar-Nelson, February, 12, 1918. Alice Dunbar-Nelson papers. University of Delaware.

10 Ibid.

11 Letter from Alice Dunbar-Nelson to W. E. B. Du Bois on May 20, 1917. University of Massachusetts-Amherst Library.

12 Folder 461. Alice Dunbar-Nelson papers. University of Delaware.

13 As the name suggests, Dunbar High was renamed in honor of Paul Laurence Dunbar. It was built as the first school for "colored" children in Washington, DC. http://www.dunbardc.org/home/about-us.

14 See Box 6 Folders 152-154 of the Alice Dunbar-Nelson papers. University of Delaware.

15 Hull, *Color*, 67.

16 "War Work of Colored Women," 4.

17 Ibid.

18 Ibid.

19 Chapman, *Prove It on Me*, 5.

20 Ibid.

21 A prominent leader in higher education, he served as president of Morehouse College and Atlanta University.

22 "Pres. Harding Receives Committee and Petition," 1.

23 Hull, *Diary*, 81.

24 Ibid.

25 Ibid.

26 Ibid.

27 Ibid.

28 Ibid. Also see "President Harding receives Committee, 1." For Johnson's full speech.

29   Ibid.

30   Hull, *Volume 2*, 81–2.

31   Hull, *Diary*, 82.

32   Reference to Hallie Q. Brown who was the national president from 1920 until 1924.

33   The article does not give the publishers' information, only that it was published in Wilmington, Delaware. This may have been published by the *Wilmington Advocate*.

34   Approximately 300 African Americans of Black Tulsa were killed by White rioters following a report that a Black man had touched a White elevator operator in 1921. http://tulsahistory.org/learn/online-exhibits/the-tulsa-race -riot/.

35   *Sunday Morning Star*, January 30, 1927.

36   Ibid.

37   Ibid.

38   "Columbus: A Play" is an unpublished manuscript located in Box 20, Folder 13, in the ADN archives.

39   Brooks-Higginbotham, "Wrestling with Respectability," *For Harriet*.

Chapter 9

1   Hull, *Diary*, 164.

2   Ibid., 166–7.

3   A respected Black theater group cofounded by W. E. B. Du Bois in 1925.

4   Hull, *Diary*, 167.

5   Ibid., 43.

6   As I will discuss later, Alice and her husband edited a newspaper. She met with Micheaux in the office of the *Wilmington Advocate*.

7   Ibid., 74.

8   Ibid., 75.

9   In reference to the unpublished manuscript in Box 20, F367, in the Alice Dunbar-Nelson papers at the University of Delaware.

10   Name of Robert Niels was likely inspired by Robert Nelson.

11   In reference to the unpublished manuscript in Box 20, F372, in the Alice Dunbar-Nelson papers at the University of Delaware.

12   Ibid., manuscript p. 2.

13   Ibid., 4.

14   Ibid., 6.

15 Ibid., 7.

16 Ibid., 16.

17 The date this was written is unknown, but references put it after the First World War.

18 Brooks-Higginbotham, 199.

19 Washburn, *The African American Newspaper*, 22.

20 Ibid., 116.

21 Ibid., 118.

22 Hull, *Diary*, 62.

23 Ibid., 26.

24 Ibid., 129.

25 Probably Bessie Bowser, who was a fellow club member.

26 Hull, *Diary*, 129.

27 Ibid., 55.

28 Ibid., 43.

29 Ibid., 127.

Chapter 10

1 Box 26, F477 in the Alice Dunbar-Nelson papers at the University of Delaware.

2 Emery, *Writing to Belong*, 291.

3 Ibid., 292.

4 Washburn, *The African American Newspaper*, 133.

5 Hull, *Volume 2*, 110.

6 Ibid.

7 Ibid., 111.

8 Ibid.

9 Ibid., 124.

10 Ibid., 125.

11 Mitchell, "Silences Broken," 103.

12 Letter from Alice Dunbar-Nelson written to W. E. B. Du Bois on Jan. 7, 1923. W. E. B. Du Bois papers. University of Massachusetts-Amherst.

13 Jean, "'Warranted' Lynchings," 354.

14 An article titled "Klan Menace to U.S. says Former K.K.K. Official" in *The Niagara Falls Gazette* gives details of the letter.

15 Hull, *Volume 2*, 118.

16 Vandiver reports that he was also known as Chandler Colding by the press.

17 Jean, "'Warranted' Lynchings," 354.

18 Vandiver, *Lethal Punishment*, 25.

19 Ibid., 73.

20 Jean, "'Warranted' Lynchings," 364.

21 Hull, *Volume 2*, 122.

22 The Emmett Till Anti-Lynching Bill was passed by the US House of Representatives and, as of July 3, 2020, stalled in the US Senate. Till was lynched by two men at the age of fourteen while spending his summer break in Mississippi in 1955. Over 200 anti-lynching bills have been introduced. This latest bill was introduced as a response to the high-profiled murders of Black men, by police, most notably George Floyd of Minnesota, Minneapolis, on May 25, 2020, and the discovery of at least five Black men found hanging from trees in different parts of the country.

23 Hull, *Volume 2*, 115.

24 Ibid.

25 Ibid., 130.

26 I have been unable to find details about this bill.

27 Hull, *Volume 2*, 137.

28 Ibid.

29 Ibid., 138.

30 Ibid.

31 Ibid.,140–1.

32 Ibid., 157.

33 Ibid., 170.

34 Ibid.

35 See Jinx C. Broussard's *Giving a Voice to the Voiceless: Four Pioneering Black Women Journalists*.

36 Dr. Ossian Sweet and his brother, Henry, faced charges for the death of a White man and the shooting of another in 1925, when they defended themselves against a group of neighbors who were unhappy about Ossian's decision to move his family into their Detroit neighborhood. See Kevin Boyle's *Arc of Justice: A Saga of Race, Civil Rights, and Murder in the Jazz Age* (New York: Henry Holt, 2004).

37 Hull, *Volume 2*, 174.

38 Ibid., 193.

39 Ibid., 192.

40 Ibid.

41 See Box 9, F214. Alice Dunbar-Nelson Papers at the University of Delaware.

42 Hull, *Volume 2*, 131.

43 Ibid., 133.

44 Early, *Ain't But a Place*, 280.

45 Hull, *Volume 2*, 148.

46 Ibid.

47 Ibid.

48 Ibid., 149.

49 Ibid., 150.

50 Evelyn Preer was a well-known light-skinned African American stage and screen actress who had starred in several of Oscar Micheaux's films, most notably *Within Our Gates*.

51 Hull, *Volume 2*, 154.

52 Although Cullen's poem "Baltimore" reflects on being called a "nigger" by a Baltimorean, the poem was published in 1925, before the incident at the Emerson Hotel.

53 Hull, *Volume 2*, 152.

54 Ibid., 178–9.

55 Ibid., 178.

56 Hull, *Volume 2*, 179.

57 Ibid.

58 Ibid., 181.

59 Ibid., 181–2.

60 Ibid., 200.

61 Ibid.

62 Ibid., 201.

63 Ibid., 229.

64 Ibid.

65 Ibid., 247.

66 Ibid., 254.

67 Ibid., 223.

68 Ibid., 224.

69 Ibid., 225.

70 Ibid.

71 Ibid., 234.

72 Ibid., 235.

73 Ibid., 238.

74 Washburn, *The African American Newspaper*, 92–3.

75 Labeled as "Eulogy" in Pauline Young Papers. Atlanta University Center Robert W. Woodruff Library. Archives Research Center. This may be mislabeled as it appears to be in reference to the Wheeler photo that had been painted eight years before her death.

Chapter 11

1 References to these articles are found in Box 25, F453. Alice Dunbar-Nelson Papers, University of Delaware.

2 See *Integrating Delaware: The Reddings of Wilmington*. Newark: University of Delaware Press, 2003.

3 Letters from Du Bois are located in the Du Bois papers at the University of Massachusetts-Amherst.

4 Ibid.

5 Ibid.

6 Ibid., letter dated, Jan. 13, 1930.

7 Ibid., letter dated, Jan. 17, 1930.

8 See Box 26, F454. Alice Dunbar-Nelson papers, University of Delaware.

9 Ibid.

10 Ibid., dated February 22, 1930.

11 Ibid., dated March 1, 1930.

12 Ibid., March 22, 1930. Jennie Dee Booth Moton was the wife of Tuskegee's second president.

13 Hull, *Diary*, 355.

14 Ibid.

15 Ibid., 357.

16 Ibid., 358.

17 Ibid.

18 *Pittsburg Courier*, 6.

19 Hull, *Diary*, 358.

20 Ibid., 356.

21 Ibid., 92.

22 Hull, *Diary*, 365.

23 Nelson, 266.

24 See Ma Rainey, "Prove It on Me Blues," 1928.

25 Vogel, *The Scene of Harlem Cabaret*, 21.

26 Hull, *Diary*, 255.

27 Ibid., 309.

28 Hughes-Watkins, "Fay M. Jackson and the Color Line," 119.

29 Hull, *Diary*, 359.

30 Letter to Callis, Howard University.

31 Hull, *Diary*, 360.

32 Lorde, "Uses of Erotic," 59.

33 Richardson, *The Queer Limit of Black Memory*, 11.

34 Pearl, "Sweet Home," 298.

35 Somerville, *Queering the Color Line*, 92.

36 Hull, *Diary*, 362.

37 Ibid.

38 Ibid., 54.

39 Ibid., 362.

40 Ibid., 363.

41 Ibid.

42 Ibid., 366.

43 Ibid.

44 Hart, "A Cry in the Wilderness," 75.

45 Hull, *Diary*, 367.

46 Ibid., 374.

47 Pearl, "Sweet Home," 299.

48 See Box 30, F481 of the Alice Dunbar-Nelson papers at the University of Delaware for copies of articles about her visit.

49 Ibid., *The Recorder*, October 17, 1931.

50 Hull, *Diary*, 324.

51 Ibid., 324.

52 Ibid., 326.

53 Ibid.

54 Ibid.

55 Ibid., 122.

56 Ibid., 210.

57 Ibid., 202.

58 See the W. E. B. Du Bois papers, University of Massachusetts-Amherst.

59 Ibid., Dunbar-Nelson to Du Bois, dated October 23, 1930.

60 Hull, *Diary*, 418.

61 Ibid., 459.

62 Box 23, F442 of the Alice Dunbar-Nelson papers. University of Delaware.

63 Hull, *Diary*, 461.

64 Ibid.

65 Ibid., 58.

66 Ibid., 319.

67 Redding, *On being Negro*, Chapter 3, parga 2.

68 Hull, *Diary*, 374.

Chapter 12

1 Ibid., 413.

2 Ibid., 103.

3 The speech and letters to Alice Dunbar-Nelson and from Robert Nelson to "A friend" are located in Box 23, Folder 431, in the ADN papers at the University of Delaware.

4 Mary Leila Young to Pauline Young. Atlanta University Center. Robert W. Woodroff Library Archives Research Center.

5 Du Bois to ADN, December 15, 1934. *W. E. B. Du Bois Papers (MS 312).*

6 Labeled as "Eulogy" in Pauline Young Papers. Atlanta University Center Robert W. Woodruff Library. Archives Research Center.

7 Hull, *Diary*, 325.

8 In reference to her Pennsylvania Death Certificate.

BIBLIOGRAPHY

"A Gracious Lady Passes Away." *The Pittsburgh Courier*, October 5, 1935, n.p.

"A Celebrated Case." *The Evening Star*, January 13, 1902, 14.

Alexander, Eleanor. *Lyrics of Sunshine and Shadow the Tragic Courtship and Marriage of Paul Laurence Dunbar and Alice Ruth Moore: A History of Love and Violence among the African American Elite*. New York: New York University Press, 2001.

"Alice Dunbar Nelson's Death Shocks Nation." *The Pittsburgh Courier*, September 28, 1935, 10.

Alice Dunbar Nelson Papers. Newark: University of Delaware Library.

"Alice Dunbar Nelson Thrills Great Los Angeles Audience on World Peace and the Negro." *The California Eagle*, March 14, 1930, 1.

"Alice Takes to the Air." *The Pittsburgh Courier*, April 3, 1930, 6.

American Interracial Peace Committee, Letter from the American Interracial Peace Committee to W. E. B. Du Bois, October 23, 1930. In *W. E. B. Du Bois Papers (MS 312)*. Univ. of Mass: Special Collections and University Archives.

Aslakson, Kenneth. "The 'Quadroon-Plaçage' Myth of Antebellum New Orleans: Anglo-American (Mis)Interpretations of a French-Caribbean Phenomenon." *Journal of Social History* 45, no. 3 (2012): 709.

Bell, Lillian. *From a Girl's Point of View*. New York: Harper & Brothers Publishers, 1897.

Battle, Juan, and Sandra L. Barnes, eds. *Black Sexualities: Probing Powers, Passions, Practices, and Policies*. New Brunswick: Rutgers University Press, 2009.

Blassingame, John. Black New Orleans, *1860–1880*. Chicago: University of Chicago Press, 1973.

Bloomberg, Kristel M. *Tracing Arachne's Web: Myth and Feminist Fiction*. Gainesville: University Press of Florida, 2001.

Boylan, Anne M. *Biography of Mary J. Johnson Woodlen, 1870–1933*. Alexandria: Alexander Street database.

Bradley, Stefan. "Progenitors of Progress: A Brief History of the Jewels of Alpha Phi Alpha." In *Alpha Phi Alpha: A Legacy of Greatness, the Demands of Transcendence*, edited by Gregory S. Parks and Stefan M. Bradley, 67–92. Lexington: University Press of Kentucky, 2012.

Broadnax, Anna. "Howard High Pride of Wilmington," *Philadelphia Tribune*, September 19, 1940.

Brooks, Kristina. "Alice Dunbar-Nelson's Local Colors of Ethnicity, Class and Place." *MELUS* 23, no. 11 (1998): 3–26.

Brooks-Higginbotham, Evelyn. "The Black Church, A Gender Perspective." Essay. In *African American Religious Thought: An Anthology*, edited by Cornell West and Eddie S. Glaude, 187–208. Louisville: Westminster John Knox Press, 2003.

Brooks-Higginbotham, Evelyn. Interview with Kimberly Foster. "Wrestling with Respectability in the Age of #BlackLivesMatter: A Dialogue." *For Harriet*, October 13, 2015. forharriet.com

Broussard, Jinx C. *Giving a Voice to the Voiceless: Four Pioneering Black Women Journalists*. Oxfordshire: Routledge, 2004.

Brown, Elsa Barkley. "To Catch the Vision of Freedom: Reconstructing Southern Black Women's Political History, 1865–1880." In *African American Women and the Vote, 1837–1965*, edited by Ann Gordon, Bettye Collier-Thomas, John H. Bracey, Arlene Avakian and Joyce Berkman, 66–99. Amherst: University of Massachusetts Press, 1997.

Carbado, Devon W, Dwight A McBride, Donald Weise, and Evelyn C White. *Black Like Us : A Century of Lesbian, Gay and Bisexual African American Fiction* (2nd ed.). Berkeley, CA: Cleis, 2011.

Carlson, Shirley J. "Black Ideals of Womanhood in the Late Victorian Era." *The Journal of Negro History* 77, no. 2 (1992): 61–73.

Cash, Floris B. *African American Women and Social Action: The Clubwomen and Volunteerism from Jim Crow to the New Deal, 1896–1936*. Westport: Greenwood, 2001.

Chapman, Erin. *Prove it On Me: New Negroes, Sex, and Popular Culture in the 1920s*. Oxford: Oxford University Press, 2012.

"A Complete And Comprehensive Narrative Of Racial Courage, Capacity And Rare Qualities As A 100." Broad Ax (Chicago, Illinois), April 5, 1919: 6. *Readex: America's Historical Newspapers*.

Cooper, Brittney C. *Beyond Respectability: The Intellectual Thought of Race Women*. Champaign: University of Illinois Press, 2017.

Cornell Handbook, Alice Dunbar-Nelson papers, Special Collections, University of Delaware Library, Newark, Delaware.

Curwood, Anastasia. *Stormy Weather: Middle Class African American Marriages Between the Two Worlds*. Chapel Hill: University of North Carolina Press, 2013.

Davidson, Adenike M. "Marginal Spaces, Marginal Texts: Alice Dunbar-Nelson and the African American Prose Poem." *Southern Quarterly* 44, no. 1 (2006): 51–64.

Davis, Thadious M. *Southscapes: Geographies of Race, Region, and Literature*. Chapel Hill: University of North Carolina Press, 2011.

"Delta Sigma Theta Data." *The California Eagle*, September 22, 1933.

Distinguished Women to Meet in Baltimore. New York Age (New York), June 22, 1916: 2. *Readex: America's Historical Newspapers*.

Drury, Doreen. "Love Ambition and 'Invisible Footnotes' in the Life and Writing of Pauli Murray." In *Black Genders and Sexualities*, edited by Shaka McGlotten and Dana-Ain Davis, 69–84. Palgrave Macmillan, 2012.

Du Bois, W. E. B, Letter from W. E. B. Du Bois to Nina Du Bois, May 20, 1929. In *W. E. B. Du Bois Papers (MS 312)*. University of Massachusetts: Special Collections and University Archives.

Du Bois, W. E. B. Letter from W. E. B. Du Bois to The American Interracial Peace Committee, May 26, 1930. In *W. E. B. Du Bois Papers (MS 312)*. University of Massachusetts: Special Collections and University Archives.

Du Bois, W. E. B. Letter from W. E. B. Du Bois to the American Interracial Peace Committee, April 30, 1930. In *W. E. B. Du Bois Papers (MS 312)*. University of Massachusetts: Special Collections and University Archives.

Du Bois, W. E. B. Letter from W. E. B. Du Bois to Alice Dunbar Nelson, December 15, 1934. In *W. E. B. Du Bois Papers (MS 312)*. University of Massachusetts: Special Collections and University Archives.

duCille, Ann. *The Coupling Convention: Sex, Text, and Tradition in Black Women's Fiction*. Oxford: Oxford University Press, 1993.

duCille, Ann. "The Occult of True Black Womanhood: Critical Demeanor and Black Feminist Studies." *Signs* 19, no. 3 (1996): 591–629.

Dunbar-Nelson, Alice, Letter from Alice to Arturo Schomburg, September 23, 1913.

Dunbar-Nelson, Alice. *The Dunbar Speaker and Entertainer: Containing the Best Prose and Poetic Selections by and About the Negro race, With Programs Arranged for Special Entertainments*. London: Forgotten Books, 2017.

Dunbar-Nelson, Alice. *Laughing to Stop Myself from Crying*. Baltimore: Black Classics, 2000.

Dunbar-Nelson, Alice. "Little Excursions Week by Week." *The California Eagle*, December 6, 1929.

Dunbar-Nelson, Alice. *Masterpieces of Negro Eloquence, 1818–1913*. Mineola: Dover Publications, 2000.

Dunbar-Nelson, Alice. "People of Color." *Journal of Negro History* 2, no. 1: 51–78.

Dunbar-Nelson, Alice. "So it Seems." *The Pittsburgh Courier*, February 22, 1930.

Dunbar-Nelson, Alice. "So it Seems." *The Pittsburgh Courier*, March 15, 1930.

Dunbar-Nelson, Alice. "So it Seems." *The Pittsburgh Courier*, March 22, 1930.

Dunbar-Nelson, Alice. "So it Seems." *The Pittsburgh Courier*, March 29 1930.

Dunbar-Nelson, Alice. "So it Seems." *The Pittsburgh Courier*, April 4, 1930.

Dunbar-Nelson, Alice. "Violets and Other Tales." *The Monthly Review*, 1895.

Dunbar-Nelson, Alice. *The Women's Era*. Emory Women Writers Resource Project. http://womenwriters.digitalscholarship.emory.edu

Early, Gerald. *Ain't But A Place: An Anthology of African American Writings about St. Louis*. St. Louis: Missouri Historical Society Press, 1998.

Eckman, Jeannette, and Henry G. Alsberg, eds. Delaware: *A Guide to the First State*. Hastings House, 1955.

Elam, Michele and Paul C. Taylor. "DuBois' Erotics." In *Critical American Studies: Next to the Color Line: Gender, Sexuality, and W. E. B. Du Bois*, edited by Susan Gillman and Alys Eve Weinbaum, 209–33. South Minneapolis: University of Minnesota Press, 2007.

Emery, Jacqueline. "Writing to Belong: Alice Dunbar-Nelson's Newspaper Columns in the African American Press." *Legacy: A Journal of American Writers* 33, no. 2 (2016): 286–309.

"Fisk Schools." *Weekly Pelican* (New Orleans, Louisiana), January 29, 1887: 2. *Readex: America's Historical Newspapers*.

"Fisk School." Weekly Pelican (New Orleans, Louisiana), March 12, 1887: 2. Readex: America's Historical Newspapers.

Feimster, Crystal N. *Southern Horrors: Women and the Politics of Rape and Lynching*. Cambridge: Harvard University Press, 2009.

Foster, Frances S. *"Til Death or Distance Do Us Part": Love and Marriage in African America*. Oxford: Oxford University Press, 2010.

Gaines, Kevin K. *Uplifting the Race: Black Leadership, Politics, and Culture in the Twentieth Century*. Chapel Hill: University of North Carolina Press, 1996.

Garvey, Ellen Gruber. "Alice Moore Dunbar-Nelson's Suffrage Work: The View From Her Scrapbook." *Legacy: A Journal of American Women Writers* 33, no. 2 (2016): 310–35.

Gebhard, Caroline. "Masculinity, Criminality, and Race: Alice Dunbar-Nelson's Creole Boy Stories." *Legacy: A Journal of American Women Writers* 33, no. 2 (2016): 336–60.

Gentry, Tony. *Paul Laurence Dunbar: Poet*. Chelsea, VT: Chelsea Publishing, 1989.

Giddings, Paula. *In Search of Sisterhood: Delta Sigma Theta and the Challenge of the Black Sorority Movement*. New York: William Morrow Paperbacks, 1988.

Giddings, Paula. *When and Where I Enter: The Impact of Black Women on Race and Sex in America*. New York: Bantam Books, 1985.

Gordon, Ann D., and Bettye Collier-Thomas. *African American Women and the Vote, 1837–1965*. Amherst: University of Massachusetts Press, 1997.

Hammonds, Evelynn. "Black (W)holes and the Geometry of Black Female Sexuality." In *The Black Studies Reader*, edited by Jacqueline Bobo, Cynthia Hudley, and Claudine Michel, 301–15. London: Taylor & Francis Group, 2004.

Hart, Betty. *Women's Studies Quarterly* 17, no. 3/4 (1989): 74–8.

Holland, Sharon. *The Erotic Life of Racism*. Durham: Duke University Press, 2012.

Hughes-Watkins, Lae'l. "Fay M. Jackson and the Color Line: The First African American Foreign Correspondent for the Associated Negro Press." *Journal of Pan African Studies* 3, no. 2 (1999): 119–34.

Hull, Gloria (Akasha) T. *Color, Sex & Poetry: Three Women Writers of the Harlem Renaissance*. Bloomington: Indiana University Press, 1987.

Hull, Gloria (Akasha) T. *Give Us Each Day: The Diary of Alice Dunbar Nelson*. New York: WW Norton & Co., 1986.

Hull, Gloria (Akasha) T. *The Works of Alice Dunbar-Nelson: Volumes 1–3*. Oxford: Oxford University Press, 1988.

Hull, Gloria (Akasha) T. "Researching Alice Dunbar-Nelson: A Personal and Literary Perspective." *Feminist Studies* 6, no. 2: 314–20.

Irwin-Mulcahy, Judith. "American Heteroglossia: Open-Cell Regionalism and the New Orleans Short Fiction of Alice Dunbar-Nelson." *Discourse* 21, no. 1 (2007): 120–39.

Jean, Susan. "Warranted Lynchings: Narratives of Mob Violence in White Southern Newspapers, 1880–1950." *American Nineteenth Century History* 6, no. 3 (2005): 351–72.

Jones Bumbry, Julia. "Talk O' Town." *The Pittsburgh Courier*, September 26, 1935.

Kellor, Francis. "The Problem of the Young Negro Girl from the South." *New York Times*, March 19, 1905.

Kramer, Steve. "Uplifting Our 'Downtrodden Sisterhood': Victoria Earle Matthews and New York City's White Mission, 1897–1907." *The Journal of African American History* 91, no. 3 (2006): 243–66.

Lee, Shayne. *Erotic Revolutionaries Black Women, Sexuality, and Popular Culture.* New York: Hamilton Books, 2010.

Lewis, Christopher S. "Cultivating Black Lesbian Shamelessness: Alice Walker's The Color Purple." *Rocky Mountain Review* 66, no. 2: 158–75.

Molesworth, Charles, ed. *The Works of Alain Locke.* New York: Oxford University Press, Incorporated, 2012.

Lorde, Audre. "Uses of the Erotic." *Sister Outsider: Essays and Speeches.* Crossing Press, 1984.

"Los Angeles To Hear Alice Dunbar Nelson." *The California Eagle*, February 28, 1930.

Martin, Joan. "Placage and the Louisiana Gens de Couleur Libre: How Race and Sex Defined the Lifestyles of Free Women of Color." In *Creoles: The History and Legacy of Louisiana's Free People of Color*, edited by Sybil Kein, 42–56. Baton Rouge: Louisiana State University Press, 2000.

Marks, Carole C., ed. *A History of African American of Delaware and Maryland's Eastern Shore.* Wilmington: Delaware Heritage Press Book, 1996.

Moore, Alice. *The Women's Era. Mary Church Terrell Papers, 1851–1962.* Washington, DC: Library of Congress.

Materson, Lisa G. *For the Freedom of Her Race: Black Women and Electoral Politics in Illinois, 1877–1932.* Chapel Hill: UNC Press, 2009.

"Meeting Minutes." 21 July 1896. Microform. *Records of the National Association of Colored Women's Clubs, 1895–1992* (1993): Reel 1, Frame 0028.

Metcalf, Eugene. "The Letters of Paul and Alice Dunbar: A Private History." Dissertation. Irvine: University of California, 1973.

"Mrs. Alice Dunbar Nelson Injured." *The Pittsburgh Courier*, March 24, 1934.

Mitchell, Michele. "Silences Broken, Silences Kept: Gender and Sexuality in African-American History." *Gender and History* 11, no. 3. (1999).

Nelson, William E. "Criminality and Sexual Morality in New York, 1920–1980." *Yale Journal of Law & the Humanities* 5, no. 2 (1993): 265–341.

Neverdon-Morton, Cynthia. *Afro-American Women of the South and the Advancement of the Race, 1895–1925.* Knoxville: University of Tennessee Press, 1989.

O'Malley, Lurana Donnels. "Staging the Color Line: Alice Dunbar Nelson's Imagined Hawai'i as African-American Allegory." *Comparative Drama* 47, no. 1 (2013): 1–30.

Parker, Allison. *Unceasing Militant: The Life of Mary Church Terrell.* Chapel Hill: UNC Press, 2020.

Pearl, Monica B., "'Sweet Home': Audre Lorde's Zami and the Legacies of American Writing." *Journal of American Studies* 43, no. 2: 297–317.

Perkins, Linda M. "The Impact of 'The Cult of True Womanhood' on the Education of Black Women." *Journal of Social Issues* 39, no. 3 (1983): 17–28.

"Pres. Harding Receives Committee and Petition For 50 Thousand Names Most Representative Group of Race Ask Clemency for Imprisoned Members of 24th Infantry." *Plaindealer*, no. 39, September 30, 1921: 1. *Readex: America's Historical Newspapers.*

"Race Represented On Charter Committee." *Washington Bee*, January 15, 1921: 3. *Readex: America's Historical Newspapers.*

Redding, Saunders J. *On Being Negro in America.* Newport: Charter Books, 1962.

Richardson, Matt. *The Queer Limit of Black Memory: Black Lesbian Literature and Irresolution.* Columbus: Ohio State University Press, 2013.

Shepard, Reginald. "The Other's Other: Against Identity Poetry, for Possibility." *Orpheus in the Bronx: Essays on Identity, Politics, and the Freedom of Poetry,* 41–55. Ann Arbor: University of Michigan Press, 2007.

Sielke, Sabine. *Reading Rape: The Rhetoric of Sexual Violence in American Literature and Culture, 1790-1990.* Princeton, NJ: Princeton University Press, 2009.

Somerville, Siobhan B. *Queering the Color Line: Race and the Invention of Homosexuality in American Culture.* Chapel Hill: Duke University Press, 2000.

Southwestern Christian Advocate. New Orleans, LA, 1873.

Spillers, Hortense. "Mama's Baby, Papa's Maybe: Am American Grammar Book." *Diacritics* 17, no. 2: 64–81.

Stouck, Jordan. "Identities in Crisis: Alice Dunbar-Nelson's New Orleans Fiction." *Canadian Review of American Studies* 34, no. 3 (2004): 269–89.

Tate, Claudia. *Domestic Allegories of Political Desire: The Black Heroine's Text at the Turn of the Century.* Oxford: Oxford University Press, 1992.

Tanritanir, Bülent Cercis, and Hasan Boynukara. "Letter-Writing as Voice of Women in Doris Lessing's The Golden Notebook And Alice Walker's The Color Purple." *Journal Of Graduate School Of Social Sciences* 15, no. 1 (2011): 279–98.

Terborg-Penn, Rosalyn. *African American Women in the Struggle for the Vote, 1850-1920.* Bloomington: Indiana University Press, 1998.

Vandiver, Margaret. *Lethal Punishment: Lynchings and Legal Executions in the South.* Piscataway: Rutgers University Press, 2005.

Vogel, Shane. *The Scene of Harlem Cabaret.* Chicago: University of Chicago Press, 2009.

Wall, Cheryl. *Women of the Harlem Renaissance.* Bloomington: Indiana University Press, 1995.

"War Work of Colored Women. Mrs. Alice Dunbar Nelson Named as Field Representative for Women's." Broad Ax (Chicago, Illinois), August 24, 1918: 4. *Readex: America's Historical Newspapers.*

"Wilmington, Del.,-Oct. 8." Plaindealer (Topeka, Kansas) 22, no. 40, October 1, 1920: 1. Readex: America's Historical Newspapers.

Washington, Margaret Murray. "The New Negro Woman." In *The American New Woman Revisited: A Reader, 1894-1930,* edited by Martha H. Patterson, 54–9. New Brunswick: Rutgers University Press, 2008.

Washburn, Patrick S. *The African American Newspaper: Voice of Freedom.* Evanston: Northwestern University Press, 2006.

Weir-Soley, Donna. *Eroticism, Spirituality, and Resistance in Black Women's Writings.* Gainesville: University Press of Florida, 2009.

West, Elizabeth. "Religion, Race, and Gender in the 'Race-less' Fiction of Alice Dunbar-Nelson." *Black Magnolias Literary Journal* 3, no. 1 (2009): 5–19.

"White Rose Mission Settlement." *New York Age,* July 6, 1905.

White, Deborah Gray. *Too Heavy a Load, Black Women in Defense of Themselves, 1894-1994.* New York: W.W. Norton & Company, 1999.

White, E. Francis. *Dark Continent Of Our Bodies: Black Feminism & Politics Of Respectability*. Philadelphia: Temple University Press, 2010.

Williams, Lillian S, and Randolph Boehm. *Records of the National Association of Colored Women's Clubs, 1895–1992*. University Publications of America, 1993.

Williams, Sylvanie F. "Report to the President, Officers and Members of the National Association of Colored Women." *Microform*, September 15, 1895.

Records of the National Association of Colored Women's Clubs, 1895–1992 (1993): Reel 1, Frame 0114.

Wiggins, Lida Keck. *The Life and Works of Paul Laurence Dunbar; Containing His Complete Poetical Works, His Best Short Stories, Numerous Anecdotes and a Complete Biography of the Famous Poet*. Naperville, IL: J.L. Nichols & Company, 1907.

Wilson, James F. *Bulldaggers, Pansies, and Chocolate Babies: Performance, Race, and Sexuality in the Harlem Renaissance*. Ann Arbor: University of Michigan Press, 2010.

Wooten, H. Ray, Letter from H. Ray Wooten to W. E. B. Du Bois, December 6, 1920. In *W. E.B. Du Bois Papers (MS 312)*. University of Massachusetts: Special Collections and University Archives.

Wright, Richard. "Blueprint for Negro Literature." In *Within the Circle*, edited by Angelyn Mitchell, 97–106. Durham: Duke University Press, 1994.

Young, Leila Mary, Letter to Pauline Young, July 26, 1935. Atlanta Center Robert W. Woodruff Library.

INDEX